THE NATURE OF CITIES

THE NATURE OF CITIES

Ecocriticism and Urban Environments

Edited by
Michael Bennett and David W. Teague

THE UNIVERSITY OF ARIZONA PRESS   TUCSON

The University of Arizona Press
© 1999 The Arizona Board of Regents
First Printing
All rights reserved

⊗ This book is printed on acid-free, archival-quality paper.
Manufactured in the United States of America

04   03   02   01   00   99   6   5   4   3   2   1

Library of Congress Cataloging-in-Publication Data
The nature of cities : ecocriticism and urban environments / Edited by
Michael Bennett and David W. Teague.
   p. cm.
Includes bibliographical references (p.   ) and index.
ISBN 0-8165-1947-1 (alk. paper)
ISBN 0-8165-1949-8 (pbk. : alk. paper)
  1. American literature—History and criticism.   2. Nature in
literature.   3. Environmental literature—History and criticism.
4. English literature—History and criticism.   5. City and town life in
literature.   6. Cities and towns in literature.   7. Ecology in literature.
8. Popular culture.   9. Urban ecology.   I. Bennett, Michael, 1962–
  II. Teague, David W. (David Warfield), 1964–
PS163.N38   1999   99-6284
810.9′355—dc21   CIP

British Library Cataloguing-in-Publication Data
A catalogue record for this book is available from the British Library.

Publication of this book is made possible in part by the proceeds of a
permanent endowment created with the assistance of a Challenge Grant
from the National Endowment for the Humanities, a federal agency.

CONTENTS

ACKNOWLEDGMENTS

The editors would like to acknowledge all those who have enabled a relatively smooth transition to the urban environments that we now call home: New York City for Michael and Philadelphia for David. First, we would like to thank the staff, students, colleagues, and administrators at our respective institutions, Long Island University (Brooklyn) and the University of Delaware Parallel Program. In particular, Michael would like to acknowledge the support of the Research Released Time Committee at Long Island University's Brooklyn campus and the Trustees of Long Island University and David wishes to recognize Deans Helen Williams and Raymond Callahan for their unflagging support. Second, we would like to give thanks to those friends and colleagues at other metropolitan institutions who have helped in building our own community of urban ecocritics, especially to those who shared their work with us. Above all, we would like to acknowledge the love and support of our respective spouses, Juan Battle and Marisa de los Santos, who have joined in our urban adventures as we moved from small-town existence to big-city life. Wherever we are with you, that is the center of our universe.

1

THE NATURE OF CITIES

URBAN ECOCRITICISM
An Introduction
Michael Bennett and David W. Teague

Over the last few years, ecocriticism—which might loosely be defined as the study of the mutually constructing relationship between culture and environment[1]—has developed from a sparsely populated area of study into a busy intersection of cultural analyses, literary criticism, environmental anthologies, and guides to the field.[2] Whether it is seen as an opportunity to break through the solipsism of poststructuralism into real-world activism or as another political scourge violating the disinterested purity of the humanities, ecocriticism has moved from the academic hinterlands into the mainstream.[3] The number of journals, presses, and academic programs devoted to the new environmental studies has mushroomed.[4] In a way, this development seemed inevitable; what is surprising is that it has taken so long for environmentalism to translate into the arena of cultural criticism. Movements for civil rights, women's liberation, and gay/lesbian rights quickly fed into the development and semi-institutionalization of Black/African American studies, feminist criticism, and queer theory. It has taken somewhat longer for the environmental movement to produce ecocriticism, but the discipline is certainly making up for lost time.

However, even as the community of ecocritics grows from a hamlet into a bustling metropolis, the movement itself has been slow to survey the terrain of urban environments. This has been particularly true in the field of literary studies, where ecocriticism has come to be associated with a body of work devoted to nature writing, American pastoralism, and literary ecology.[5] A parallel tradition of studying the city in literature was forged by works like Blanche Housman Gelfant's *The American City Novel* and Raymond

Williams' *The Country and the City.* Only in a very few works did literary studies of the city cross paths with the study of pastoralism and literary ecology to build the foundation for an urban ecological cultural criticism.

The closest these traditions have come to one another has probably been on the turf of Marxist environmental theory. "Classic" works in Marxist social geography and ecosocialism have created the groundwork for a recent flourishing of ecological Marxism.[6] These works built on the development of urban sociology earlier in the century in confluence with Georg Simmel's analysis of the ways in which urban living transformed human consciousness and in reaction to the rise of the Chicago School in the 1920s (see Ross, chapter 2).[7] However, these various sociological and philosophical approaches to urban ecology have tended to lack a thoroughgoing *cultural* analysis of urban environments. Such an analysis was evident in the work of Lewis Mumford and Paul Goodman. More recently, works by Andrew Ross, Will Wright, and Timothy W. Lukes have appeared to fill the cultural gap. Special issues of *Orion, Terra Nova,* and *American Book Review* have focused on what the last calls "urban nature."

The purpose of the current volume is to sharpen this focus on the nature of cities by exploring the components of an urban ecocriticism. One goal of this volume is to point to the self-limiting conceptualizations of nature, culture, and environment built into many ecocritical projects by their exclusion of urban places. However, the main objective is to remind city dwellers of our placement within ecosystems and the importance of this fact for understanding urban life and culture. We begin with an interview with Andrew Ross that explores the general parameters of an urban ecocriticism and frames the particular essays included in this volume. From there, two or three essays explore each of five related topics: urban nature writing, city parks, urban "wilderness," ecofeminism and the city, and theorizing urban space.

Troping on the close association between ecocriticism and nature writing, the first section (Part 2) focuses on urban nature writing. The authors in this section trace the ways in which the generic components and social meaning of nature writing are transformed when its subject is the city. Gary Roberts's "London Here and Now: Walking, Streets, and Urban Environments in English Poetry from Donne to Gay" notes that the poetic representation of the city is a complicated and neglected topic in the criticism of urban literature, which has tended to focus on prose genres. Conversely, the criticism of poetic environments has developed its most interesting and advanced arguments by reading and working with "nature" poetry, which variously shores up or troubles the limits of that category. Roberts's essay focuses on the early history of English urban poetry because that period offers a particularly rich set of responses to new environments created during a time of rapid urbanization. In "'All Things Natural Are Strange': Audre Lorde, Urban Nature, and Cultural Place," Kathleen Wallace analyzes how Audre Lorde explores both the geographical and cultural aspects of place and identity in an urban setting—specifically, what it means to be black, lesbian, feminist, and an artist in her native New York City. Audre Lorde ritually identified herself as a black lesbian feminist poet, but Wallace argues that her unbreakable string of identifiers should also include another—nature writer. Lorde articulated an ecological literacy of place that is both primal and historically informed: blood bound her to her environment of "brick and shitty stone," a bond that Lorde argued could not easily be disregarded. At a physical, and even metaphysical, remove from Lorde's inner-city environment, the suburbs have played an important, if sometimes overlooked, part in the outpouring of American nature writing in recent years. This literature examines how both the natural and the human components of the environment fare in the face of the relentless suburbanization of America. Terrell Dixon's "Inculcating Wildness: Ecocomposition, Nature Writing, and the Regreening of the American Suburb" looks at three major figures in contemporary literary environmentalism—Rick Bass, John Hanson Mitchell, and Robert Michael Pyle—whose writing seeks to redefine the role of nature in the American suburb.

The word "nature" usually calls to mind open spaces, perhaps with a few trees, wild animals, or bodies of water. We often forget that these gifts from Mother Nature are also found in the midst of cities. The next section (Part 3) examines planned efforts to provide such green spaces in the form of city parks. Adam Sweeting makes a crucial connection between cultural production and urban park design in his essay "Writers and Dilettantes: Central Park and the Literary Origins of Antebellum Urban Nature." This essay is informed by an apparently simple claim: Central Park and other large urban parks of the nineteenth century were works of literature as much as they were works of architecture. Sweeting's examination of park space uncovers a narrative of power and gentility, a story in which comfortable New Yorkers use their literary sensibilities to alter the streetscape. The story is also a sentimental one that reflects a restricted view of the natural order. By reading the park as a text, one comes to an understanding of the origins of urban nature. Richard Heyman's "Postindustrial Park or Bourgeois Playground? Preservation and Urban Restructuring at Seattle's Gas Works Park" traces the cultural history of a very different urban park by examining the development of Brown's Point from park to industrial plant and back to park again. Heyman argues that the passive, Victorian, escapist park embraced by the public in 1968 was the product of the manufacturing-dominated urban landscape and social structure of industrial capitalism, embodied in the factory, that existed in the United States prior to the crisis and restructuring of the early 1970s. However, Richard Haag's successful 1971 plan for an "active urban park" that preserves remnants of the old plant is the product of the restructured service-oriented urban landscape of the contemporary social structure of capitalism, embodied in the corporate office tower.

Part 4 examines the trope of the urban "wilderness," which, as Andrew Ross notes in chapter 2, has been used to justify the treatment of minority inhabitants of the inner city as "savages" to be contained by the forces of civilization. In "Boyz in the Woods: Urban Wilderness in American Cinema," Andrew Light tracks this malicious representation of the city as an urban wilderness in recent American cinema. First, Light looks at films, such as *Falling Down,* that portray the wild city from the perspective of whites unfortunately trapped in the urban environment. Second, and more hopeful, are the appeals to an urban wilderness in portrayals of the inner city by African American film makers like Spike Lee, John Singleton, and the Hughs brothers. With both types of film, Light maintains that the successful description of the inner city as a kind of wilderness relies on the historical misperception of wild nature as fulfilling the traditional role of classical wilderness—a savage space separate from and inferior to the realm of civilization. In "Central High and the Suburban Landscape: The Ecology of White Flight," David Teague looks at the fallout from whites' fears of the urban wilderness: white flight and suburbanization. Teague notes that although these two processes have been seen as separate, they are actually parts of the same process—the "cultural" dimension of white flight is inseparable from the "ecological" dimension of suburbanization. He argues that the same solipsistic ideology that drives a white family to be terrified of sending its children to mingle with other ethnicities at Little Rock's Central High also drives that family to demand the sort of insularity, autonomy, and cultural intolerance found in suburban life. Michael Bennett's "Manufacturing the Ghetto: Anti-urbanism and the Spatialization of Race" argues that the anti-urban sentiment evident in the cultural analyses of Light and Teague has had a very real sociopolitical component: the collapse of a coherent urban policy in the United States over the last twenty years. This same period witnessed the rise of the environmental justice movement to combat the disproportionate placing of toxic sites and other ecological hazards in minority communities. Bennett maintains that these historical developments are both manifestations of the spatialization of race—discrimination against urban communities that *happen* to be populated almost exclusively by people of color. He suggests that this form of "racism without race" could best be addressed within the framework of an expanded environmental justice movement that combines the best of the 1960s War on Poverty with 1990s ecological activism.

Part 5 invokes another strand of political philosophy woven into the environmental movement by taking up the issue of urban ecofeminism. From the movement's beginning, women have played an important role within modern environmentalism, both literally (as political leaders and ideological gurus) and figuratively (as in Mother Nature or the Earth goddess Gaia). In this tradition, Catherine Villanueva Gardner's "An Ecofeminist Perspective on the Urban Environment" suggests that a feminist approach to ecology can examine the ethical problems of urban environments. Ecofeminists call for shifts in perception of the nonhuman world, from an instrumentalist and exploitative gaze to loving or respectful perceptions of that world; indeed this shift is part of the perception necessary for a transformation of values. However, can this nonhuman world be meaningfully understood as an inner city or are we talking only of the pastoral—that part of the world not created by humans? Gardner's essay explores this question and suggests that ecofeminism can provide an inclusivist, pluralist account that magnifies the voices of protest against "environmental racism" and the social injustices of urban environments if the movement is understood as a social and moral strategy offering an alternative to a deep-ecological environmental ethics. In contrast, Laura Sullivan's " 'You Make Me Feel Like a Natural Woman': The Political Economy of Contemporary Cosmetics Discourse" critiques the ways in which First World women appropriate environmental rhetoric in a beauty discourse that either commodifies indigenous peoples or renders them invisible. In the latter case, the so-called Third World is depicted as a place of "pure nature," contrasted with the urban, "civilized" First World. Similarly, the Third World "natural" woman is counterposed to the First World urban consumer of beauty products. By building on the logic of ecofeminism, Sullivan analyzes these texts— print advertisements, television commercials, infomercials, brochures, and company-produced books—as depictions of a prelapsarian world in which the Western Anglo woman has been inserted into the habitat of the contemporary Third World "natural" woman. These constructions are based upon racist assumptions and serve to perpetuate myths of the superiority of the urban North over the "uncivilized" South.

The final section (Part 6) takes up the question of how, ultimately, we are to comprehend the nature of cities by examining where our conception of urban ecology comes from and where it is headed. Joanne Gottlieb's "Darwin's City, or Life Underground: Evolution, Progress, and the Shapes of Things to Come" traces the trope of the evolutionary deformation of the technological utopia from its appearance in late-nineteenth-century science fiction (particularly in the work of H. G. Wells) to three recent re-articulations *(The X Files, Jurassic Park,* and *12 Monkeys).* Gottlieb explores the relation between the status of the city and the notion of the future that resides in the imaginative possibility of utopia as a technological environment fostering the improvement of social life. This analysis of the status of utopia also relates to recent diagnoses of the contemporary city in terms of dispersal and placelessness and the possible loss of a modernist urban orientation toward purpose and legibility altogether. Gottlieb asks, if the city has become dispersed and defined by the flow of information, what happens to its traditional orientation as a site of social experiment or its potential to embody social progress? David R. Shumway focuses on a much more constrained urban environment and its inhabitants in "Nature in the Apartment: Humans, Pets, and the Value of Incommensurability." As the most familiar fauna inhabiting urban space, pets are animals that we are socially licensed to anthropomorphize. Shumway argues for the social and ecological value of this anthropomorphism. He contends that because human and animal worlds are incommensurable, we can understand them only in our terms. However, by understanding animals as like us, we recognize our own naturalness and provide a point of emergence for the recognition of the value of other species. Finally, Michael Branch's "Cosmology in the Casino: Simulacra of Nature in the Interiorized Wilderness" examines the proliferation of artificially constructed and highly controlled representations, simulations, and simulacra of nature in urban spaces by focusing on the accelerated "sky" housed within the colossal dome of the Silver Legacy Casino in downtown Reno, Nevada. By invoking the insights of space- and place-theorists including Gaston Bachelard, Yi-Fu Tuan, and Jean Beaudrillard, Branch explores the cultural significance of such artificial monuments to nature as they appear in urban settings. He speculates, finally, that "satisfactory" urban simulations and simulacra of nature may lead to the perceived superfluity of the natural world itself. The modern construction of urban space that Gottlieb argues arose with the Industrial Revolution, and especially the railroad, comes full circle in the simulated mining disaster that highlights the virtual reality of the Silver Legacy Casino.

As a group, these essays provide the parameters for an urban ecocriticism that offers the ecological component often missing from cultural analyses of the city and the urban perspective often lacking in environmental approaches to contemporary culture. The editors of this volume are especially attuned to the sociopolitical construction of all environments—"natural" and manmade—because of our experience as transplanted ruralites now dwelling in urban ecosystems, where the human determinants of the environment are too present to be ignored. Coming from small towns in eastern Washington and central Arkansas, we both ended up in major urban areas: New York City and Philadelphia. Urban environments have reshaped our perceptions of nature and ecology. Moving to urban areas has both sharpened our appreciation for "unspoiled, natural" habitats, which we took for granted while growing up in out-of-the-way places, and increased our suspicion of ecocritical perspectives that privilege "unspoiled, natural" environments while excluding the kinds of places that we now occupy. We prize the "rural splendors" that we have fled, even more now that they no longer fit into our day-to-day existence. However, like other sometimes-disaffected urbanites and many ecocritics, we must be careful not to idealize these places and clear out the original soil and trees to make room for the imaginary spaces we need in our very different current environments. It turns out that the apple fields of Orchard Drive, where Michael grew up, were downwind from the planned radioactive releases of the Hanford Nuclear Facility during the 1950s and 1960s. The sleepy town where David spent his early years became a haven for white flight from nearby Little Rock. We are forced to recognize that even the pristine settings that we remember were and are shaped by decisions and policies made in urban centers. If it is sometimes easy to overlook this fact in the seemingly tranquil environs of our rural youth, it is almost impossible to forget the sociopolitical determinants of the landscape in our new urban homes.

Based on this perspective, we have chosen the essays that follow because they endeavor to reconceive nature and its cultural representations in ways that contribute to understanding the contemporary cityscape. These essays avoid the tendency of discussions of culture and environment to exclude those who have not been privileged to embrace pastoral or wild nature. Instead they explore the theoretical issues that arise when one attempts to adopt and adapt an environmental perspective to analyze urban life. By addressing the historical gap between environmentalism, cultural studies, and urban experience, we hope that this book will prove to be especially relevant to the development of the ecocritical movement.

NOTES

1. For a more extensive effort to define the term ecocriticism and trace the history of the movement, see Glotfelty and Fromm's *The Ecocriticism Reader.* The essays by Glotfelty and Howarth provide particularly useful introductions to the "field." Ecocriticism has usually been associated with literary analysis of nature writing. We hope to expand that domain to include cultural study of urban environments, although this expanded domain would not exactly overlap with the terrain traversed by the long sociological and philosophical traditions associated with thinking about urbanicity (which tend to downplay, or bypass, the process by which cultural production is implicated in human adaptation to urban habitats).

2. For a bibliography of ecological literary criticism, see Glotfelty and Fromm's *The Ecocriticism Reader.* Some additional environmental readers are *Being in the World*

(Slovic and Dixon), *Constructing Nature* (Jensoth and Lott), *The Diversity of Life* (Wilson), *The Endangered Earth* (Morgan and Okerstrom), *The Environmental Predicament* (Verburg), *A Forest of Voices* (Anderson and Runciman), *This Incomparable Lande* (Lyon), *The Literature of Nature* (Begiebing and Grumbling), *The Norton Book of Nature Writing* (Finch and Elder), *Reading the Environment* (Walker), *Sisters of the Earth* (Anderson), and *Writing Nature* (Ross). Donald Edward Davis's *Ecophilosophy* provides, as the subtitle states, a "field guide to the literature" from Rachel Carson's *Silent Spring* in the 1960s to efforts in the 1980s to create a "new culture of wholeness and harmony with Nature" (ix). *Teaching Environmental Literature: Materials, Methods, Resources,* edited by Frederick O. Waage, was the first guide to appear that acknowledged the development of ecocriticism as a "field." The attempt to provide an updated account of "environmental teaching" was undertaken by the 1996 publication of Collett and Karakashian's *Greening the College Curriculum.*

3. See, for example, Erik Davis's "It Ain't Easy Being Green: Eco Meets Pomo"; Jay Parini's "The Greening of the Humanities," which was attacked by Jonathan Yardley in the *Washington Post;* Jonathan Collett and Stephen Karakashian's "Turning Curricula Green"; and Karen J. Winkler's "Inventing a Field: The Study of Literature about the Environment."

4. *Environmental Ethics, The Environmental History Review, ISLE: Interdisciplinary Studies in Literature and the Environment, Organization and Environment, The Orion Society Magazine, Philosophy and Geography, Terra Nova,* and *Western American Literature* are some of the more significant journals and magazines associated with the ecocritical movement. Schools with a focus on environmental criticism in their graduate programs, presses, or both include the universities of Arizona, Georgia, Nevada (Reno), Oregon, Utah, and Wisconsin.

5. The "classic" works on American pastoralism are Henry Nash Smith's *Virgin Land* and Leo Marx's *The Machine in the Garden.* The development of "literary ecology" could be traced to Joseph Meeker's *The Comedy of Survival* and Yi-Fu Tuan's *Topophilia.* Building on this foundation, a "new pastoralism" has been constructed by such popular works of ecocriticism as Neil Evernden's *The Social Creation of Nature,* Jonathan Bate's *Romantic Ecology,* and Lawrence Buell's *The Environmental Imagination.*

6. The Marxist influence in social geography is evident in works by Manuel Castells, David Harvey, and Ira Katznelson. Peter Dickens, David Pepper, and others have made important contributions to ecosocialism. Other signs of the productivity of Marxist environmental theory include the well-respected journal *Capitalism, Nature, Socialism;* a flurry of articles in various other journals *(Cultural Critique, New Political Science, Telos);* and the popular Guilford Press series on "Democracy and Ecology": *Is Sustainable Capitalism Possible?* (O'Connor), *Green Production: Toward an Environmental Rationality* (Leff), and *Minding Nature: The Philosophers of Ecology* (Macauley). Although sharply critical of Marxist ecology while

sharing many of its insights, social ecology has also developed a sociopolitical analysis of the ways in which environments are constructed, following the lead of the prolific Murray Bookchin.

7. In addition to those works of the Chicago School, which share a formalist approach that Andrew Ross critiques (see chapter 2) for its tendency to equate social and natural processes, the development of urban sociology was also influenced and codified by works like Nels Anderson and Eduard Lindeman's *Urban Sociology,* Niles Carpenter's *The Sociology of City Life,* and the essays of Louis Wirth.

Works Cited

American Book Review 18.2 (December–January 1996–97).

Anderson, Chris, and Lex Runciman, eds. *A Forest of Voices: Reading and Writing the Environment.* Mountain View, Calif.: Mayfield, 1995.

Anderson, Lorraine, ed. *Sisters of the Earth: Women's Prose and Poetry about Nature.* New York: Vintage, 1991.

Anderson, Nels, and Eduard Lindeman. *Urban Sociology: An Introduction to the Study of Urban Communities.* New York: A. A. Knopf, 1928.

Bate, Jonathan. *Romantic Ecology: Wordsworth and the Environmental Tradition.* New York: Routledge, 1991.

Begiebing, Robert J., and Owen Grumbling, eds. *The Literature of Nature: The British and American Traditions.* Medford, N.J.: Plexus, 1990.

Buell, Lawrence. *The Environmental Imagination: Thoreau, Nature Writing, and the Formation of American Culture.* Cambridge, Mass.: Harvard UP, 1995.

Carpenter, Niles. *The Sociology of City Life.* New York: Longmans, Green, and Co., 1945.

Carson, Rachel. *Silent Spring.* Boston: Houghton Mifflin, 1962.

Collett, Jonathan, and Stephen Karakashian, eds. *Greening the College Curriculum: A Guide to Environmental Teaching in the Liberal Arts.* Washington, D.C.: Island Press, 1996.

——. "Turning Curricula Green." *The Chronicle of Higher Education* 23 February 1996: B1–B2.

Davis, Donald Edward. *Ecophilosophy: A Field Guide to the Literature.* San Pedro, Calif.: R. & E. Miles, 1989.

Davis, Erik. "It Ain't Easy Being Green: Eco Meets Pomo." *Voice Literary Supplement* February 1995: 16–18.

Evernden, Neil. *The Social Creation of Nature.* Baltimore, Md.: Johns Hopkins UP, 1992.

Finch, Robert, and John Elder, eds. *The Norton Book of Nature Writing*. New York: W. W. Norton & Co., 1990.

Gelfant, Blanche Housman. *The American City Novel*. Norman: U of Oklahoma P, 1954.

Glotfelty, Cheryll, and Harold Fromm, eds. *The Ecocriticism Reader: Landmarks in Literary Ecology*. Athens: U of Georgia P, 1996.

Goodman, Paul, and Percival Goodman. *Communitas*. New York: Columbia UP, 1990.

Jensoth, Richard, and Edward E. Lott, eds. *Constructing Nature: Readings from the American Experience*. Upper Saddle, N.J.: Prentice Hall, 1996.

Leff, Enrique, ed. *Green Production: Toward an Environmental Rationality*. New York: Guilford, 1995.

Lukes, Timothy W. *Ecocritique: Contesting the Politics of Nature, Economics, and Culture*. Minneapolis: U of Minnesota P, 1997.

Lyon, Tomas J., ed. *This Incomparable Lande: A Book of American Nature Writing*. Boston: Houghton Mifflin, 1989.

Macauley, David, ed. *Minding Nature: The Philosophers of Ecology*. New York: Guilford, 1996.

Marx, Leo. *The Machine in the Garden: Technology and the Pastoral Ideal in America*. New York: Oxford UP, 1964.

Meeker, Joseph. *The Comedy of Survival: Studies in Literary Ecology*. New York: Scribner's, 1972.

Morgan, Sarah, and Dennis Okerstrom, eds. *The Endangered Earth: Readings for Writers*. Needham Heights, Mass.: Allyn & Bacon, 1992.

Mumford, Lewis. *The Culture of Cities*. San Diego: Harcourt Brace, 1996.

———. *The Lewis Mumford Reader*. Athens: U of Georgia P, 1995.

O'Connor, Martin, ed. *Is Sustainable Capitalism Possible?* New York: Guilford, 1994.

Orion Magazine 13.4 (Autumn 1994).

Parini, Jay. "The Greening of the Humanities." *New York Times Magazine* 29 October 1995: 52–53.

Ross, Andrew. *The Chicago Gangster Theory of Life: Nature's Debt to Society*. London: Verso, 1994.

Ross, Carolyn, ed. *Writing Nature: An Ecological Reader for Writers*. New York: St. Martin's, 1995.

Simmel, Georg. *The Sociology of Georg Simmel*. Trans. Kurt H. Wolff. Glencoe, Ill.: Free Press, 1950.

Slovic, Scott, and Terrell Dixon, eds. *Being in the World: An Environmental Reader for Writers*. New York: Macmillan, 1993.

Smith, Henry Nash. *Virgin Land: The American West as Symbol and Myth*. New York: Vintage, 1950.

Terra Nova: Nature and Culture 1.4 (Fall 1996).

Tuan, Yi-Fu. *Topophilia: A Study of Environmental Perception, Attitudes, and Values.* 1974. New York: Columbia UP, 1990.

Verburg, Carol J., ed. *The Environmental Predicament: Four Issues for Critical Analysis.* Boston: Bedford–St. Martin's, 1995.

Waage, Frederick O., ed. *Teaching Environmental Literature: Materials, Methods, Resources.* New York: MLA, 1985.

Walker, Melissa, ed. *Reading the Environment.* New York: W. W. Norton & Co., 1994.

Williams, Raymond. *The Country and the City.* New York: Oxford UP, 1973.

Wilson, Edward O., ed. *The Diversity of Life.* New York: W. W. Norton & Co., 1992.

Winkler, Karen J. "Inventing a Field: The Study of Literature about the Environment." *The Chronicle of Higher Education* 9 August 1996: A9, A15.

Wirth, Louis. "Urbanism as a Way of Life." *American Journal of Sociology* 44 July 1938: 1–24.

Wright, Will. *Wild Knowledge: Science, Language, and Social Life in a Fragile Environment.* Minneapolis: U of Minnesota P, 1992.

Yardley, Jonathan. " 'Ecocriticism,' Growing Like a Weed." *Washington Post* 13 November 1995: B2.

2

THE SOCIAL CLAIM ON URBAN ECOLOGY

Andrew Ross (Interviewed by Michael Bennett)

Q : Given that the central concern of this volume is "urban ecocriticism," let me start by asking what this term means to you. Many would see it as an oxymoron.

A: There's a long history behind the oxymoron, but one could start as recently as the period immediately following Earth Day in 1970, when it became clear that a huge gulf of understanding existed between environmentalists, whose activism was explicitly tied to the protection of open-space areas affecting white, middle-class suburbia, and social justice activists in inner city areas, concerned with affordable housing, sustainable income, and environmental security of a sort that simply did not register with the elite power base of the environmental movement at that time. The distance between these two wings of movement politics was as profound as anything in the historical conflict of country and city. Then as now, the priorities of mainstream environmentalism are wilderness and natural-area preservation, wildlife protection, water-quality control, land-use planning and control, outdoor recreation, and the like. Last on the list come the environmental priorities that affect urban residents, like sanitation, rat and pest control, noise pollution, hunger, malnutrition, poor health, premature death, not to mention the conditions that underpin these hazards, like the slashing of public services and the savage inequities of public housing policy. Then as now, mainstream environmentalists fail to understand how and why the values and activities close to the heart of the population that goes hiking, camping, and bird watching and has easy access to outdoor recreation, simply do not rate so highly among urban dwellers whose access to income and employment and health is persistently endangered by policies that continue to direct resources to the suburban classes and voters. It's no coincidence that the environmental crisis only achieved widespread recognition at a time when pollution, traffic congestion, crowding of recreational space, and resource degradation were finally taking their toll upon suburban dwellers.

Prescient commentators in the early 1970s foresaw that environmental legislation would place a higher burden on the poor, since the social and the economic costs of this legislation would be factored into consumer prices that claimed a much higher portion of low-income salaries. Land-use regulation in the name of environmental conservation would have a similarly punitive effect on low-income groups seeking affordable housing, or, just as insidiously, on the emerging black middle class already seeking ex-urban space that had been denied to them by forty years of racist federal housing legislation. Now that a substantial number of African Americans were leaving the city in search of green space and clean air, those areas adjoining white suburbs that remained undeveloped were suddenly being declared by conservationists to be protected zones. It's hard not to be cynical about some of this history, but it's very much where we are today, in the latest installment of this long conflict between country and city. Of course, there are many cases to show that coalitions are possible and that they can be effective, but the pressure of single-issue politics has tended to maintain and solidify the differences.

As for criticism more narrowly defined, the literature of conservation—almost wholly devoted to nature worship in the "cathedral of pines"—is persistent in its demonization of the city. In the dominant environmental literature, the city is sick, monstrous, blighted, ecocidal, life-denying, parasitical, you name it. . . . In the face of that tradition, it's easy to see why "urban ecocriticism" is considered an oxymoron.

Q: How does the focus on urban ecosystems affect the notion of what you have called "green criticism"?

A: Well, there may not be a vast urban literature of green criticism, but there is a strong tradition of urban ecology dating back to the work of the Chicago School in the 1920s. In fact, it is a dominant strain within urban studies, a formalistic strain that Marxists and other critics have long combatted. The basic thesis, as formulated by Park, Burgess, and Mackenzie, was that the growth of cities was analogous to principles of plant ecology. Just as plant ecology is determined by the struggle of species for space, food, and light, so too the spatial organization of city life can be explained as the products of competition and selection. According to this model, the growth of a city proceeds through successional phases when some invasive element—a new population group or industry—tips the balance and establishes territorial dominance. A climax point is reached when the dominant species can withstand all invasions; subdominants fit into available niches as best they can. This view of city space as an evolving, contested habitat had an immense influence on urbanist scholarship. This description of collective adaption to a given environment became a favored model for explaining the organization of urban space. In fact, the sociology of social relations, in this tradition, was often reduced to measuring the distance between groups and populations.

The result, of course, was to naturalize, or provide a biological gloss, for the experience of social conflict within cities. Everything could be explained within the framework of assumptions provided by evolutionary organicism in the mold of Herbert Spencer—social Darwinism, in other words. Criticism of this model has appealed to alternative models. Those influenced by classical Marxism, for example, see metropolitanization as a product of uneven development and economic concentration of capitalist investment. In this view, there was nothing natural about urbanization, unless, of course, you view the workings of capitalism as akin to the laws of nature. The record of legislation and political sponsorship that supports vested interests in land and industrial speculation might still be viewed as behavior that is endemic to the species, but I don't believe this is a useful way of explaining what is, in every respect, a complex social process.

This tradition of urban ecology isn't simply an academic outlook. It's very much in sympathy with the rhetorical image of the city as an immense biological organism, hopelessly overextended, of course, and totally beyond any carrying capacity or sustainable organization of resources. So you see, there is already a history of critical attention to urban ecosystems—to the city as an ecosystem—much of it unfortunate in my view. It's only recently that we have begun to compensate for those unfortunate associations and move in a different direction. Part of this involves the movement devoted to the greening of cities in ways that directly affect the material environment; green spaces, green architectural design, human-scale neighborhood planning, traffic mitigation, pedestrian-friendly development, waste management, and energy efficiency. But other parts have to relate to social ecology—shouldn't a green outlook on urbanism include attention to the redistribution of wealth, de facto racial desegregation, extension of community board power, safeguarding of public services and education, reforms of political decision-making at city, state, and federal levels, and the like? Unless you attend to these social features you can't fully understand the effects upon the material environment. Nor can you understand the culture of cities, the folklore and psychology of urbanism, the local humor, human loyalties, and so on, which are even less conventionally the objects of green criticism.

Q: You note that cities can only exist on the basis of surplus resources from elsewhere, yet in certain ways they are environmentally friendly. In comparison to suburbs, cities certainly waste less space, require less water resources, and promote greater use of mass transit. And a city's population density is what allows large areas of the countryside to remain relatively free of human interference (after all, if everyone went back to nature, there would be no nature left to go back to). On balance, what do you make of the environmental impact of cities and what can be done to soften that impact?

A: There's more than enough evidence to suggest that postwar suburbanization—a movement as rapid, in terms of sheer population growth, as urbanization had been in the late nineteenth century—had a much more decisive environmental impact than anything that happened in cities during that same period. The infamous, placeless sprawl created by the massive federal subsidization of suburban highways and the single-family home on a large lot was not only directly responsible for the loss and deterioration of open land and wilderness, but also the severe toll exacted on ecosystems, both regional and global, by high-octane automobile culture. Nothing in the city compares with this kind of environmental impact. Suburban development was not only at the expense of urban taxpayers, it also drained cities of investment, political clout, and all kinds of other resources. With this in mind, it's clear that it's the suburbs that have been parasitical upon cities, rather than vice versa—especially since cities traditionally provide workplaces and recreational and cultural amenities for the surrounding populace and absorb the costs of providing these benefits. But now there is a less clear-cut relation between the two; it no longer corresponds to a core-periphery type relationship. A third of U.S. suburbs face "urban" type problems—an eroding tax base, plummeting house prices, pollution, rising poverty and crime rates. Many suburbs are declining faster than the core cities.

The urban planning movement that has sprung up to address these issues—the New Urbanism (Duany and Plater-Zyberg in Florida, Calthorpe in northern California, Moule and Polyzoide in southern California)—has tried to blend the best of high-density urbanism with the best of the tradition of greenbelt, garden-city suburbs dating back to Howard and Unwin. High-density residency combined with light-rail transit development, on the one hand, and mixed-use, mixed-income, postsuburban plans, on the other. The result is more or less aimed at a mix of sustainable green space and traffic efficiency and traditional aesthetics. City and state policymakers are increasingly taking up the principles of the movement, and the planners themselves are turning their attention to center-city projects. This is an interesting development, and if it is combined with effective regional planning, we may see some surprising results. The biggest obstacle remains the massive industrial complex—builders, developers, banks, and highway-auto-rubber interests—that is committed to maintaining the national cult of the single-family house and its half-acre lot. So much of the economy is invested in that cult in the form of public subsidies and tax breaks that it will take more than the evangelism of the New Urbanism to dislodge. From a cultural point of view, the associations that people have with higher-density environments today are ingrained with noxious stereotypes. These associations are the result of a half century of racist propaganda on the part of the suburban lobby depicting the dangers of center-city life. But the evidence of the growing taste for post-suburban "downtowns" is that people are beginning to rediscover the benefits of older forms of urbanism: sociability, walkability, cosmopolitanism, spontaneity, and diversity.

Q: So far we have talked about how cities have been conceptualized in environmental movements, urban sociology, and urban planning. How does urban culture fit into the mix? The second section of this volume considers the ways in which the literary genre most closely associated with the environment, nature writing, is transformed within the context of urban culture. What role does the kind of cultural criticism that you have engaged in and that is on display in this volume play in understanding these and other urban cultural productions and the ways in which these productions reveal and shape the nature of cities?

A: One instructive approach is to compare some of the traditional urban genres—the detective, crime, and gangster stories—with the more recent ones, like dystopian science fiction and the disaster genre. The early ones see the city as the "natural" site of habitation for modern people. In these genres, the city is the obvious backdrop for tales of power and corruption and other stylized struggles over territory and turf. Insofar as the urban geography is a moral landscape, it functions more like a Greek chorus, reflecting and supporting the judgements passed upon the protagonists. The play of light and darkness in the streetscapes of film noir would be a classic example. In the more recent genres, the city as a whole has become the object, not just of judgement (in the biblical tradition), but of radical ecological transformations. Citizens, in these genres, are often passively at the mercy of an urban environment that has been turned against them. To some extent, this shift reflects our consciousness about ecosystems and our doubts about their carrying capacity. In other, more literal ways, it reminds us, in the United States at least, of the political war on cities that has been raging since the backlash against the Great Society programs of the 1960s. In the bestiary of politics, the post-1960s city became an endangered species as a result of public disinvestment, capital flight, and other active forms of "benign neglect." For all their complexity, cities are treated in a terribly simplistic and transparent manner by policymakers. That's why my favorite urban culture flows from films like *Batman* and *Ghostbusters,* cartoonish stories about control over environmental macrosystems.

Q: The fourth section in this volume focuses on the trope of "urban wilderness" to explore the racialization of space in cities and their suburbs. You have commented on this phenomenon in your discussion of gentrification and its accompanying tropes on the inner city as a "jungle" inhabited by "wildlife." The title of your book *The Chicago Gangster Theory of Life* refers to the use of a social stereotype—the cigar-chomping, sadistic mafioso—to explain a supposedly natural fact—the genetics of selfish behavior. What about the opposite phenomenon: the use of nature imagery to explain dubious social facts? Perhaps you could comment more on what might be called "A Wildlife Theory of Chicago Gangstas."

A: I am reminded of the Florida congressman whose debating contribution to the 1996 rubbishing of the welfare state consisted of holding up a sign that said "Don't Feed the Alligators." Welfare dependency was being compared to the undesirable dependency of wildlife on resource-rich humans. A shockingly racist analogy, of course, but not untypical of the Republican class of '94. This kind of rhetoric is common enough in elite and redneck circles and is always infused with a more virulent strain of prejudice when applied to urban patterns (remember the nonsense about "wilding" among African American youth after the Central Park jogger rape a few years back). As you point out, the principle of the Chicago Gangster Theory is that nature and society often are commutable categories. The "theory" refers to the tendency of sociobiologists to take descriptions of social behavior, find some derivation for them in the natural world (selfish genes, in Richard Dawkins's infamous example) and then reapply this description to the social world as if it had always existed in nature and carried the authority of nature as a result. You can see the theory in action in any piece of science journalism that informs us that a gene has been found for arrogance, shyness, adventurousness, you name it. There's a vicious metaphorical circle at work here.

Q: In the overwhelming built environment of New York City and other urban areas, it's easy to forget that the images we usually associate with nature—trees, rivers, wildlife—are also part of the cityscape in the form of urban parks. The third section of this volume examines the design and function of two of these parks—Seattle's Gas Works Park, and, most famously, New York's Central Park. Here in New York, various parks—including those in Washington Square, Union Square, and Tompkins Square (the site of riots during the forced removal of homeless park dwellers)—have been part of the planned "revitalization" of public spaces. Is this redesign just another example of the displacement of "undesirables," an offshoot of gen-trification, or does it also represent a salutary desire to commune with the "great outdoors"?

A: Most urban parks are soaked in the history of irony. In the nineteenth century, a good deal of urban reform was based on the moral influence of pastoralism, and so the great landscape gardeners like Olmsted were moral engineers. Gardens, parks, and green spaces were considered to be civilizing agents, even when they were designed to evoke "wilderness," which in pre-Romantic times was associated with barbarism. Urban greenery was in-tended to take the rough edge off the immigrant soul. As with the attempts to cordon off "wilderness" in national parks, the actual inhabitants of these spaces had to be evicted—Native Americans in Yosemite and African Americans in Central Park, where residents of a thriving black township were displaced in New York's first example of urban renewal/removal.

Today, urban green space is a primary battleground not necessarily because it is green, but because it is rare, public space, and thus the invest-ment home of a variety of interested claims. Urban green space is fought over in ways that are quite different from the preservation of wilderness space. For one thing, it is accepted that these parks are a place of intense socialization and cohabitation, not a *cordon sanitaire* to be kept free from human influence. To the extent to which environmentalists are involved in these battles, they necessarily share the field with homeless advocates, com-munity activists, antidevelopment groups, and a whole host of other pro-moters of social justice. It seems to me that these are the kinds of coalitions, however fraught and unstable, that the ecology movement needs to embrace and champion.

Q: And, of course, there are the city's built environments that we are much less likely to think of as "natural" in comparison to city parks—apartment complexes, ghettos, skyscrapers, sports arenas—but that are equally amena-ble to ecological analysis. The final section of this volume looks at some of these urban spaces, from the nineteenth-century urban underground to late-twentieth-century imagineered interior wilderness. Some of your most recent work focuses on one such urban interior space—the sweatshop. Perhaps you could comment on the ways in which this recent work on sweat-shops jibes with your ongoing interest in green criticism.

A: Well, one of the more surrealistic features of the global city is its ability to recycle the past. In a postindustrial metropolis like New York, patterns of work for large portions of the population increasingly resemble those in the early years of the century, before industrial democracy and progressive taxation and the welfare infrastructure were adopted into law. Nowhere is this more visible than in the so-called return of the sweatshop to the core (in fact, the sweatshop was never eradicated, it simply was driven further underground or overseas). Recent disclosures about these sweatshops summon up the misery and filth of turn-of-the-century workplaces, plagued by chronic health problems (tuberculosis, the scourge of the sweatshop has also made a return of late) and home to the ruthless exploitation of greenhorn immigrants. Indeed, the repugnance attached to the term "sweatshop" commands a moral power, second only to slavery itself, to rouse public opinion into a collective spasm of abhorrence. As it happens, the juxtaposition of technocultures in today's two-tier city is also strikingly similar to turn-of-the-century workplaces. Then, the sweatshop's primitive mode of production and the cutter's artisanal loft coexisted with semiautomated workplaces that would very soon industrialize into economies of scale under the pull of the Fordist factory ethic. Today, the sewing machine's foot pedal is still very much in business, no longer competing with steam power but with the CPU.

The preindustrial sweatshop sector flourishes in proximity to postindustrial, high-tech workplaces, often within the same block, and this proximity makes all the difference to fast turnaround, just-in-time production that keeps the fashion industry in business. Sweatshop technology hasn't changed much since the invention of the sewing machine, and the conditions under which this sector is thriving again are dependent on a vast influx of immigrant labor. Just as garment companies scour the globe for the lowest wage floor to produce offshore, the creation of a low-wage metropolitan sector in the garment trade and other industries explains and supports the vast migration of populations in our time. These have obvious environmental consequences. For one thing, "population" and "immigration" are always touchy subjects for some environmentalists, and no more so than today. But, more generally, the flourishing of these low-wage atrocities helps to normalize the urban workplace, yet again, as unsafe, unsanitary, unregulated, and inhuman. For urban workers and dwellers, it lowers the threshold of tolerance for substandard habitation.

Q: Do you think that racial and sexual minorities have a unique relationship to urban environments because so many of us came to the cities in search of a kind of freedom lacking in our previous locales—for example, African Americans escaping the Jim Crow South during the Great Migration or lesbians and gay men leaving oppressive hometowns for the relative safety of so-called gay ghettos?

A: City life has always promised a relief from the stifling strictures of parochialism, tribalism, and the "idiocy of rural life." The absence of moral fundamentalism or communitarianism has played a large role in the urban version of citizen freedoms. It's odd, these days, when cities are considered to be centers of ungodliness, to consider the city's centrality to the Christian traditions—the Celestial City, the City on a Hill, and so on. To be a good Christian was to live in a city. Odd, and yet, if you look at Mayor Giuliani's quality-of-life campaign in New York City and at related developments like the Disneyfication of Times Square and Forty-Second Street, you actually do find that majoritarian morality exerting its sway over the urban agenda. Just as urbanism is now affecting the suburbs, so too we see values associated with anti-urban sentiment asserting themselves within the cities: in particular, the puritan rage for decency, orderliness, safety, and hygiene. All of this has its socially repressive side to it, and minorities suffer disproportionately when a moral high-pressure zone comes to visit. Subcultural toleration, respect for difference, and public rights to the city are increasingly illegal in my hometown.

Q: A dominant concern in *Chicago Gangster Theory* is that nature will be used as an authority dictating certain social and cultural policies. This insight underlies much of your writing about the relationship between the natural and social sciences, technology, and politics. Do you believe that the misuse of nature in this way is becoming more or less prevalent?

A: Perhaps not so prevalent as it was in the earliest part of the century, when eugenics was at the height of its influence on social policy. But under the subsequent ascendancy of the party of nurture over nature in social thought we enjoyed a half-century of relief until the rise of the New Right was accompanied by a revival of biologism in the form of sociobiology and in resurgent forms of social Darwinism. This revival, which has had a dramatic impact on social legislation and political culture, occurred in a context quite different from the earlier period. Discoveries in molecular biology, gene splicing, and recombinant DNA had changed the nature of nature, for one thing, rendering it more ductile, less inflexible—subject to revision. Genetic determinism has become all the more powerful as a result. In addition, we were witnessing the rise of the environmentalist movement, whose appeal to the authority of nature was profoundly benign in principle. And yet, the influence of Malthusianism upon sectors of the movement—especially in the enthusiasm for population control—emphasized draconian limitations that reminded many of race theories of Lebensraum and the like. Even on the Left, we hear complaints these days that "culturalism" has gone too far and that some rethinking of biologism is needed. All of this, to my mind, is sad at best and dangerous at worst. I believe we have to be vigilant in the struggle against what Marx diagnosed as the ceaseless attempt to present social relations as if they were a state of nature.

Q: You have critiqued theories that seem to posit elemental, natural gender roles as part of their ecocritical project. At the same time, you have praised certain types of ecofeminism. This same conflicted vision is on display in the essays in this volume by Catherine Gardner and Laura Sullivan, who point to the complications in applying ecofeminist principles to urban environments. What, for you, distinguishes positive and negative attempts to analyze the ways in which gender gets played out in green criticism? For instance, from an ecological perspective do you see certain positive elements within the men's movement, of which you have been a harsh critic?

A: The environmental movement has been a haven, within the landscape of the new social movements, for straight, white, middle-class males who may feel uncomfortable with the obligation to acknowledge their sexuality, race, and gender in other areas of social activism. Guys have felt they could simply be themselves and that they could play leadership roles that would not be so legitimate elsewhere. Notwithstanding that women have played a leading role in the movement, as intellectuals (Rachel Carson, Helen Caldicott, Petra Kelly, Vandana Shiva) and as frontline activists, men have had the license to indulge in unreconstructed behavior in some sectors—most notoriously in Earth First! and in wilderness activism generally, where male engagement with the extremities of nature are much heroicized and where city slickers are cast as effeminate types. This is ironic, given that powerful feminist critiques have linked patriarchal privilege to the domination of nature in ways that are often quite persuasive and always provocative.

Q: You sometimes speak of a "postscarcity society" as a worthy goal for ecological movements, although such a concept is anathema to many environmentalists. Could you describe such a society and explain why the concept worries so many critics and policymakers?

A: In the period since Bookchin and others spoke up for this concept in the early 1970s, "postscarcity" has become a dirty word. In fact, ever since the OPEC oil embargo of 1974, it has been almost heretical to think in this utopian mode. People look at you as if you had two heads. For me, it's not such a matter of a postscarcity utopia (although I have no real problem with that), as a natural extension of the fight against the kind of pro-scarcity politics that was launched locally in the mid-1970s in the city fiscal crises and systematically applied to the national and global economy ever since. With recognition of the global ecology crisis in the 1970s, awareness about the "earth's natural limits" brought a new paradigm of scarcity into the world: a concept of scarcity that had hitherto not existed. This could be characterized as "this-time-we-really-mean-it" scarcity and has to be distinguished from the perennial social manufacture of scarcity, through which elites have always sought to monopolize resources, control markets, and suppress the demographic majority.

For more than two decades now, public consciousness has sustained mistaken assumptions about both kinds of scarcity—confusing them, in effect. In that period of time, we have seen the near-triumph of neoliberalism's austerity regimes, distinguished, economically, by deep concessions and cutbacks and, politically, by the rollback of "excessive" rights. As a result, the new concerns about natural scarcity have been paralleled, every step of the way, by a cruel imposition of socially generated scarcity. More often than not, then, the two kinds of scarcity have been confused, either deliberately, in order to reinforce austerity measures against the working poor, or else inadvertently, through a lack of information and education about how natural resources are produced and distributed. Such conditions are ripe for neo-Malthusian politics—operating on the myth that there's simply not enough to go around. Data about the massive upward redistribution of wealth tell us a different story. Analysis of hunger created purely by our crazy global food markets also tells us a different story.

I don't deny that natural scarcity exists, I just don't think it can, and should, ever be divorced from attention to the manipulation of social scarcity for human gain. If we don't make this link then we fail in our thinking about social and natural sustainability and, ultimately, in our utopian vision of a world where the concept of scarcity (and abundance) no longer makes sense.

Q: Even as we speak, I can hear many environmentalists objecting that this position downplays sacrosanct ecological principles concerning Earth's "carrying capacity" and our common destiny on "spaceship Earth." These critics would object that you reify the natural world to the point that it has no more priority than any other tool for the improvement of the human condition. Could you respond in more detail to this criticism?

A: I'm not sure if that would be the form of the criticism. It's not that difficult to distinguish the basic principles of social ecology, which are concerned with the social roots of environmental justice, from the kind of technocratic management of "resources" that views the natural world as a utilitarian setting for human comfort or profit. Anyone who is confusing these two tendencies is simply not listening.

The more interesting form of criticism would be political. There is considerable suspicion among environmentalists that a green politics that leans toward social-justice issues often amounts to the political equivalent of corporate greenwashing, or, more precisely, camouflaging red with green. All of us are guilty, at times, of simply paying lip service to environmental issues—nature is the ultimate people-pleaser after all—but it's also undeniable that the ecology movement has enriched and transformed the radical and Marxist traditions in ways that are no longer possible to ignore. The North-South equity debate among global environmentalists is one of the outcomes of that transformation, and the fact that it is still not really on the radar screen of the American wilderness environmentalist says more about the social blindnesses of the northern nature cult than about any "neglect of nature" on the part of the social ecologist.

Q: No doubt, many would find it odd that the eco-utopian aims that you outline in the conclusion of *Chicago Gangster Theory* have little to do with ideas conventionally associated with environmentalism—preserving endangered species, saving the wilderness, etc.—and more to do with sociopolitical hopes—common prosperity, transnationalism in balance with local self-sufficiency, and hedonism replacing asceticism in green conduct. This last aim must strike some environmentalists as particularly bizarre. What does it say about the fundamental difference between green cultural criticism and traditional environmentalism?

A: I'm not sure what you mean by traditional environmentalism unless social ecology is not considered traditional at this point in time. It's always frustrating when the full spectrum of ecological views is not acknowledged. Media shorthand that refers to "environmentalists" has a very limited referent—usually the views of the big ten mainstream organizations, not grassroots activists, and least of all the host of other actors—ecofeminists, eco-urbanists, bioregionalists, social ecologists, socialist ecologists, and indeed the whole movement in the South, often quite remote from the wilderness-obsessed priorities of northern environmentalists.

More than any other social movement, I think, environmentalism harbors a diversity of positions that are not easy to reconcile and many of which are publicly suppressed. (Isn't this why you are taking on the urban issues in this book?) That's not unhealthy, although it makes it easier to divide activism. Whatever it is, however, environmentalism is not, and cannot afford to be, single-issue politics.

Q: Actually, this leads to my next question. Given the variety of forms environmentalism can take, what effect has the rather fundamental split between those forms associated with deep ecology and those springing from social ecology had on green criticism? Like many other contributors to this volume, your own work seems to be more influenced by the social ecological camp. What are the connections between your work and that of others who have been interested in social ecology, like Murray Bookchin, Alexander Wilson, or David Pepper?

A: Alex was a friend, a beautiful person who managed to combine all of his exemplary enthusiasms with a quiet zeal that was adorable. Although it's not evident in his book *The Culture of Nature,* he always saw the links between his ecological work and his work on gay politics in Toronto. The "body politic" was an integral part of attention to ecological matters. Interestingly enough, the only time I have met Bookchin—whose ideas have had an enormous influence on all of us—was at a conference in Vermont where we had a little dispute about the role of masculinity in the ecology movement. Basically from an Old Left formation, he just doesn't see such matters as all that important. Maybe they're not. And I'm not suggesting that we always approach major thinkers from the standpoint of what they neglect or exclude from their systems of thought. But everyone has their conceptual limits, and modernizing and renewing our politics is about facing up to them. As Keynes used to say, we learn new facts and we change our mind.

Q: Much of your work has to do with technoculture, yet some would argue that there is an irreconcilable opposition between a cybernetic and ecocritical worldview. How would you respond to this claim?

A: I think this illustrates the problem with seeing ecology as a single-issue politics rather than as a comprehensive worldview in federation with others. The Greens in Germany have had to grapple with this problem at the most advanced level—within a parliamentary system—and often in coalition with more traditional left groupings. There's every good reason why we should be thinking about sustainability in all areas of social life, including the technological. That means attending to everything from the nature of material production—the environmental costs of machine manufacture—to the social ecology of a high-speed information society. Two examples might suffice. According to a study by the Wuppertal Institute, the fabrication of each PC requires the consumption of from 15 to 19 tons of energy and materials. The high-grade minerals used for PC components can only be obtained through major mining operations and energy-intensive transformation processes. By contrast, an average automobile requires about 25 tons—not much difference, in other words. All of this runs contrary to the mythology of an information age that is supposed to have left behind the damaging ecological costs of industrial manufacturing. Moreover, the rate of worker illness, including toxic poisoning, in the postindustrial workplace is higher than in industrial sites.

As for social ecology, we need to be thinking inventively about how the speed of information technology governs the division of labor—how, for example, most of the readers of this book want their computers and software to go faster and yet most people who work with computers on the job want them to go slower. Now there's a thought to end with.

2

URBAN NATURE WRITING

3

LONDON HERE AND NOW
Walking, Streets, and Urban Environments in English Poetry from Donne to Gay
Gary Roberts

Urban poetry in English is abundant, but it has received surprisingly little critical attention. The few comprehensive studies of it do not make their best points about its early history, if that history is mentioned at all. Literary critics have tended to begin the story of urban poetry in the eighteenth century, during the formation of what Jürgen Habermas has taught us to call the "public sphere." It was then, presumably, that capitalist mass culture started to shape the consciousness and behavior of urban dwellers, especially of middle-class urbanites, in ways that still affect us today. Although reference to the eighteenth century is much more than an academic convenience, we should acknowledge that it is a relatively late focus, in part resulting from our common notion of urban literature as defined principally by novels. The crowded and sooty world of Charles Dickens, for example, skews our generic and historical frames of reference toward a later "bourgeois" mode of literary representation developed in English approximately 150 years after the beginning of London's urban literature and almost a century after its first urban poetry.

The critical neglect of urban poetry before the eighteenth century is also a consequence of our historical interest in finding sources for the stylistic innovations and moral judgments that matter most to twentieth-century urban poets. We have reasonably assumed that the rhetorics, tropes, and dictions that were important for these poets were derived from poetry that represented "modern" types of social contradiction and psychological experience.[1] Obligatory references are made to Blake and Baudelaire, Wordsworth and Whitman.[2] Working from such precedents, T. S. Eliot, William Carlos Williams, and W. H. Auden defined the modernist city, which in turn was revisited and revised by postmoderns such as Frank O'Hara and Allen Ginsberg. But these poets, our contemporaries, do not necessarily provide the best point of departure for reading the first fully urban poets in English, such as John Donne or Ben Jonson—poets who wrote at a formative moment in the early history of urban literature in English.

These native Londoners were among the first poets to grapple with the problems of how to write poems about their hometown as an urban place. Their responses to preindustrial London, however, do not contain the kinds of information about city life that we typically expect from urban poets. Consider, for example, Donne's epigram on the "Fall of a Wall":

Under an undermined, and shot-bruised wall
A too-bold captain perished by the fall,
Whose brave misfortune, happiest men envied,
That had a town for tomb, his bones to hide.
(149)

Absent from this short poem is the intensely subjective and problematic experience of individuality (or its loss) defined in Georg Simmel's classic essay on "The Metropolis and Mental Life" (324–39) and represented in canonical modernist urban poems such as "The Waste Land." The deceased "captain" here is singled out, but he is not individualized by the possession of a recognizably urban psychology; nor is the epigrammatist himself meant to be read as an enunciative consciousness imbued with a particular sense of self.

We also do not find a familiar urban space in Donne's epigram. A wall has been weakened by the shot of a cannon used against it in an unspecified military conflict. The sixteenth-century Londoner would have recalled more readily than his twentieth-century counterpart that the technology of cannons was developed to overcome walled cities. However, because we no longer live within walled cities, we have lost the special understanding of inside/outside created by the material boundary of the epigram's wall. Whatever the symbolic significance of different kinds of boundaries (such as a highway) to our own urban experience, our city limits themselves do not physically embody the ritual definition of difference so important to medieval and Renaissance towns. Thus, both the space of this environment and the wit of this poem are specific to a time and place that are not immediately accessible to us. The epigram's joke relies on the felicitous rhyme of "wall" and "fall" and on the alliteration between "town" and "tomb," so that these arbitrary correspondences among graphemes carry out conceptual and figurative relationships assumed by the city's inhabitants. The very alacrity of the conflation of metaphor and metonymy in "town for tomb" underscores how much the poem's wordplay takes for granted. That the important matter of the city wall is being treated comically and offhandedly told Donne's audience something about their relationship to older notions of local environment, which were then coming under fire not just by warfare but also by the urbanization process itself. These specific changes, of course, are no longer present to us as innovations and thus are unlikely to seem a compelling part of a twentieth-century history of urban poetry, because we take for granted different things about the relationships of space to walls and walls to cities.

A less obvious reason for the paucity of adequate criticism about the origins of urban poetics is found in some of the first critical works on urban poetry. Raymond Williams's influential book *The Country and the City* made an auspicious start in defining a transhistorical English tradition of urban poetry by relating literary production to political economy, social transformation, and technological change. His way of reading "the city" with *and* against "the country" remains important because it posits their economic and ideological interdependence: "a city eats what its country neighbours have grown" (50). This relationship, however, is not equally beneficial because city dwellers have historical ties to the secular structures of state power and its nonagrarian forms of work; city dwellers provide services in the form of "political authority, law and trade, to those who are in charge of rural exploitation, with whom [they are] organically linked in a mutual necessity of profit and power" (51). In reading poetry for evidence of ideological concealment or revelation, Williams discovers an ecology of literary representation in which pastoral and urban genres respond not only to each other, but also to those social changes whose effects never remain isolated either to the country or to the city alone.

Despite the range of his argument, Williams overlooks some important poems and crucial features of urban poetics. It should be noted that his work has a specific goal: to tell the political truth about the relationship between the country and the city in England. Given the necessary discussion of prose as well as poetry, Williams cannot be expected to define the full scope of urban poetics. Nonetheless, it is unfortunate that he does not mention some of the greatest English poems of the city—Jonathan Swift's "A Description of the Morning" (1709) and "A Description of a City Shower" (1710), John Gay's "Trivia: or the Art of Walking the Streets of London" (1720), and Alexander Pope's "The Dunciad" (first version 1728)—especially because these early-eighteenth-century texts rendered in verse an unprecedented and unsurpassed amount of information about London's environment, its sensory reality, and the habits and jargons of its residents. Although probably neither accidental nor polemical, Williams's omissions are telling. Because he does not discuss earlier poetic representations of urban London, he cannot account for what makes the poems of Swift, Gay, and Pope possible, let alone exceptional. We therefore can only assume that, for Williams's purposes, these important poems are *too* urban—that is, insufficiently in-volved in the fate of the countryside despite the fact that they borrow extensively from earlier pastoral poetics. Although Williams is well aware of the history and literature of the sixteenth and seventeenth centuries, his narrative is focused on the mid-eighteenth century and its aftermath. Dur-ing this period, the centuries-long legal, political, and economic struggles for control of the English landscape intensified to the point that they perma-nently altered its human geography and displaced thousands of rural inhabi-tants, most of whom flocked to London and thereby helped to turn it into the world's largest city.

This very specific history of urban poetry has set precedents that have misled subsequent critics. Williams plausibly asserts the historical impor-tance of the pastoral mode of description, which focuses on human labor and environmental details, while he usefully emphasizes the topographical rhetoric of urban representation. For example, the first poem that Williams refers to (Wordsworth's "Sonnet Composed upon Westminster Bridge, September 3, 1802") employs a visual, panoptic perspective gained by phys-ical distance from the city. Williams is also justified in this focus because there is a poetic tradition that observes both the country and the city, or that invokes the pastoral to talk about the urban; his other examples include

Charles Jenner's "Town Eclogues," James Thomson's "Seasons," and Book 7 of Wordsworth's "Prelude." Defining urban poetry according to hybrid poems such as these is a good idea, but it is limited to the extent that it gives tacit priority to visual rhetorics of description over other kinds of rhetoric and thereby distracts us from poetic modes of representation that are specifically urban instead of nostalgically or ironically pastoral.

Following Williams's lead, John Johnston's *The Poet and the City* grounds the poetic city in the topographical tradition of the pastoral. His canon of English urban poetry is restricted to those poems that have "viewed the city primarily as a physical place" (xvii). This principle of selection sounds promising because it is predicated on the importance to urban poetics of the loco-descriptive techniques of Virgil's *Georgics*. However, the focus on the poet's ability to represent, from the perspective of the country, "the actualization of the city in terms of its relationship to the physical and moral totality of which it is necessarily a part," leads Johnston to exclude the satirist's depiction of the city "from within." The urban satirist, although "powerfully engaged with [his] subject," is omitted from Johnston's literary history because satire is "limited in motivations and perspectives" and is "unable to create a vision of the city apart from the range of [its] imperfections" (15). That the satirical mode does not represent metropolitan London in its fullest environmental context is not a sufficient reason for leaving it out of a history of English urban poetry and thereby excluding all specifically urban poems written before the eighteenth century. Like Williams before him, Johnston has a specific interest in urban poetry, from which he adeptly derives an important, although partial, tradition of representation; and like his predecessor, Johnston consequently neglects the early history of urban poetics. Both critics, for example, omit Donne entirely and restrict Jonson's contribution to his country-house poem "To Penshurst." Similarly, neither have anything to say about "The Dunciad," and, astonishingly, Pope is represented by Johnston only with "Windsor-Forest."

The merits and limitations of Johnston's critical take on early urban poetics can be seen in his discussion of Swift's mock-georgic "A Description of the Morning." Because this poem relies on the fiction of an overlooking perspective, it can be read as an extension of the seventeenth-century tradition of topographical poetry. As Johnston shows (42), an important type of rural or, more accurately, cultivated description—exemplified in poems such as Jonson's "To Penshurst" (1616), John Drayton's "Poly-Olbion" (1622), and John Denham's "Cooper's Hill" (1642)—finds its urban "inversion" in Swift's visual tours of London. In "A Description of the Morning," the vantage of Swift's describer is ostensibly that of an elevated (literally and poetically) viewer who has or is looking for moral and intellectual control of his environment:

> Now hardly here and there a hackney coach
> Appearing, showed the ruddy morn's approach.
> Now Betty from her master's bed has flown,
> And softly stole to discompose her own.
> The slipshod prentice from his master's door
> Had pared the dirt, and sprinkled round the floor.
> Now Moll had whirled her mop with dexterous airs,
> Prepared to scrub the entry and the stairs.
> The youth with broomy stumps began to trace
> The kennel-edge, where wheels had worn the place.
> The smallcoal man was heard with cadence deep;
> Till drowned in shriller notes of chimney-sweep.
> Duns at his Lordship's gate began to meet;
> And Brickdust Moll had screamed through half a street.
> The turnkey now his flock returning sees,
> Duly let out a-nights to steal for fees.
> The watchful bailiffs take their silent stands;
> And schoolboys lag with satchels in their hands.
> *(107–8)*

Johnston appropriately emphasizes that the poem handles its "tawdry details" with "something like a tolerant Virgilian sense of the whole" (43). Although Johnston does not describe how this "whole" is created, we can see that it depends on a metonymic series in which the named and anonymous inhabitants of the poem represent the city, which itself is not named but represented as "Morning."

It is worthwhile to examine more closely how metonymy works in Swift's poem because this trope is important to urban poetics in general. A careful analysis of metonymy's mechanism is therefore warranted whenever a critic makes generalizations about an urban poet's predilections for certain rhetorical patterns and goals. Johnston claims that Swift here "has unlocked a moment in the street life of London—a typical moment which encompasses the morning 'business' of people high and low, good and bad" (43). This "moment" is available for description because the poet exercises control over his vision of the urban environment with a rhetoric based on "point of view, perspective, distance, proximity, selection, focus" (45). The visual terms in this list reveal the representational priorities of Johnston's study. I would suggest that they also indicate how he misreads "Morning" when he interprets it as "a" moment, and in turn, why Johnston's reading of Swift's "description" as an ironic version of georgic "perspectives" begs the related questions of why the poet chooses morning instead of any other time of day and how the reader knows where the poem is supposed to be taking place.

The pleasure and success of Swift's realism is a function of the way in which the textual unfolding of the description reinforces its rhetorical tactics. The conceit of the poem's fragmentary pseudoimprovisation is to use a list to organize the contents in such a way that our motion through/past the items in the text performs the temporal onset of its titular subject. As we read down the lines, an empty city fills up before our eyes. The key to the poem is its anaphorical deployment of the temporal adverb "now": It marks the beginning of the world and initiates the poem's motion toward its fulfillment. As the first word, indeed the first syllable, "now" establishes an origin point before which the morning and the poem do not exist; the reader by implication exists in some other solitary realm. The beginning of our reading of the poem, therefore, is simultaneously coincident with the beginning of the poem and of the day. The three subsequent uses of "now" throughout the poem mark successive moments, not, as Johnston suggests, the same moment: Every event in the description does not happen at the same time, each "now" is not the same "now." The subtle changing of verb tenses reinforces the temporal progression: "has flown," "had pared," "had whirled" (lines 3–7); "began to trace," "was heard . . . till drowned," "began to meet" (9–13); "sees," "take," "lag" (15–18). The description is therefore a diachronic recapitulation of the process of creating the metonym that replaces "morning" for London, not a synchronic spatialization of that metonym. Unlike the totalizing glimpse of sublime morning clarity that Wordsworth represents in his sonnet "Composed upon Westminster

Bridge," Swift's description privileges motion over stasis, and the working population coheres gradually, not instantaneously, from individual activities into social significance.

This is not to say that a visual, topographic rhetoric is not a crucial feature of early urban poetics. However, what is missing from criticism such as Johnston's, despite its insights, is a way of reading the textual spaces of the poetic city not just as they are surveyed, but also, and more importantly, as they are produced and used as part of what David Harvey has called the "built environment" (36). The visibility of Swift's urban dwellers is, after all, a function of their *doing* something within and to the city and not a function of their discrete positions. In fact, what several of them are doing is tracing out the spaces of the built environment to prepare them for use, that is, for the production and consumption of urban goods and services. For these Londoners, the setting of their lives is not a given in the way that the Thames River is, but it is something that they themselves create in part out of their mundane activities of mopping, sweeping, and making deliveries. These preparations open up, set in motion, make legible the urban world, and without such maintenance the built environment degrades into invisibility. Critics of urban poetry need to consider ways of defining environmental space other than by reference to landscape if they are to avoid unwittingly hypostatizing notions of place in terms of natural fact (and/or wish) rather than analyzing them in terms of social process. Such critical analysis is especially relevant to urban poetics because the indigenous "perspective" on the city is often rendered from a mobile, ground-level vantage point that is contained within variably useable social spaces defined by structural and conceptual limits, such as walls, streets, and walking people.

Henri Lefebvre's immensely suggestive work on urbanism argues for a concept of space as a contingent totality made, excreted, projected by collective human endeavors. This argument resists the Western and capitalist tendencies to think of space as an already present emptiness filled by things and data, as a paradoxically negative object to be described best by an abstract coordinate system, or as a transparency laid out over the ground of reality. Instead, Lefebvre builds process and motion into his theoretical description of urban space by designating it as "social space." "(Social) space is not a thing among other things, nor a product among other products: rather it subsumes things produced, and encompasses their interrelationships in their coexistence and simultaneity—their (relative) order and/or (relative) disorder. It is the outcome of a sequence and set of operations, and thus cannot be reduced to the rank of a simple object. . . . Itself the outcome of past actions, social space is what permits fresh actions to occur, while suggesting others and prohibiting yet others" (73). The move from seeing space as a container or remainder to understanding it as the continual result of actions (including linguistic actions) is, I would suggest, crucial for critics interested in the relationship of literature to environments. This reorientation has the advantage of encouraging us to think simultaneously about how poems and cities work and are related. The concept of social space also makes available for critical study a greater number of situations, arrangements, and places because it insists that we read the spatial aspect of urban environments not as the neutral absence of structure, but as itself a structure in motion, a structure that in fact makes possible the motion of other dynamic systems.

Lefebvre provides three dialectically related concepts with which to "see" social space as procedural environment instead of as static objectivity: (1) *spatial practice,* which "propounds and presupposes" social space and which "embodies a close association, within perceived space, between daily reality (daily routine) and urban reality (the routes and networks which link up the places set aside for work, 'private' life and leisure)"; (2) *representations of space,* which are more or less official, "dominating" constructions and definitions of space, such as maps, produced by those who "identify what is lived and what is perceived with what is conceived"; and (3) *representational spaces,* which are "directly *lived* through associated images and symbols" and are "the space of 'inhabitants' and 'users' " as well as those unofficial "dominated" spaces that "the imagination seeks to change and appropriate" (38–39). These abstract terms, which designate both a city's physical infrastructure and its cultural self-knowledge, can be adapted for literary criticism because they are predicated on the assumption that the means of spatial production use and are mediated by "representations," that is, by signs and codes including language. Because linguistic representations, in turn, can be understood in terms of the structuralist distinction of *langue/parole* (competence/performance), literary critics should be able to read individual examples of urban literature according to how they rehearse implicit knowledge of the production of urban space.

If we read Swift's "A Description of the Morning" in these terms, the poem reveals other aspects of its encompassing metonym. The "spatial practices" of mopping, scrubbing, sweeping, screaming, and watching establish a "representation of urban space" metonymically signified by "a hackney coach," "the master's door," "the entry and the stairs," "the kennel-edge," "his Lordship's gate," "a street," and the jail. These bits of furniture and architecture make visible the implicit London of commerce and regulation that dominates the new day. The dominated "representational spaces," however, have been virtually obliterated; their only true remnants are the two beds at the start of the poem, which signify the private, illicit activities that had occurred during the night that has just ended. Therefore, the overarching "morning" may be read as a conception of totalized social space displaced onto temporalized nature. This displacement, however, reinforces the reader's everyday knowledge of procedural social space, not just, as Johnston might have it, a literary knowledge of irony and pastoral poetics.

The difference between a Lefebvrian reading of an urban poem and one that leaves a poem's spatial knowledge untheorized can be more clearly understood if we compare Swift's description of morning to one of Gay's versions in "Trivia: or the Art of Walking the Streets of London." In his prefatory remarks to "Trivia," Gay acknowledges that he owed "several hints . . . to Dr. Swift," thereby crediting his friend with the concept of a mock-georgic treatment of London life (134). Even more so than Swift, Gay does not settle for visual/topographical description, but also elaborates the didactic potential of the georgic approach. Thus, the context for the sights-and-sounds rhetoric in the following self-contained section on "Morning" is a full-blown instruction manual for urban walking and, by implication, for urban living:

> For Ease and for Dispatch, the Morning's best:
> No Tides of Passengers the Street molest.
> You'll see a draggled Damsel, here and there,
> From *Billingsgate* her fishy Traffick bear;
> On Doors the sallow Milk-maid chalks her Gains;
> Ah! how unlike the Milk-maid of the Plains!
> Before proud Gates attending Asses bray,
> Or arrogate with solemn Pace the Way;

These grave Physicians with their milky Chear,
The Love-sick Maid, and dwindling Beau repair;
Here Rows of Drummers stand in martial File,
And with their Vellom-Thunder shake the Pile,
To greet the new-made Bride. Are sounds like these,
The proper Prelude to a State of Peace?
Now Industry awakes her busy Sons,
Full charg'd with News the breathless Hawker runs:
Shops open, Coaches roll, Carts shake the Ground,
And all the Streets with passing Cries resound.

(143–44)

Where Swift uses "now" four times, Gay uses it once. While Swift seems to merely describe, Gay recommends, explains, compares, digresses, questions, and observes. Thus the anaphorical series of metonyms in the former poet's description is rhetorically thwarted here, on the level of the single-verse paragraph; the logic of London's contents in the entire poem is similarly discursive. However, "Trivia" is explicitly framed, as its subtitle suggests and as is alluded to throughout the poem, by a totalizing representation of space called "the Streets of London." In this section, for example, London is metonymically signaled by a variety of places: "the Street," "here and there," "proud Gates," "the Way," "the Ground," and "all the Streets." These are places where ideals of one spatial order, "Ease" and "Dispatch," give way to the commands of other ideals: "Now Industry awakes her busy Sons." The reference to "Industry," a traditional personification of London's mercantile power often featured in the famous Lord Mayor's pageants of the previous century, awakens the poem out of its digression into the representational space of the newlyweds' home ("the Pile"). Swift's faint allusion to a personification of dawn ("ruddy morn's approach") is comic in the context of his couplet's syntax, but as Aurora she is merely a marker of classical genre and is left behind as the poem moves into its other details. Gay, however, replaces Aurora with Industry, who does not approach from anywhere, but rather manifests herself seemingly spontaneously as an inhabiting maternal metonym for the social space of commerce.

When we recall that the ostensible audience for the poem is a visitor from the country, we realize that the ironic inversion of a passage such as this is not so much an effect of treating an urban scene in a classically pastoral mode, but of inviting the poem's actual audience, the native Londoner, to pretend that he or she is unfamiliar with the most familiar daily scenes. The imagined immigrant reader presumably would be without an established residence, that is, without a representational space from which to read the city. Thus, the urban resident who has purchased "Trivia: or the Art of Walking the Streets of London" has also purchased a text that represents him or her as homeless to reintroduce the urban resident to spaces and environments that are known and yet are not known. This strange self-deception augments the dominating representation of space because it displaces the urban reader's individual spatial position into a fluctuating system of signs gathered together into the "nowhere" of London. Regardless of the authenticity or quantity of the metonyms and synecdoches adduced, the reader cannot stand still among them to lay claim to a nonurban perspective.

The critic of urban poems who attempts to read their depictions of urban environments will need to be aware of the complicated ways in which the practices of procedural social space are represented and themselves represent. Lefebvre's terms are useful in this respect, but they say nothing about how Londoners learned to write *urban* poetry as opposed to poetry about place. Lawrence Manley's recent study *Literature and Culture in Early Modern London* synthesizes an impressive amount of criticism, history, and political economy to define "fictions and techniques of settlement" developed from the early sixteenth to the late seventeenth centuries; during this time London experienced prodigious growth at a uniquely accelerated rate. Manley discusses in great detail the literary responses to this growth as one kind of "behavioral urbanization," in which "evolving moral technologies . . . helped to organize and discipline populations for cohabitation and cooperation in settlements of massive scale" (14). These moral technologies included a wide range of poetry about London life, not all of which was also necessarily "urban" in our sense of the term. According to Manley, earlier native traditions of "complaint" relied on feudal and Christian tropes of inversion that in their most sophisticated constructions formed catalogues of fools and vices, or carnivalesque allegories of a collective plight; this mode of representation was dominant at least until the mid-sixteenth century (77–91).

Although such poems were "about" London, they cannot be considered specifically "urban" because London was not yet thought of as an "urban" place. In 1500, London was still only a large medieval town of about 35,000 people, rather than anything we might with precision call a city. Its growth was slow and its cultural position relative to continental cities was marginal. Furthermore, the absence of urban poetry at this time was not just a function of London's relatively small size. As Manley reports, the concept of an "urban" city was unavailable to English poets until after the beginning of the sixteenth century. Even then, the word itself was not immediately naturalized and remained rare until the nineteenth century. For Londoners in their quickly growing city, "urban" was not an inevitable description of their new environmental situation, but instead a totalizing abstraction or, in Lefebvre's terms, a "representation of space" imported by the humanist movement.

In 1516, the *Utopia* of "Thomas More, Citizen and Undersheriff of London," first presented to an English audience some of the ideas—such as ordered space and rational government—with which "citizens" could apprehend, describe, and criticize an urban city as opposed to a feudal or religious city. This imagined urban city was intentionally constructed by its inhabitants in such a way as to facilitate and at the same time to symbolize their urban lives. What is important about this city for our purposes is that its urban structure required new environmental concepts, that is, new representations of space: "While More's *Utopia* surveys a host of problems besetting the contemporary world, it imagines their solution within a conceptual framework whose material counterpart is a perfectly ordered urbanistic space" (Manley 30). The radical abstractness of More's concept can be seen in his various erasures of local difference. As his spokesman, Raphael Hythloday, explains of the Utopians' world: "If you know one of their cities you know them all, for they're exactly alike, except where geography itself makes a difference" (115). Physical similarity, in turn, manifests itself in the fantastical deliberateness of the Utopians' architecture: "The streets are conveniently laid out both for use by vehicles and for protection from the wind. Their buildings are by no means shabby. Long unbroken rows of houses face each other down the whole block. The housefronts are separated by a street twenty feet wide (119)."[3] Such a user-friendly environment, located in the capital city (i.e., London's Utopian equivalent) presents a planned space that is reproducible in any location without regard for historical or natural vicissitudes. Its ideological function is to imply, but leave unstated, several things: a social need for such a layout, a social structure organized to build it, and social technologies available to accomplish its realization. Over the next one hundred years, Londoners witnessed and participated in the establishment of a centralized state apparatus that, if it could not deliver the fabricated space of More's Utopia, did nevertheless produce a variety of new ideological and physical environments. Early urban representation was not just a matter of topographical description, but also of a comparison between local ways of doing things "on the ground level," as it were, and ideal concepts of social spaces. Pastoralism, as defined by Williams and Johnston, also makes this kind of comparison, but it comes later and does not necessarily account for the native Londoner's experience of the urbanization process.

Late-sixteenth-century urban poetics can be read as a response to the need for such accountability because, according to Manley, "early modern England was an urbanizing society lacking indigenous traditions of urbanism" (15). To literary urbanites, traditional and popular verse forms, such as street ballads, as well as their means of creation and distribution could only signify the older feudal mode of complaint and thus the pre-urban spatiality of London, which was still extant but in the process of transformation.[4] If London poets wanted to claim an interest in the project of defining the representational and critical possibilities of their city's urban literature, then they would need specifically urban modes of contextualizing social space, modes that by their form signified an unmistakable contemporaneity and that through their ethos articulated an enunciative position independent from earlier discursive hierarchies.

Enter the satire, the epigram, and the classical poetics of the city as an urban capital, known to the sixteenth century primarily from the work of Horace, Juvenal, Catullus, and Martial. These cosmopolitan Roman poets gave Londoners several attitudes and schemas with which to compose their own urban poetry in the context of the slowly emerging confidence in the authority of vernacular, secular, and noncourtly literature. Renaissance imitation of classical forms is a complicated story that I will not retell here. However, it is worth recalling that the sixteenth-century project of modernizing English according to ancient examples was predicated on the ability of writers and readers alike to make continual conceptual comparisons between the old and the new. As Jonson says "To [His] Mere English

Censurer": "To thee, my way in epigrams seems new, / When both it is the old way, and the true" (40). Jonson's joke is that his "way" is both old and new because he approximates Martial's cagey urban style (ancient/old) and at the same time emphasizes his own contemporaneity through his witty use of rhyme (modern/new).

This type of comparison functions as the literary corollary to the structural comparisons that London's urbanization required of its inhabitants, whether poets or not. Such comparisons brought together the old and new spaces of the city in an attempt to comprehend how they overlap and interfere with each other, a technique on view in Jonson's epigram on "The New Cry," which, along with his many other urban poems, depicts London's environment as a network of social exchange upon which the urbanization process depends. In the opening of "The New Cry," for example, Jonson burlesques the "new" phenomenon of "statesmen" by appropriating the exemplary London folk tradition of "crying" wares through the streets: "Ere cherries ripe, and strawberries be gone, / Unto the cries of London I'll add one; / Ripe statesmen ripe: they grow in every street." The new capitalist social structure requires and trades upon these men—users of urban space who, by their practice of walking through "every street," signify the contradiction between official and unofficial assumptions about the purpose of London's social spaces. Jonson's sense of urban space cannot be divorced from the activities of buying and selling. However, as Manley and Lefebvre's claims suggest, it is important for the critical consumer of Jonson's poems not to reduce the production of space to economic activity alone because the needs of settlement and dwelling more profoundly create the space of the urban environment. On the other hand, focusing on the most obvious procedures of habitation, the basic *techné* of everyday life such as eating or sleeping, does not reveal much of interest in the early history of urban poetry. Not until the eighteenth century, when Gay's "Trivia" borrows Virgil's didactic method of describing how things work, do we find urban poetry with a special interest in urban living.

With "Trivia," we move to a later moment in the tradition of urban poetry and risk skipping over the poems that have led up to it. However, this same poem gives us an important clue to how to approach the urban poetry of Donne, Jonson, and their successors. Gay's interest in "walking" does not come to him *ex nihilo,* but is the culmination of a transhistorical poetic interest in representing this basic type of what Lefebvre has named "spatial practice." Walking is a fundamental social action for urban dwellers, so fundamental that such an obvious statement does not at first seem to merit mention. But although it may be taken for granted, walking, like other such human activities, has its own history and its cultural meanings change in response to other historical transformations.[5] The walking poem allows the city dweller to represent the city by simultaneously engaging mind and body and their relationships to the structures of the environment. In this way, the poetics of walking reveal, as the philosopher Maurice Merleau-Ponty explains, a phenomenology of experience by which historical differences and specificities may be measured: "By considering the body in movement, we can better see how it inhabits space (and, moreover, time) because movement is not limited to submitting passively to space and time, it actively subsumes them, it takes them up in their basic significance" (102). Poetry representing motion requires the poet to articulate his own changing spatial positions and thus to recapitulate, with varying degrees of awareness and confidence, the meaning of his activity in the context of its location.

We can designate this kind of representation as "kinesthetic" to distinguish it from both the earlier use of allegorical narrative and the later use of pastoral topographic observation. Defining a tradition of urban poetry in this way has the advantage of enabling us to gather together poems from radically different eras, such as Horace's Ninth Satire, Book I (historically, a favorite of English translators), which opens with its speaker being accosted during a stroll, and contemporary poems by Frank O'Hara such as "A Step Away from Them," which begins "It's my lunch hour, so I go / for a walk among the hum-colored / cabs" (110). It is important to remember that the walking poem is not exclusively urban—the wilderness walk is also a major transhistorical poetic subject.[6] However, the difference between them is more subtle than the difference between being alone in nature and being surrounded by people and their culture. Unlike kinesthetic nature poems, kinesthetic urban poems in English, at least since the sixteenth century, allude to mental maps of the city that are derived from being a resident on foot with the ability to perform the secular cognition of space and time in the service of urbanization. This mapping is not a mere reflection of an unproblematic and static arrangement of physical space; it is an active linguistic construction of that space every time that it is performed. As

Lefebvre's theory of space suggests, we should think of poetic walking as a process that, instead of taking place *inside* an inevitably preexisting urban space, produces urban space itself.

In *The Practice of Everyday Life,* Michel de Certeau persuasively argues that there is a more than analogical relationship between walking in a city and performing speech acts. He thereby opens up the possibility that close readings of walking poems can display their specifically urban and kinesthetic rhetoric of space. Because urban footsteps have a continually changing "qualitative character" that is defined in relation to the different rules of changing places and positions, urban walking can be usefully defined in a "space of enunciation" as a set of variously improvised or rehearsed "pedestrian speech acts" (de Certeau 97–98). In turn, these moves inscribe a new and spontaneously meaningful text over the official topographic text of the urban system. For example, if we look again at Swift's "A Description of Morning," we see that the sleepy schoolboys, as they "lag" in the last line, quietly announce their resistance to the authority of the bailiff's surveillance in the penultimate line. With de Certeau's claims in mind, we should not find it difficult to connect the rhetoric of walking to the use of poetic figures such as metonymy, nor should we be surprised to find that urban poets tend to represent walking when they want to represent an urban environment.

The rhetoric of poetic walking can be divided into three main types of tactical moves for organizing a poem's performance: (1) the use of spatial and temporal adverbs such as "here" and "now," which situate the urban speaker in a narrative that is parallel to his walking; (2) the use of a rich idiomatic vocabulary for the wide range of walking styles; and (3) the use of proper names for local places, especially street names, which situate the speaker in or in relation to socially significant locations. These locations imply the position of the London reader at the time of reading as well, if only because the reader is *not* wherever the poem's speaker is, but is nonetheless involved in the production of urban space. For example, when Jonson concludes his epigram "To [his] Bookseller" with the mock advice that his unsold poems be sent to "Bucklersbury" Street (so that they might be used as packing paper for that area's grocers and apothecaries), he invokes a provisional map of the city in which orientation and criticism are possible. The joke here depends on the contrast between the bookseller's indiscriminate use of social space to advertise books (by walking their title pages through the streets or attaching them to the city walls) and the poet's witty allusion to a specific place. To understand the joke, Jonson's reader needs to know that London's spaces are produced and thus how he or she is implicated in that production process. When used in the context of a poetics that is self-consciously urbanizing itself, deictic adverbs, idiomatic verbs, and street names become primary devices for representing a practical and spatially productive knowledge of the city. These tactical linguistic moves are part of a complex metonymical system standing in place of a London that is in constant motion.

Donne's first satire borrows the kinesthetic satirical method of Horace's Ninth Satire, Book I. The premise of Donne's poem is that a silent companion has invited the wary speaker for a walk in the city; after trying his "conscience" and the companion's faithfulness, the satirist capitulates. The opening dramatizes its high-toned speaker insisting on the security of his own dwelling compared to the moral risk of cruising the streets. Tellingly, he prefers the conceptual spaces of texts to the social spaces of the city:

Away thou fondling motley humourist,
Leave me, and in this standing wooden chest,
Consorted with these few books, let me lie
In prison, and here be coffined, when I die;
Here are God's conduits, grave divines; and here
Nature's secretary, the Philosopher;
And jolly statesmen, which teach how to tie
The sinews of a city's mystic body;
Here gathering chroniclers, and by them stand
Giddy fantastic poets of each land.
Shall I leave all this constant company,
And follow headlong, wild uncertain thee?
(155)

Donne's emphatic use of "here" discriminates from an implied "there" that the reader must fill in as the poem progresses. Throughout the poem, the deictic adverbs "here" and "now" situate a supposedly stable personal enunciative position in a moving and "wild uncertain" space. On their walk, speaker and friend encounter numerous other walkers, who the former eschews but who the latter moves toward as often as he can. These distractions are the result of the aggressive, homosocial politicking engaged in by the new class of upwardly mobile urbanites who are practicing various arts of urban self-fashioning. The difference between them and the speaker is spatialized as the difference between here and there, such that the narrative's textual movement forward corroborates the moral steadfastness of the speaker and the moral wandering of his companion. Equally notable here is the impressive catalogue of verbs describing the styles, or what the anthropologist Marcel Mauss would call the "body-techniques" (114), of city walking: "leave," "go," "follow headlong," "come in the way," "creeps," "skip forth," "stoops," "move," "leaps," "dance," "drooped," "overtakes," "go on the way," "flings from me," "came to me hanging the head." This set of expressive idioms reveals how impossible it is to reduce urban walking to mere ambulation because the movement through physical space requires the performance of legible gestures that use and create social spaces.

The kinesthetic rhetoric of this satire moves the reader out of the private, stationary space of the individual into a relentlessly social representation of space and back again. In Donne's London, the relationship of experience to environment is mediated by performative codes—gestures, manners, and clothing—that shape the human body itself into a walking transcription of the urban text. The poet frames this spatial practice within a representational space, his speaker's bedroom, which is called at the beginning of the poem "this standing wooden chest" as well as a "prison" and a coffin; at the end of the poem, the bedroom is reduced to a "bed" (the last word of the poem) to which the speaker's beaten and debauched companion has returned and in which he "must keep" himself "constantly a while." The caveat in the last line should not be missed: Presumably, at some time a little "while" later, after the bruises have healed and the poem has concluded, the speaker and the companion must venture once more to walk outside, to negotiate again the representation of the city from which they had retreated.

Donne's early, innovative satire launches a critical representation of urban London with the active reading of its mobile sign systems. Although the poem does not contain street names, it should be read, along with Jonson's epigrams, as a part of the historical development of the kinesthetic rhetoric of urban poetry. Its example was not lost on the following generation of poets, for example, Henry Vaughan's 1646 poem "Rhapsody. Occasionally written upon a meeting with some of his friends at the Globe

Tavern in a chamber painted overhead with a cloudy sky and some few dispersed stars, and on the sides with landscapes, hills, shepherds, and sheep" uses a similar kinesthetic rhetoric. At the center of this convivial exhortation to fellow Royalist drinkers is a brief reverie imagining night scenes that the poem's speaker might encounter in "every street" and "each narrow lane" if he were to leave the tavern and walk around London. Vaughan's use of specific street names frames the walk with a mental map of urban space, a map in which locations are defined by activities and motions assumed to occur there.

It is from poems such as Donne's first satire, Jonson's epigrams, and Vaughan's "Rhapsody," that Swift, Gay, and Pope learned to build their grand urban creations. However, as long as all of this urban poetry is approached with a critical eye focused only on visual imagery, its kinesthetic rhetoric will remain unnoticed and thus its understanding of urban environment misunderstood. If we accept the theoretical claims of Lefebvre and de Certeau, then we can posit that urban environments are socially produced spaces in which walkers perform a set or series of metonymical moves to represent a "here and now." A process of selection that gathers together names and gestures ends up producing representational space that allows the walker to inhabit an official representation of space. When poets map the city with kinesthetic rhetoric, they thereby define it as the spatial outcome of their representational practice. Therefore, a critical reading of urban environments should understand them as the buzzing outcome of continuously produced and inherently contradictory social space. Urban dwellers, some of whom are also poets, use totalized representations of urbanicity to create their own critical walks through the modern city.

NOTES

1. We should remember that twentieth-century poets and critics alike have also been greatly influenced by the nineteenth-century inventions of the social and behavioral sciences. Marx and Freud, among many others, have taught us all what to look for in urban culture.

2. See, for example, Sharpe and Thesing.

3. The idea of twenty-foot-wide streets was "lavish, by sixteenth-century standards," as Logan et al. point out (see More 119).

4. Street ballads are an especially important kind of poetry about place, thus a fuller discussion of their relevance to urban poetics is warranted. However, their origins are not "urban" in the specialized sense of the term that I am using in this essay. For an introduction to their form and history, see Würzbach.

5. That the meaning of walking can respond to anything at all is not obvious, especially in our time, when its significance has become attenuated. Since the transportation revolutions of the nineteenth and twentieth centuries, walking no longer has a comparable importance in overland travel as do our trains and automobiles. For suburban residents, who now are wholly dependent on machines to do their traveling for them, the experience of walking is practically vestigial, as the absence of sidewalks in many such areas makes clear. The computer revolutions of the twentieth and twenty-first centuries will likely make walking still more irrelevant to daily home economy. However, we do not have to put forward a narrative of decline in which some Golden Age of Walking has been supplanted by an Iron Age of combustion to claim that this activity no longer has the same basic priority in our spatial practices. Nothing is more indicative of this change than the debased functionality of walking when it was relegated to the meaningless status of a repetitive exercise for the sake of stress reduction, calorie expenditure, and cardiovascular fitness.

6. See Gilbert and Wallace.

WORKS CITED

de Certeau, Michel. *The Practice of Everyday Life.* Berkeley: U of California P, 1984.

Donne, John. *The Complete English Poems.* Ed. A. J. Smith. London: Penguin, 1971.

Gay, John. *Poetry and Prose.* Ed. Vinton Dearing and Charles Beckwith. Oxford: Oxford UP, 1974.

Gilbert, Roger. *Walks in the World: Representations and Experience in Modern American Poetry.* Princeton, N.J.: Princeton UP, 1991.

Harvey, David. *Consciousness and the Urban Experience: Studies in the History and Theory of Capitalist Urbanization.* Baltimore, Md.: Johns Hopkins UP, 1985.

Johnston, John. *The Poet and the City: A Study in Urban Perspectives.* Athens: U of Georgia P, 1984.

Jonson, Ben. *The Complete Poems.* Ed. George Parfitt. London: Penguin, 1975.

Lefebvre, Henri. *The Production of Space.* Trans. Donald Nicholson-Smith. Cambridge, Mass.: Blackwell Publishers, 1991.

Manley, Lawrence. *Literature and Culture in Early Modern London*. Cambridge: Cambridge UP, 1995.

Mauss, Marcel. *Sociology and Psychology: Essays*. London: Routledge & Keegan Paul, 1979.

Merleau-Ponty, Maurice. *The Phenomenology of Perception*. Trans. Colin Smith. London: Routledge & Keegan Paul, 1962.

More, Thomas. *Utopia: Latin Text and English Translation*. Eds. George Logan, Robert Adams, and Clarence Miller. Cambridge: Cambridge UP, 1995.

O'Hara, Frank. *The Selected Poems*. Ed. Donald Allen. New York: Vintage Books, 1974.

Pope, Alexander. *The Poems of Alexander Pope*. Ed. John Butt. New Haven, Conn.: Yale UP, 1961.

Sharpe, William. *Unreal Cities: Urban Figuration in Wordsworth, Baudelaire, Whitman, Eliot, and Williams*. Baltimore, Md.: Johns Hopkins UP, 1990.

Simmel, Georg. *On Individuality and Social Forms*. Ed. Donald L. Levine. Chicago: U of Chicago P, 1971.

Swift, Jonathan. *The Complete Poems*. Ed. Pat Rogers. London: Penguin, 1983.

Thesing, William B. *The London Muse: Victorian Poetic Responses to the City*. Athens: U of Georgia P, 1982.

Vaughan, Henry. *The Complete Poems*. Ed. Alan Rudrum. New Haven, Conn.: Yale UP, 1976.

Wallace, Anne D. *Walking, Literature, and English Culture: The Origins and Uses of Peripatetic in the Nineteenth Century*. Oxford: Clarendon Press, 1993.

Williams, Raymond. *The Country and the City*. New York: Oxford UP, 1973.

Würzbach, Natascha. *The Rise of the English Street Ballad, 1550–1650*. Cambridge: Cambridge UP, 1990.

4

``ALL THINGS NATURAL ARE STRANGE''
Audre Lorde, Urban Nature, and Cultural Place
Kathleen R. Wallace

In the center of a harsh and spectrumed city
all things natural are strange.
I grew up in a genuine confusion
between grass and weeds and flowers
and what colored meant
except for clothes you couldn't bleach
and nobody called me nigger
until I was thirteen.
(61)

With these words from Audre Lorde's poem "Outside," collected in *The Black Unicorn,* the self-described "Black lesbian feminist poet" points to the abundant ironies in attempting to distinguish between what is and is not natural in her home environment, the urban landscape of New York City. Unlike much nature writing, Lorde's poetry and nonfiction repeatedly describe places where the division between nonhuman and human-made environments is confused. Rather than celebrating the great outdoors, Lorde's poetry suggests that although humans are always part of nature (the "outside"), they also determine who and what is considered natural. Lorde's work repeatedly shows how others who criticize her identities as an African American, lesbian, feminist, and writer/lover of urban landscapes label her as being "unnatural," an outsider.

However, Lorde's awareness of her outsider status gives her an interesting vantage point from which to write about the environment. But is Audre

Lorde a nature writer? I believe she is. Lorde's position as a black, lesbian, feminist resident of one of the densest urban areas of the world influences her relationship with that landscape, and her poetry and nonfiction reflect how she works out that often troubled but committed relationship. While Toni Morrison, Barbara Christian, and Melvin Dixon have written about African American women writers' interest in place because of the very real spatial implications of the African diaspora, Lorde engages these issues within the added displacement that occurs because of her sexual orientation.

By being committed to helping those who have been silenced find their voices, Lorde goes to considerable trouble to write herself into urban and cultural spaces that trap or ignore her—or at least those parts of the black, female, lesbian, poet self she refuses to dissect. In dedicating herself to this complex identity, Lorde argues that each aspect is an integral part of the whole. For instance, she resists pressure to emphasize being black over being lesbian. Doing so would result in a kind of psychic violence. She clarified her position in an interview with Karla Hammond: "There's always some-one asking you to underline one piece of yourself—whether it's *Black, woman, mother, dyke, teacher,* etc.—because that's the piece that they need to key into. They want you to dismiss everything else. But once you do that, then you've lost because then you become acquired or bought by that particular essence of yourself, and you've denied yourself all of the energy that it takes to keep all those others in jail" (15).

Scholars have often been guilty of this charge. Audre Lorde has been read mostly for her lesbian and feminist politics, readings that have obscured her very real interest in issues of place and environment. Although even Lorde herself may not have recognized the centrality of these interests, other readers have. In the Hammond interview, Lorde expressed surprise that a reader had described her as a "nature poet" (24). Given the standard reception and use of her work, Lorde's surprise is understandable. Yet, it is not difficult to see how a reader might conclude that Lorde was a nature poet given the themes in Lorde's poetry and her lyrical/critical descriptions of New York City and the Caribbean in her nonfiction, particularly *Zami* and *The Cancer Journals.* While being an activist for many of her other constituencies, Lorde may have regarded the kind of environmentalism popularized during the early 1970s as detracting from more pressing social problems facing women, African Americans, and the poor. As Norman Faramelli put the problem in 1972, "To the poor and the low-income families, ecology may appear to be a cop-out, a flight from social realities, and a digression from dealing with the real issues of racism and social justice" (Smith 2). However, our tendency to read Lorde's work for its application to feminist, racial, or sexual politics has kept most readers from seeing how she regularly extended her art and politics to her surroundings—both natural and human-made—in New York. A close ecocritical reading of Lorde's work reveals her keen interest and care for these environments, particularly as they pertain to issues of social and environmental justice.

In this essay, I analyze Lorde's poetry and her autobiographical *Zami: A New Spelling of My Name* to illustrate how ecocritics might better address literature written by people of color about urban environments. As my starting point, I take what many might consider an overly generous view of Cheryl Glotfelty's definition of ecocriticism as "the study of the relationship between literature and the physical environment" (xviii). I see this definition as including the study of nature writers like Audre Lorde who might turn expected notions of "wild" or "natural" upside-down. If we are to see Lorde as a nature writer, we need to understand the importance of community and context in her work. Until recently, these concepts have been better handled in the literature of the environmental justice movement than they have in the literary scholarship on nature writing. As literary ecocritics begin more systematically to consider other writers and literatures, we need different lenses through which to view this material. We need, as Giovanna Di Chiro puts it in her essay "Nature as Community: The Convergence of Environmental Justice," to comprehend "nature [as] historically dynamic and culturally specific. What counts as nature is therefore different among various people of color groups that have very different cultural histories" (311).

In an early and important poem, "To the Girl Who Lives in a Tree" (1974), Lorde identifies with a woman who moves away from New York City to work to protect the natural environment. However, the extent of Lorde's empathy is colored by the legacies of racism, sexism, and homophobia, with their attendant restrictions of free movement:

My mothers [sic] nightmares are not yours but just as binding.
If in your sleep you tasted a child's blood on your teeth
while your chained black hand could not rise

to wipe away his death upon your lips
perhaps you would consider then
why I choose this brick and shitty stone
over the good earth's challenge of green.

.   .   .   .

. . . I think you will be back soon from Honduras
where the woods are even thicker than in Oregon.
You will see it finally as a choice too
between loving women or loving trees
and if only from the standpoint of free movement
women win
hands down.
(New York 21)

Lorde renders her position here within the dynamics of choice: between flight and staying put, between the "good earth" and the city's "shitty
stone," and between "loving trees" and "loving women." However, this
decision should not be subjected to a simple interpretation, one that reads
Lorde as rejecting the natural world while privileging the human, specifically female, presence. When this poem is read within the context of Lorde's
nearly three decades of published work, it reads differently. It reads more as
an ecological decision to remain committed to one's home place, even if
that place is an atypical environment—an urban area that can be hostile to
people of color, women, homosexuals, and even trees. For Lorde, humans
and culture are as natural as trees: The degradation of people and places is
unnatural. This poem is the closest articulation of what I see as Lorde's
vision of ecological literacy, a sense and experience of place that is immediate, historical, and primal. In his essay "The Trouble with Wilderness,"
William Cronon articulates a similar idea as he calls for us to cultivate the
means for "discovering what an ethical, sustainable, honorable human place
in nature might actually look like" (81). He argues that if we continue to
"pretend to ourselves that our real home is in the wilderness, to just that
extent we give ourselves permission to evade responsibility to the lives we
actually lead" (81). Lorde honors such a sense of home. Blood binds her to
this urban environment of "brick and shitty stone," and she cannot easily
disregard this bond.

What does it mean, then, to love New York City as an African American lesbian poet and mother? Audre Lorde considers this question throughout her work, but especially in her poetry collections *New York Head Shop and Museum* (1974), *Our Dead Behind Us* (1986), and *The Marvelous Arithmetics of Distance: Poems 1987–1992*, which was published posthumously in 1993. Lorde writes often about the environment from within the bounds of human affection and desire. However, a fuller and ecocritically informed understanding of Lorde's work must simultaneously attend to the cultural/political aspects of physical environments—urban and wild—that appear in her work. Lorde expresses interest in natural and built environments repeatedly, but nearly always with an eye toward how racism and sexism are implicated in them.[1]

Lorde writes from a doubled perspective as nature writer and social critic. Two of her poems illustrate this enterprise particularly well. "Every Traveler Has One Vermont Poem" reveals the tension Lorde sees between what might and might not be considered natural. "Every Traveler" moves from her appreciation of the rural landscape to several abrupt, but not unexpected, final lines:

> Spikes of lavender aster . . .
>
> .   .   .   .
>
>
> .   .   .   .
> . . . already the hills are turning
> curved green against the astonished morning
> sneeze-weed and ox-eye daisies
> not caring   I am a stranger
> making a living choice.
>
> Tanned boys I do not know
> .   .   .   .
> wave from their father's tractor
> one smiles as we drive past
> the other hollers
> nigger
> into cropped and fragrant air.
> (Our Dead 41)

When Lorde identifies the natural elements in this landscape as "not caring," she defines nature as something different from and indifferent to humans, who obviously do care about her presence in the Vermont hills. This poem reveals Lorde's familiarity with a nonurban landscape when she identifies plants, such as "sneeze-weed," by their colloquial names, but this insider status is abruptly disrupted when the boy yells "nigger" as she passes in her car. This offensive name-calling highlights how Lorde uses visibility and invisibility as tropes expressing interconnections between human and natural elements. When the boy censures Lorde because of her blackness, which identifies her as an outsider in what is presumably a white rural area, he relies upon his whiteness to ensure his invisibility as someone who belongs. Earlier in the poem, Lorde uses another less incendiary but equally ominous example to question such culturally imposed determinations. In the middle of a stanza describing the route of her travels, the quote, "I remember when air was invisible," appears. I read this line as acknowledging air pollution as yet another unexpected, unwelcome, and visible feature of the Vermont landscape. Although the line implies a longing for an earlier and more pristine era, by placing it early in the poem and creating a parallel with the name-calling in the final stanza, Lorde accounts for how social and economic cultural practices impact natural landscapes.

In a later nature poem, "Making Love to Concrete" (1993), Lorde again challenges conventional thinking about what constitutes the natural, particularly in urban areas:

> You cannot make love to concrete
> if you care about being
> non-essential   wrong or worn   thin
>
> . . . .
>
> if you cannot pretend
> concrete needs your loving
>
> To make love to concrete
> you need an indelible feather
> white dresses before you are ten
>
> . . . .
>
> and air raid drills in your nightmares
> no stars till you go to the country

and one summer when you are twelve
Con Edison pulls the plug
on the street-corner moons   Walpurgisnacht
and there are sudden new lights in the sky
(Marvelous 5–6)

An unlikely love object, concrete is nonetheless an ubiquitous urban material and, as such, is a "natural" choice for the subject of a nature/love poem by a writer who publicly acknowledged her commitment to urban environments, especially those of New York City and particularly her home on Staten Island, which is also the site of the world's largest landfill. Lorde conflates natural and human elements in this poem; the street lights, for example, are "moons" hiding the stars. But when the lights go out and the stars appear, Lorde regards them with mixed feelings because their sudden appearance in the city landscape requires a new relationship between herself as an urban dweller and this newly revealed natural environment. Unlike many nature writers who might regard stars as reassuring natural features of the nighttime sky, Lorde personifies these stars as "stone chips that forget" she is the one who must create a relationship between the human-made and the natural. To do so, she needs "to become a light rope [and] a hammer," tools that can help her build connections between her immediate urban circumstances and the expansive natural environment she also finds resistant to love. Lorde seeks to "become . . . a repeatable bridge" that helps her navigate her environment while establishing connections with it.[2]

Lorde's collected work reveals how such a commitment to urban places is continually tested and affirmed. In the early poem "Equinox" (1973), in *From a Land Where Other People Live,* Lorde connects news of Malcolm X's assassination with "the dark mangled children / . . . streaming out of the atlas / Hanoi Angola Guinea-Bissau Mozambique Pham-Phen / merged into Bedford-Stuyvesant and Haselhurst Mississippi / haunting my New York tenement that terribly bright / summer / while Detroit and Watts and San Francisco were burning" (11–12). By omitting the commas in this list of city names, Lorde emphasizes the connections between her New York tenement and foreign and domestic locations. All these places are linked by violence, a violence that typically has dire consequences for "dark mangled children."

Children appear regularly in Lorde's cityscapes, especially in connection with those environments that both harm and strengthen them. *New York Head Shop and Museum,* for instance, presents New York City in terms of its youngest human inhabitants. It is a bleak portrait. Several poems—especially "A Sewerplant Grows in Harlem or I'm a Stranger Here Myself When Does the Next Swan Leave" (9) and "The American Cancer Society or There is More Than One Way to Skin a Coon" (7)—document the environmental and psychological hazards disproportionately deposited in poor or minority neighborhoods. In "New York 1970," Lorde records the city's brutality, but commits herself and her children to witnessing "the grim city quake to be reborn perhaps / blackened again but this time with a sense of purpose"; she describes herself as "bound like an old lover—a true believer— / to this city's death by accretion and slow ritual" (1). Although as an adult she chooses to be bound to the city, she finds that she must submit her children to its "death throes and agony / and they are not even the city's past lovers . . . which if survived / will teach them strength or an understanding of how strength is gotten / and will not be forgotten: It will be their city then" (1). Her children, then, must be tested by fire, just as she was, before they can become native to place, before the city will become theirs and they, the city's.

Lorde's autobiographical *Zami* can be profitably read within and against two literary fields concerned with issues of place—ecocriticism and immigrant and migrant literatures. The significance of place provides a foundation for the overall construction of *Zami*. Its narrative map runs through the real and metaphysical spaces of Carriacou, Harlem, Mexico, and the gay-girl bar scene in Greenwich Village in the 1950s. Underpinning Lorde's representation of these locations is an idea of home that gradually comes to encompass physical places and personal, communal, and sexual identities. *Zami* provides Lorde's most sustained description and discussion of the urban environment she inhabited as a child and young adult. Except for a brief trip to Mexico in 1953–54, which Lorde describes as a sojourn from political activism and the site of her first fully conscious and reciprocal lesbian relationship, most of *Zami* takes place within the confines of the largest, densest urban area in the United States—New York City.

The story of a daughter of parents who immigrated from the Caribbean to New York in 1924, *Zami* can be read as a second-generation immigrant autobiography written to make sense of that experience. *Zami* focuses upon two primary loci—New York City and Carriacou, a small island off Grenada and the birthplace of Lorde's mother—while articulating Lorde's struggle with those two radically opposed sites. In this sense, *Zami* follows the form of a journey to and from home. In an essay on ethnic literature in New York, Mario Maffi observes that "the act of marking out a territory is a crucial step in the process of defining an identity" (160). *Zami* marks out territories that critic Katie King describes as having multiple dimensions, just as Lorde's identity is multifaceted.

However, the first sections of *Zami* show the strain of a disrupted sense of place. Lorde's parents eventually take up residence in Harlem, but stories about Grenada and the small island of Carriacou provide a legacy, a specifically matrilineal one, with which Lorde must grapple. Carriacou, which Lorde knows out of her "mother's mouth," functions within *Zami* as both geographic site and locus for cultural and individual memory. But it is through Lorde's experiences of New York that she comes to understand Carriacou. Lorde depicts New York as a sensual entity, differing in degree, rather than in kind, from the tropical sensuality she typically associates with the Caribbean. Rather than charting an uncomplicated linear progression from Lorde's ancestral origins in Carriacou to various sites during her childhood, adolescence, and adulthood in New York, she represents these places as contingent, not only in horizontal space, but in the vertical spaces suggested by memory.[3] Lorde's mother Linda's memories and stories make Carriacou a place despite the island's absence from the official space of two-dimensional maps. Linda's stories, in fact, actually constitute narrative maps that provide models for the ways Lorde uses writing to render the urban place—New York—that she knows intimately.

Lorde listens to her mother's stories about Carriacou and gradually incorporates that women-centered, tropically lush, and "natural" place with her women-centered and created environments in New York. This process of incorporation is complicated by Carriacou's mythic qualities. As a child, Lorde searches for it on her school maps to no avail. It is not until she is twenty-six and working on a library-science research project that she finally locates Carriacou on a published map. In the absence of such standard documentation, the word "Carriacou" evoked both distrust and longing for an Edenic landscape. She writes, "When I hunted for the magic place during geography lessons or in free library time, I never found it, and came to believe my mother's geography was a fantasy or crazy or at least too old-fashioned, and in reality maybe she was talking about the place other people called Curacao, a Dutch possession on the other side of the Antilles" (*Zami* 14).

Until she locates Carriacou on a map, Lorde distrusts her mother's stories and memories, but she cannot disregard their power. As a child and young adult, Lorde's developing relationship with her urban environment is filtered through the Edenic lens created by her mother's stories. Carriacou becomes "home . . . a far way off, a place I had never been to but know well out of my mother's mouth" (13). In the absence of external verification, Lorde draws a narrative map of her ancestral homeland, a sensual map created by the combination of the mother's experience and the child's imagination. Lorde describes her mother as a woman who "breathed exuded hummed the fruit smell of Noel's Hill morning fresh and noon hot, and I spun visions of sapadilla and mango as a net over my Harlem tenement cot in the snoring darkness rank with sweat" (13).

This passage, which is laced with paradoxical visions and scents, negotiates Lorde's complex sense of place. Although Linda's narratives of Carriacou are politically expedient because they reveal an attractive reality beyond Lorde's stories of her "Harlem tenement cot," the Carriacou narratives hide as much as they reveal. The contents of these narratives—the explicit romanticism of Carriacou and the violence of New York City—need to be decoded. Carriacou exists for Lorde in childhood primarily as a fantasy home place and New York exists as violent terrain, and Lorde critiques these assumptions by the end of *Zami* as she draws survival strategies from each environment. Carriacou takes on increasing symbolic importance as Lorde explores how home and place, even the most Edenic of places, are inextricably linked with human, and specifically female, presences.[4]

Without undercutting the importance of Lorde's matrilineal connections to Carriacou, *Zami* reveals the consciousness of a daughter of New York City. Like most New Yorkers, Lorde describes the city by its boroughs, neighborhoods, street coordinates, and subway stops. Her depiction of her Harlem childhood illustrates how geographic boundaries reflect cultural dictates about race and class. When she describes the years she spent exploring what it meant to be a black lesbian poet, she focuses upon what she calls the "gay-girl bar scene" in Greenwich Village and several homes, hers and those of others, that functioned as safe havens. During the mid to late 1950s, the Village reasserted its bohemian image, which was promoted in the *Village Voice* (founded in 1956).[5] Lorde lived on Seventh Street and described the Village as "at the time . . . a state of mind extending all the way from river to river below 14th Street, and in pockets throughout the area still known as the Lower East Side" (178). It is in the Village that Lorde forges communal ties and tests her identity in "the Village gay-girl scene" (177), including various lesbian bars: the Bagatelle, Laurel's, the Mermaid, the Riviera, Swing, Snooky's, the Grapevine, the Sea Colony, the Pony Stable Inn. The Bagatelle reigned as the most popular lesbian bar, where Lorde learns that being "an outsider in the Bagatelle had everything to do with being Black" (220). Because the Bagatelle was meant to be a safe haven where difference could safely be explored, the bouncer's racism and that of her white lesbian friends who refused to acknowledge that being black created a division within their "sacred bound of gayness" was all the more brutal. Lorde resists these neat categories in her writing and remaps an urban environment crisscrossed with the paths of young lovers traversing a dense and often treacherous natural and built terrain.[6]

In *Zami,* Fourteenth Street takes on multiple layers of meaning. In Lorde's personal geography, it represents the silence she must maintain in the Village about her college work uptown at Hunter College. Although uptown is generally understood as beginning about forty blocks north, near Central Park, Lorde is definite about her designation of Fourteenth Street as her meaningful boundary between uptown and downtown, between blacks and whites, between college life and the coded lifestyles stylized in Village lesbian bars. The Village is home for Lorde, and home ends at Fourteenth Street.[7] Fourteenth Street, however, is not impenetrable; it becomes a physical and symbolic landmark for Lorde's relationships with black women: "During the fifties in the Village, I didn't know the few other Black women who were visibly gay at all well. Too often we found ourselves sleeping with the same white women. We recognized ourselves as exotic sister-outsiders who might gain little from banding together. Perhaps our strength lay in our fewness, our rarity. That was the way it was Downtown. And Uptown, meaning the land of Black people, seemed very far away and hostile territory" (177). Uptown is literally terra incognita—wilderness. Uptown is also the land of inscrutable institutions of higher education. By comparison, Lorde's home territory downtown is concrete and sensual, much like her ancestral homeland in Carriacou, but without the Edenic overtones. Lorde works out the relationship between her urban environment and matrilineal heritage in the final sections of *Zami,* particularly through several important human figures and objects, such as fruit, that are typically associated with the tropics.

In a scene from the latter part of *Zami,* Lorde describes how she and a lover "stood eyeing the ripe melons piled high on the sidewalk stands in front of Balducci's. Cartons and cartons of beautiful and expensive fruits and vegetables extended out onto the sidewalks of Greenwich Avenue" (206). The two end up copping a melon. Fruit, as it turns out, is a fundamental link between Lorde's relationship to Carriacou and New York City. Anna Wilson argues that Lorde rejects "her mother's home [while] rescuing it for herself. She must rework the originary myth, putting it at a different relation with 'here' to construct, between the two, a new 'fruitful' country" (83).

Kitty, or Afrekete (a name that plays between the boundaries of an actual person and the African goddess/trickster/linguist), is central to this construction. Lorde's relationship with Kitty/Afrekete brings Lorde back to the sensuality of the body, nature, and urban life following the breakup of a long-term relationship. Through Kitty/Afrekete, Lorde learns that roots are not necessarily in geography, but are also in the body. Rootedness is a physical state of both body and mind, according to Lorde: "Afrekete taught me roots, new definitions of our women's bodies—definitions for which I had only been in training to learn before" (250).

Kitty/Afrekete also takes Lorde back to the territory of Lorde's childhood, a journey uptown that she had been reluctant to make. After accepting Kitty/Afrekete's invitation for a drink at her uptown apartment, Lorde feels panic at "crossing 59th Street" (246). She is crossing into what she earlier called "hostile territory," a wilderness of sorts. In his critique of that concept, environmental historian William Cronon remarks that wilderness "is entirely a creation of the culture that holds it dear, a product of the very history it seeks to deny. In virtually all its manifestations, wilderness represents a flight from history. . . . [W]ilderness offers us the illusion that we can escape the cares and troubles of the world in which our past has ensnared us"

(78–80). Lorde's panic subsides when she comes to terms with her history, when she embraces her place in the wilderness, when she "comes home," a phrase Lorde also uses to describe making love to a desired woman.

Zami is framed by these acts of coming home, but it is only in the final chapter that Lorde seems truly "at home"—with another woman who gives as much as she takes, with the past and the present, and with Carriacou and New York City. Lorde highlights and ultimately reconciles these dichotomies in prose ranging from the lyrical to the didactic, rendered, respectively, in italic and roman typographies. In the final chapter, Lorde incorporates italicized and roman passages within the same paragraphs, suggesting a merger between the actual and the mythic, between New York City and Carriacou. The following passage provides an important illustration of how Lorde uses Kitty/Afrekete to work out these polarities:

> How many times into summer had I turned into the block from Eighth Avenue, the saloon on the corner spilling a smell of sawdust and liquor onto the street, a shifting indeterminate number of young and old Black men taking turns sitting on two upturned milk-crates, playing checkers? I would turn the corner into 113th Street towards the park, my steps quickening and my fingertips tingling to play in her earth.
>
> *And I remember Afrekete, who came out of a dream to me always being hard and real as the fire hairs along the underedge of my navel. She brought me live things from the bush, and from her farm set out in cocoyams and cassava*—those magical fruit which Kitty bought in the West Indian markets along Lenox Avenue in the 140s or in the Puerto Rican *bodegas* within the bustling market over on Park Avenue and 116th Street under the Central Railroad structures.
>
> "I got this under the bridge" was a saying from time immemorial, giving an adequate explanation that whatever it was had come from as far back and as close to home—that is to say, was as authentic—as was possible. (249)

The eroticism in this passage is clear enough; Lorde identifies the origin of these fruits as simultaneously from "the bush" (the italicization gives this passage its mythical and sexual appeal) and from "under the bridge," a direct reference to the urban source of Linda's groceries mentioned in the first chapter. One sentence in the middle of this passage suggests the simultaneous existence of the mythic and the real. Lorde introduces Afrekete (italicized) as the provider of fruits from the bush and tropics (suggesting Africa and the West Indies) and Kitty, who knows where to buy them in ethnic city markets. In this passage, Afrekete elides into Kitty; the mythic, ancestral, Edenic place merges with the real, present, and urban place.

This merged place provides a deep sense of home, which is perhaps the most inclusive concept expressed in *Zami*. In the descriptions of the "Tar Beach" atop Afrekete's house, Lorde collapses the natural and urban worlds she calls home. One midsummer's evening, Lorde and Kitty go to the roof, what Lorde calls "the chief resort territory of tenement-dwellers" (252). Although not quite a Caribbean beach at night, Lorde's descriptions nonetheless capture the sensuality of a landscape that cannot easily be bifurcated into natural and urban categories:

> We jammed the roof door shut with our sneakers, and spread our blanket in the lee of the chimney between its warm brick wall and the high parapet of the building's face. This was before the blaze of sulphur lamps had stripped the streets of New York of trees and shadow, and the incandescence from the lights below faded this far up. From behind the parapet wall we could see the dark shapes of the basalt and granite outcroppings looming over us from the park across the street, outlines, curiously close and suggestive. . . . When we came down from the roof later, it was into the sweltering midnight of a west Harlem summer, with canned music in the street. . . . It was not onto the pale sands of Whydah, not the beaches of Winneba or Annamabu, with cocopalms softly applauding and crickets keeping time with the pounding of a tar-laden, treacherous, beautiful sea. It was onto 113th Street that we descended after our meeting under the Midsummer Eve's Moon, but the mothers and fathers smiled at us in greeting as we strolled down to Eighth Avenue, hand in hand. (252–253)

This passage presents the city as deep and dark but not frightening or threatening. The city's built environments, chimneys, walls, and tar echo natural—actually tropical—elements: the moon, basalt and granite outcroppings, and the ocean. When Lorde and Kitty descend back into their urban environment, back into the street, the city welcomes them through parental figures who smile greetings. Human connections provide the sense of home Lorde seeks throughout her poetry and nonfiction as she plumbs the seemingly irreconcilable polarities between Carriacou and New York City, between the tropics and asphalt.

Her poem "Home," from *Our Dead Behind Us,* more fully describes Lorde's realization that home and affirmation do not lie in Carriacou. The search for origins no longer matters:

> We arrived at my mother's island
> to find your mother's name in the stone
> we did not need   to go to the graveyard
> for affirmation .
> our own genealogies
> the language of childhood wars.
> *(49)*

Zami reflects Audre Lorde's search for depth and belonging; yet, as the poem "Home" and others suggest, this search cannot only be backward. As she puts it in another New York poem, memory and history must be "restitched . . . with living" (*Our Dead* 54–57). Lorde renders survival as a forward movement. In this sense, she has moved beyond the immigrant's inclination to look back to the homeland. Lorde's collected work represents her attempt to live fully and deeply in her present home place, New York City.

Each significant place in Lorde's personal geography functions within women-centered networks; each place is associated with particular women—friends, lovers, and family. It is among women that the effects of lax environmental standards and inequitable distribution of environmental hazards most hit home for Lorde. In *The Cancer Journals,* Lorde writes about her experience of breast cancer, which was diagnosed in 1978. She intended the book to express her "thoughts and feelings about the travesty of prosthesis, the pain of amputation, the function of cancer in a profit economy, [her] confrontation with mortality, the strength of women loving, and the power and rewards of self-conscious living" (10). That last phrase, about the benefits of "self-conscious living," expresses a theme woven throughout

Lorde's prose and poetry, one that puts her in the company of Thoreau and other nature writers who are as interested in exploring and documenting their lives and motives as they are in surveying the surrounding environment. In *The Cancer Journals,* Lorde steps up her critique of what she sees as unself-conscious living and implicates those industries, governmental agencies, and the capitalist economic system for fostering environmental hazards that lead to disease.[8]

Several pointed passages about these hazards exist in *The Cancer Journals.* In one such passage, Lorde writes that the "socially sanctioned prosthesis is merely another way of keeping women with breast cancer silent and separate from each other" (16). She asks, "What would happen if an army of one-breasted women descended upon Congress and demanded that the use of carcinogenic, fat-stored hormones in beef-feed be outlawed?" (16). This passage connects poignantly with the work of another contemporary nature writer, Terry Tempest Williams, who, in her essay "The Clan of One-Breasted Women," writes about the prevalence of breast cancer in her family and its probable connection with nuclear testing in the Intermountain West in the 1950s (281–90). Lorde goes on to question the American Cancer Society's motivation and priorities, asking why the organization has not "published the connections between animal fat and breast cancer for our daughters the way it has publicized the connections between cigarette smoke and lung cancer" (59). She continues, "We must also heed the unavoidable evidence pointing toward the nutritional and environmental aspects of cancer prevention. . . . Cancer is not just another degenerative and unavoidable disease of the ageing process. It has distinct and identifiable causes, and these are mainly exposures to chemical or physical agents in the environment" (72–73).

Although Lorde does not speculate, to my knowledge, as to the possible causes of her own cancer in *The Cancer Journals* or elsewhere, *Zami* provides at least one salient possibility. *Zami* includes a substantial section describing how Lorde worked under environmentally hazardous conditions at Keystone Electronics in Stamford, Connecticut, in the early 1950s. Keystone processed quartz crystals to be used in radios and radar equipment. Men ran the cutting machines, and women read the electrical charge of each crystal on X-ray machines or washed the quartz crystals in carbon tetrachloride.

Lorde describes the plant as "offensive to every sense, too cold and too hot, gritty, noisy, ugly, sticky, stinking, and dangerous" (126). She writes that the male workers were typically Puerto Rican because the local population would not take jobs under such conditions. Furthermore, "Nobody mentioned that carbon tet destroys the liver and causes cancer of the kidneys. Nobody mentioned that the X-ray machines, when used unshielded, delivered doses of constant low radiation far in excess of what was considered safe even in those days" (126).

The plant workers were all faced with the same type of environmental blackmail: "Your health or your job. You decide." Lorde decided to stay at Keystone in large part because they hired black women and allowed them to join the union. Twenty-five years later, Lorde returns to this theme of environmental blackmail in *The Cancer Journals* by pointing out that the homophobia and racism at the root of the "public hysteria surrounding AIDS" blots out public scrutiny of the causes of CAIDS, or Chemically Acquired Immune Deficiency Syndrome, an equally ravaging disease brought upon workers exposed to trichloroethylene, which Lorde describes as "a chemical in wholesale use in the electronic sweatshops of the world, where workers are primarily people of Color, in Malaysia, Sri Lanka, the Philippines, and Mexico" (40–41).

In her collection of essays *A Burst of Light,* a discussion of the state of feminism in the 1980s, Lorde makes the following observation: "We are anchored in our own place and time, looking out and beyond to the future we are creating, and we are part of communities that interact. To pretend otherwise is ridiculous. While we fortify ourselves with visions of the future, we must arm ourselves with accurate perceptions of the barriers between us and that future" (64). If Lorde had articulated an explicit environmental ethic, I believe it would sound much like this passage. She reminds us that—as feminists, environmentalists, activists, as human beings—we are all tied to particular places and particular times. We are all interconnected. In this sense, Lorde reminds me of many American nature writers. However, Lorde's enterprise goes at least one significant step further when she writes that we need to "arm ourselves with accurate perceptions of the barriers" before we can reach the nonracist, nonsexist, environmentally healthy future we want to create.

Lorde uses interrogation throughout her work as a strategy to arm herself. She repeatedly asks, "Who is profiting from this?" She asks this question when she is told that her decision to not wear a prosthesis is lowering morale at her doctor's office; when a sewer plant takes root in Harlem; when a Vermont farm boy feels free to yell "nigger" at her as she passes in her car. In repeatedly asking this question, Lorde moves beyond the "genuine confusion" she describes in the poem used as the epigraph to this chapter. When she writes that "all things natural are strange" in the city, she is not referring only to trees and flowers and weeds. She is also referring to the "strange" practices of racism, sexism, homophobia, and environmental degradation that are so pervasive that they seem natural. Lorde's strategy for survival in such state of confusion is to learn to call things by their right name, and she starts with herself. She is not "colored," she is not a "nigger." She is what she names and claims for herself. She is Audre Lorde, Zami, black lesbian feminist poet.

The specificity that comes from such interrogation is one of the key characteristics of the texts usually considered as part of the nature writing tradition, and it is likewise a dominant feature of Lorde's poetry and nonfiction. In this sense, Lorde participates in and expands upon what other nature writers and ecocritics have called "ecological literacy" or the intimate knowledge of one's home place. One such writer, Paul Gruchow of Minnesota, laments the ecological illiteracy of high school students and writes: "Can you, I asked those students, imagine a satisfactory love relationship with someone whose name you do not know? I can't. It is perhaps the quintessentially human characteristic that we cannot know or love what we have not named. Names are passwords to our hearts, and it is there, in the end, that we will find the room for a whole world" (130).[9]

When she calls things by their right name, when she identifies the flower in the Vermont poem as a lavender aster, or when she calls concrete an appropriate object of love, Lorde demonstrates her ecological literacy. However, she also takes ecological literacy another step when she names those conditions that create or are part of her environment, when she correctly renames the "cosmetic problem" of breast cancer as the commodification of women's bodies. Asking and learning and naming lead Lorde to write environmental texts that are like "a route map . . . an artifact for survival" (*Our Dead* 57). For Audre Lorde, asking questions that lead to the naming of oneself and one's world are fundamental survival tactics that underlie her sense of ecological literacy.

NOTES

An earlier version of this chapter was published in *Phoebe: Journal of Feminist Scholarship, Theory, and Aesthetics* vol. 9, no. 1 (spring 1997) and is reprinted here by permission of the publisher.

1. With contributions from social scientists, architects, and others, Margrit Eichler's *Change of Plans: Towards a Non-Sexist Sustainable City* provides an excellent overview of these connections between racism, sexism, and urban living.

2. For useful analyses of the relationship between rural and urban places in American thought and literature, see Bremer, Dixon, and Machor.

3. I am borrowing heavily here from Homi K. Bhabha's description of the "contingent" in his essay on "Postcolonial Criticism" (451–453). Bhabha describes the contingent as "contiguity, metonymy, the touching of spatial boundaries at a tangent, and at the same time, the contingent is the temporality of the indeterminate and the undecidable" (452).

4. In *Zami*, Lorde identities Carriacou as an island where lesbianism was socially accepted. Her information appears to be drawn primarily from Donald R. Hill's 1977 ethnography because Lorde thanks Hill in her acknowledgments. Hill writes that "the relatively widespread and socially acceptable practice of Carriacou lesbianism appears to have evolved within the context of long-term absences by Carriacou men who immigrated to other islands and to the United States for work. From an islander's perspective, . . . a discreet homosexual relationship is more acceptable than a liaison between a married woman and a male lover" (281). Hill also refers to an islander's assessment of the origins of Carriacou lesbianism: "One man believed that women get the drive to become Zami from their mother's blood" (281). This phrasing has echoes in Lorde's descriptions.

5. A subscription ad in the *Village Voice*'s second issue (2 November 1955) connected the newspaper to the Village's revitalization. " 'Pretty soon it won't be Hollywood and Vine or the Astor Lobby, it will be 8th and 6th' . . . said Harvey Breit speaking of Greenwich Village and hailing the *Village Voice* in last Sunday's *New York Times*. We agree. The *Village Voice* reflects this 'new vitality' of Greenwich Village—its people and its culture . . . join us in this novel experiment in journalism" (12).

6. Sharon Zukin raises a related but ultimately unexplored point: "Lesbian novels about New York give evidence of the freedom that homosexuality, like all bohe-

mianism, finds in the city's indecipherable codes and ambiguous maps" (493). Katie King explores a similar theme when she designates the lesbian bar of the 1950s as a site of the production of historical memory and literary identity of feminist and gay movements (52). Although King never actually describes what she means by such a designation, her observation that "bar life in general stands for the possibilities of militant community" (66) has clear resonances in *Zami*.

7. The *Village Voice* supported this designation of Fourteenth Street as Greenwich Village's northern boundary. In a short feature, "Notebook for Pub Crawlers," reviewer Chester Whitehorn writes that he covers night spots "north of the border." His reviews are intended "for the braver soul who occasionally leaves the Village womb to roam above 14th Street" (2 November 1955, 10).

8. For provocative discussions of environmental justice movements, see Brown and Bullard.

9. See also Jackson.

WORKS CITED

Bhabha, Homi K. "Postcolonial Criticism." *Redrawing the Boundaries: The Transformation of English and American Literary Studies*. Eds. Stephen Greenblatt and Giles Gunn. New York: MLA, 1990. 437–65.

Bremer, Sidney H. *Urban Intersections: Meeting of Life and Literature in United States Cities*. Urbana: U of Illinois P, 1992.

Brown, Raymond Taylor. *Ecological Resistance Movements: The Global Emergence of Radical and Popular Environmentalism*. Albany: State U of New York P, 1995.

Bullard, Robert E. *Confronting Environmental Racism: Voices from the Grassroots*. Boston: South End Press, 1993.

——. *Dumping in Dixie: Race, Class, and Environmental Quality*. Denver: Westview Press, 1990.

Christian, Barbara. *Black Feminist Criticism: Perspectives on Black Women Writers*. New York: Pergamon, 1985.

Cronon, William. "The Trouble with Wilderness; Or, Getting Back to the Wrong Nature." *Uncommon Ground: Toward Reinventing Nature*. Ed. William Cronon. New York: Norton, 1995. 69–90.

Di Chiro, Giovanna. "Nature as Community: The Convergence of Environment and Social Justice." *Uncommon Ground: Toward Reinventing Nature*. Ed. William Cronon. New York: Norton, 1995. 298–320.

Dixon, Melvin. *Ride out the Wilderness: Geography and Identity in Afro-American Literature*. Urbana: U of Illinois P, 1987.

Eichler, Margrit. *Change of Plans: Towards a Non-Sexist Sustainable City.* Toronto: Garamond, 1995.

Glotfelty, Cheryl. "Introduction: Literary Studies in an Age of Environmental Crisis." *The Ecocriticism Reader: Landmarks in Literary Ecology.* Eds. Cheryl Glotfelty and Harold Fromm. Athens: U of Georgia P, 1996. xv–xxxvii.

Gruchow, Paul. *Grassroots: The Universe of Home.* Minneapolis: Milkweed Editions, 1995.

Hammond, Karla M. "Audre Lorde: Interview." *Denver Quarterly* 16 (1981–82): 10–27.

Hill, Donald R. "The Impact of Migration on the Metropolitan and Folk Society of Carriacou, Grenada." *Anthropological Papers of the American Museum of Natural History* 54.2 (1977): 191–391.

Jackson, Wes. *Becoming Native to This Place.* Lexington: UP of Kentucky, 1994.

King, Katie. "Audre Lorde's Lacquered Layerings: The Lesbian Bar as a Site of Literary Production." *New Lesbian Criticism: Literary and Cultural Readings.* Ed. Sally Munt. New York: Harvester Wheatsheaf, 1992. 51–74.

Lorde, Audre. *The Black Unicorn.* New York: Norton, 1978.

——. *A Burst of Light.* Ithaca, N.Y.: Firebrand Books, 1988.

——. *The Cancer Journals.* Argyle, N.Y.: Spinsters Ink, 1980.

——. *Chosen Poems: Old and New.* New York: Norton, 1982.

——. *The First Cities.* New York: Poets Press Inc., 1968.

——. *From a Land Where Other People Live.* Detroit: Broadside, 1973.

——. *The Marvelous Arithmetics of Distance: Poems 1987–1992.* New York: Norton, 1993.

——. "My Words Will Be There." *Black Women Writers (1950–1980): A Critical Evaluation.* Ed. Mari Evans. Garden City, N.Y.: Anchor Press/Doubleday, 1984. 261–68.

——. *New York Head Shop and Museum.* Detroit: Broadside, 1974.

——. *Our Dead Behind Us.* New York: Norton, 1986.

——. *Zami: A New Spelling of My Name, a Biomythography.* Freedom, Calif.: Crossing Press, 1982.

Machor, James L. *Pastoral Cities: Urban Ideals and the Symbolic Landscape of America.* Madison: U of Wisconsin P, 1987.

Maffi, Mario. " 'Chi Lai, Arriba, Rise Up!' Some Remarks on Ethnic Writing in New York City." *Multiculturalism and the Canon of American Culture.* Ed. Hans Bak. Amsterdam: Vu UP, 1993. 160–71.

Morrison, Toni. "Rootedness: The Ancestor as Foundation." Interview with Eleanor Traylor. *Black Women Writers (1950–1980): A Critical Evaluation.* Ed. Mari Evans. New York: Anchor Press/Doubleday, 1984. 339–45.

Smith, James Noel, ed. *Environmental Quality and Social Justice in Urban America: An Exploration of Conflict and Concord among Those Who Seek Environmental Quality and Those Who Seek Social Justice.* Washington, D.C.: Conservation Foundation, 1974.

Williams, Terry Tempest. *Refuge: An Unnatural History of Family and Place.* New York: Vintage, 1992.

Wilson, Anna. "Audre Lorde and the African American Tradition: When Family Is Not Enough." *New Lesbian Criticism: Literary and Cultural Readings.* Ed. Sally Munt. New York: Harvester Wheatsheaf, 1992. 75–93.

Zukin, Sharon. "The Postmodern Invasion." Rev. of *City of Quartz: Excavating the Future in Los Angeles,* by Mike Davis; *The Conscience of the Eye: The Design and Social Life of Cities,* by Richard Sennett; and *The Sphinx in the City: Urban Life, the Control of Disorder, and Women,* by Elizabeth Wilson. *International Journal of Urban and Regional Research* 16.3 (1992): 489–95.

5

INCULCATING WILDNESS
Ecocomposition, Nature Writing, and
the Regreening of the American Suburb
Terrell Dixon

ECOCOMPOSITION IN THE CITY

This chapter originates in a freshman class at the University of Houston Central Campus a few years ago, during a period when what we now designate as ecocomposition—classes that emphasize reading and writing about nature and the environment—was beginning to take shape. At that time, I walked into an auditorium overflowing with 180 first-semester freshmen and began to distribute the course syllabus. There were eight of us team-teaching the course: myself; a senior colleague, the winner of several teaching awards and well known for a teaching expertise that could encompass even these monster sections of composition; and six talented graduate students, all of whom were selected for their teaching abilities and many of whom had studied literature and the environment at the graduate level. Together we had formulated a course plan that we were eager to try. It featured a number of our favorite authors (Henry David Thoreau, Mary Austin, Sue Hubbell, Barry Lopez, and Edward Abbey) as nature writers from whom students could learn both ecological values and the techniques of good writing.

Unfortunately, after the first few weeks, it was clear—even to me, the local ecocritic and the instigator of this particular experiment in teaching environmental literature—that our students (a wonderfully diverse mix of African Americans, Asian Americans, European Americans, and Hispanic

Americans) did not share our enthusiasm. They were not responding as well as we had hoped either to these readings or to the class plan that we had so carefully constructed. Finally, they did come to appreciate both, but the process was certainly not automatic or easy and it came about only after we restructured the course. What follows about the ways to inculcate wildness in urban and suburban America stems directly from this intersection of my notions of nature and how best to know and teach it—that is, those held by a European American, fifty-something, long-time and resolutely antisuburban urban dweller who is also a fanatic flyfisher, backpacker, and a devotee of the Alaskan wilderness—with the concerns of my students—bright, ambitious, extremely diverse, many first-generation Americans and first-generation college attendees who commute to campus from all parts of the metropolitan sprawl of Houston and who often live in or aspire to life in the suburbs.[1]

Brazos Bend State Park and the Greatwood Subdivision

What has happened to nature and wildness with the rapid growth of Houston into the nation's fourth largest city is represented by two areas on the city's southwestern outskirts: Brazos Bend State Park and a large, still-developing subdivision named Greatwood. Both are large tracts of land near one of Houston's major highway arteries—Highway 59 South. This ten-lane highway that funnels traffic back and forth from Houston's far-flung suburbs to the downtown and inner-loop areas is one of four such major throughways in the city. Brazos Bend State Park is a few miles from the highway, and Greatwood—its signs and its greenspace—is roughly parallel to the park, but adjacent to Highway 59 and visible from it.

As its name indicates, Brazos Bend State Park is located on a bend of the Brazos, one of the major rivers in Texas; its five thousand, mostly wild acres includes forests, other rivers, creeks, marshes, ponds, and lakes, as well as a splendid observation tower and some walking paths. The park is notable not only for habitat diversity, but also for its beautiful scenery and abundant wildlife. It is one of the best places in the region to view alligators in the wild. There are also attractive and abundant snakes. Bobcats, white-tailed deer, and raccoons can sometimes be seen; cottontails, swamp rabbits, and nutria are common. The birdwatching is usually good and often spectacular, as it is on so much of the Texas coastal plain marshes and prairies. There are waterfowl, such as coots, blue-winged teal, and shovellers, and there are abundant wading birds, such as the great blue heron, Louisiana night heron, and the great egret. Songbirds are there, too; birds like painted and indigo buntings and red-eyed and white-eyed vireos often stop over as they migrate. In spring, the prairies come alive with wildflowers and the darker woods in the park are exceptionally rich in cardinals. Their streaking red flights through the dark woods have over time become as memorable and important to me as my first sight of a caribou herd crossing the Noatak in Alaska's Arctic National Wildlife Refuge or my first encounter with a wild grizzly. Despite the park's proximity to the city, the cardinals' presence, along with the alligators and the abundant waterfowl, speak volumes about the beauty of wild nature. Overall, this park is a splendid example of the best of what we now designate as an urban retreat, that is, a mostly wild place, not far from an urban center, where urbanites can go to experience the wild.[2]

Eleven miles from Brazos Bend, between the river and the highway, is the new suburban development named Greatwood, which is one of Houston's most successful "master-planned" communities. It has twenty-one hundred acres under development, and there are plans to build three thousand homes. These homes sell from $110,000 (patio homes near the golf course for empty-nesters) to $1,000,000 (mansions to be located on newly purchased land on the shore of the Brazos River). The name, as a visit makes clear, has been chosen not out of deference or honor to the forest that was once there, but as a marketing tool. The name suggests nature in abundance, and because that helps to sell houses, nature is the subdivision's most advertised amenity. Although the advertising proclaims that "Greatwood has been planned and built to preserve its identity and its most significant natural feature—its trees," neither the original forest nor many of the trees have been preserved. Instead, they have been cut down and replaced by new trees planted in accordance with the master plan, usually in rows. There are some birds, some nicely arranged flower beds, and no alligators. There are also graded and surface hike and bike trails, man-made lakes, manicured parks, and greenbelts.

However, for all of Greatwood's advertising to the contrary, there remains little of the original flora and fauna. Shots from promotional videos shown in the sales office sweep over a tract of undisturbed forest. (The precise locale is unspecified, but the hope is clearly that the viewer will associate this large forest with the Greatwood suburban development.) Newspaper advertisements depict a large family of songbirds and urge readers to "Visit Greatwood soon. It's a rare bird." Other advertisements proclaim that "Trees and families grow better in Greatwood." Clearly, Greatwood offers a particular kind of nature, one where little wildness remains. It has been replaced by an abundance of planned and managed territory, a kind of denatured nature contoured and shaped for high-end commodification. The problem, of course, is not that the notion of packaged nature sold here is so original or even unusually evil in its intent. Like the television advertisements that feature sport utility vehicles perched on the edge of the Grand Canyon, this use of nature must sell or it would be discontinued.

Rather, the problem is that the Greatwood notion of nature is now nearly ubiquitous. Greatwood in Southwest Houston is much like the Woodlands in North Houston; similar names—Tall Pines, Silver Tree, Grey Fox—and similar developments echo across the city and the nation. What we have with the two proximate, but radically different, versions of contemporary urban nature that constitute Brazos Bend and Greatwood serves as a kind of capsule history of the land, one that juxtaposes a protected version of the original landscape with a picture of where we are rapidly going. We are all—professors of environmental studies and freshman English students alike—bombarded with the notion that packaged nature is an acceptable, and in some ways preferable, substitute for the real thing; that the environment to which we should aspire today features man-made lakes and a golf course; that our master-planned and gated suburbs are, quite naturally and in more ways than one, a very light shade of green. Unless we change our thinking about city nature, landscape, and wildness, this progression from wildness to sterile, ostensibly green suburbs threatens to reconfigure what we expect from where we live and to change our expectations about how and what we learn from the natural world.

In the face of this increasingly widespread attempt to sell a packaged and sterile version of nature, there are some nature writers who speak out for city environments capable of inculcating wildness and who urge us to re-envision the nature of suburbs. Even with the recent increases in nature writing, however, the number of such writers is small. For those of us engaged with environmental literature and practicing ecocriticism, our focus is often, as it is in the larger environmental movement, on wilderness preservation. However, because we now live in a nation where over eighty percent of the population resides in urban areas, those nature writers who do deal with urban life have special importance. The three writers featured below—Rick Bass, John Hanson Mitchell, and Robert Michael Pyle—are not the only ones who know that our concern with nature should not stop once we enter an urban area, but their work does represent three central currents in contemporary urban nature writing: the elegiac meditation on what is lost; the emphasis on learning to see and, thus, to value nature in the suburbs; and the call for an urban land-use policy that fosters education through wildness and works to prevent our culture from moving further away from nature.[3]

INCULCATING WILDNESS IN URBAN NATURE WRITING

Although students of nature writing tend to view Rick Bass's work mainly in terms of his literary nonfiction about Montana wilderness (books like *Winter, The Ninemile Wolves,* and *The Book of Yaak*), his short ecofiction is equally impressive. One of its central themes is what has happened to Houston landscapes with the relentless growth of its suburbs. Bass's first collection of short fiction, *The Watch,* features two stories that explore this theme; their position as frame stories for this collection indicates their thematic importance. The first story in the collection, "Mexico," features the suburban lives of the narrator and his best friend Kirby in Houston during the oil-boom years of the early 1980s. With his recent oil wealth, Kirby has bought two big houses in one of Houston's new-growth suburbs—one house for himself and his wife and one for his best friend, this story's narrator. They escape the urban life with bogus attempts at wildness—frequent trips to Mexico, where they drink and watch the bullfights.

Like many of his wealthy neighbors, Kirby has installed a large swimming pool. However, his pool differs from the others: he puts it in the front yard and stocks it with fish. One fish—the largest bass in the pool—takes on special symbolic significance for this story and this collection. The bass lives deep in the pool, in the shadows of an automobile—that critical feature in the creation and maintenance of the Houston suburbs—that has been driven into the pool and left there for habitat. This giant fish remains uncaught, and it attains a kind of epic status in the lives of the two friends, serving as their best, but ultimately doomed, attempt to incorporate some of the wildness of nature into their affluent suburban lives. The attempt and the story end when they return from Mexico to discover that young boys from the neighborhood—the next suburban generation—have caught the fish and dragged it away.

In the last story in the collection, "Redfish," Kirby and the narrator drive out from Houston to visit one of the city's major urban retreats, the ocean wilderness of the Gulf of Mexico in Galveston Bay. They conceive of their mission in terms that are reminiscent of Hemingway characters. Their plan is to catch a huge redfish and thus prove themselves in a heroic mastery of nature. Instead, they spend all night sitting on a couch that they have brought to the beach from Houston, drinking, and boasting, but fishless. This trip and this story, however, conclude with a wonderful epiphanic moment. When morning comes, it is accompanied by that rarest of Gulf Coast weather surprises—a snow storm. The snow transforms their braggadocio into awe, and it emphasizes the survival of the unpredictability and uncontrollability of the natural world even in the face of unrelenting urbanization.

Rick Bass's later short-story collection, *In The Loyal Mountains,* also interrogates the whole concept of urban nature. In the title story, the focus is on contrast; it plays the wildness of the mountains in the Texas Hill Country against the clipped, manicured, and managed nature of city golf courses. Another story, "The Wait," features older versions of the narrator and Kirby together with a third friend, Jack, on another excursion to the Gulf Coast. After a day of fishing, Jack has his two friends haul a metal box from the back of his car to the beach. What he has trapped in the suburbs and will now release on the Gulf of Mexico's shoreline is a coyote: "A small coyote about the size of a collie shoots out without looking back and begins running down the beach in a straight line. It is running with its tail floating, running—and this is the most beautiful thing—directly toward the condominiums and townhouses, running north and into the wind, without looking back, as if it knows exactly where it is going" (127). The coyote, a wild cousin to the domestic dog, is known for its adaptability, its ability to survive, even flourish, not only in the suburbs of Houston, but in the cities of Los Angeles and New York. What happens with the release, however, certainly problematizes Jack's wish to free this suburban resident into a larger wilderness; the coyote seems eager to replicate his suburban surroundings.

"Swamp Boy" is arguably the most complex of Rick Bass's short stories about nature. Set in a Houston suburb much like the one where Bass lived as a young man, this story presents the narrator's rendition of a time when the suburban landscape still had adjacent areas of prairie, woods, and swamp. Part of what the narrator finds there is a kind of collective memory triggered by his attention to the landscape. He "remembers" buffalo, wolves, and ancient trees. He can "feel magic in this spot, feel it rise from centuries below and brush against your face like cool air from the bottom of a deep well" (26).

The narrator also finds wild nature in the suburbs as he grows up. There are copperheads, skunks, and raccoons in the forest and there is wildness in the lake water that he takes back home to study: "The water swirled and wriggled with hundreds of thousands of tadpoles—half-formed things that were neither fish nor frog, nor yet of this world. As they swirled and wriggled in the moonlight, it looked as if the water were boiling" (27). Unfortunately, Bass's sense of abundant and wild life is more memory of the suburbs as they existed decades ago than it is of present-day reality, when the narrator tells his story. The narrator is no longer the explorer of a landscape that teems with life; instead, he concludes his story from a downtown office tower where he feels "so entombed that I have *become* the giant building in which I work" (27). Rick Bass's urban nature stories want to find and honor a wilder, deeper sense of green, but they, as his move to the wilds of Montana would suggest, are finally more elegiac than celebratory. Thus far in Bass's career, his predominant attitude is a pessimism about finding or preserving wildness in the contemporary suburb.

The nature writer John Hanson Mitchell also seeks true wildness in the suburbs. Although he is best known for his two major books of literary nonfiction, *Ceremonial Time* and *Living at the End of Time,* Mitchell sets out the guiding premise of his urban nature writing in a different kind of book: *A Field Guide to Your Own Back Yard.* In his introduction to this unique blend of suburban nature field guide and a series of short nature essays, Mitchell states his credo:

> I have spent some ten to fifteen years in or near the suburbs of North America and I think I have discovered over the years that in spite of development, in spite of the so-called technological age, the same forces and the same diversity of life that are so evident in the larger wilderness areas of the world are alive and well in the suburban back yard. A watchful eye, a little extra attention to detail, and a sharpened sensitivity to seasonal changes can uncover a veritable Serengeti just beyond the bedroom window. All you have to do is learn to see. (11)

His two major works of literary nonfiction attempt to carry out precisely this task: they embody for us Mitchell's views on how we can re-envision the nature of the suburbs. In *Ceremonial Time,* Mitchell works out a more sustained and elaborate method of viewing nature than that used by Rick Bass's swamp boy to take in his environment. Mitchell seeks to evoke a kind of collective human memory and use it to understand and to write about the changes in the nature of a small piece of land near Boston over a period of fifteen thousand years, the time since the first ice age. To do this, Mitchell employs what he calls the "primitive concept of ceremonial time in which the past, present, and future can all be perceived in a single moment" (1). He uses this perspective to write a sustained natural history, including human interaction with the land, of Scratch Flat—one square mile of land near Boston that is in the process of being engulfed by suburbanization.

With his exceedingly long view of the landscape, Mitchell finally resolves his fear of encroaching development and the destruction of habitat in two different ways. One of these is simply an observant walk through the land that takes note of nature, "a genuine nature walk filled with the kind of small epiphanies that make exploration of the natural world such a continuing adventure" (178). Fortified by this resolve and by his sharp eye, Mitchell can see a landscape replete with birds, turtles, and a fox. He argues implicitly that wild nature remains in the face of suburban onslaughts, if we can but see it. However, Mitchell's second way of dealing with the sprawl of city life exhibits a somewhat darker view. He consoles himself with the thought that this current age of development will, when viewed later as part of the great stretch of geological time, be relatively brief. When another ice age remakes the land, it will all disappear.

By the end of *Living at the End of Time,* however, Mitchell's more usual optimism reasserts itself, although not without some effort and some qualification. He chronicles the advent of a computer maker's large office complex near the once-wild ridge where he has gone resolutely about his own work, studying Thoreau's life and building his own distinctive version of Thoreau's cabin. Mitchell tells about the increase in daytime automobile use, the new service station, and the new cafe, but he can still glory in the contrast between the ridge where he scythes his meadow and listens to indigo buntings and a chestnut-sided warbler and what is coming with the suburban office park: "About eight-thirty, the dull roar of the commuter traffic quieted and then ceased altogether. The sun warmed, climbed above the oaks on the lower fields, and then began to edge across the meadow. On the other side of the valley, in the great plant, the workers would be reading their electronic mail, punching up numbers on the screens, sending memos and jokes to one another across regions and continents. The light in their cubicles would be uniform, a white, unshadowed fluorescence" (211). Although we sense the increasing difficulty of his determination to find nature in the face of suburban onslaught, Mitchell goes to sleep that night listening to the howls at first of a lone wild coyote and then of the whole pack. For all of his knowledge and even his fear of the encroaching suburbs, Mitchell's resolve still remains steady. He stays with the notion that no matter what changes development brings to the landscape, we can, if we follow his example, learn to see and to keep seeing nature in the midst of development.

Robert Michael Pyle specializes in neglected environmental areas and topics, places in need of restoration and rehabilitation that lie outside the usual preservation focus of much environmental literature—logged over areas in Washington state; the cultural importance of the Bigfoot legend; and, in an important early book, *The Thunder Tree: Lessons from an Urban Wildland,* the importance of urban wildlands, especially secondhand ones. This book about growing up in the then-brand-new Denver suburb of Hoffman Heights relates both his family's joy at moving up to the Denver suburb and his own discovery of wildness and salvation in the wilds of a water transportation ditch—the Denver High Line Canal—that ran through his neighborhood. Pyle tells how growing up where he could explore the wild nature of "the big ditch" inculcated his love of butterflies, set him on a path that resulted in his doctorate in ecology (he is now one of the most respected butterfly authorities in the world), and helped shape his ideas on why suburban wildness—not parks, not golf courses, not walking paths—is crucial.

The explanation of that lesson forms the climax of Pyle's narrative and his plea for landscapes that can help inculcate wildness. In the chapter "The Extinction of Experience," which makes an extremely powerful case for urban wildlands, he summarizes:

> Everyone has at least a chance of realizing a pleasurable and collegial wholeness with nature. But to get there, intimate association is necessary. A face-to-face encounter with a banana slug means much more than a Komodo dragon on television. With rhinos mating in the living room, who will care about the creature next door?
>
> The extinction of experience is not just about losing the personal benefits of the natural high. It also implies a cycle of disaffection that can have disastrous consequences. As cities and metastasizing suburbs forsake their natural diversity, and their citizens grow more removed from personal contact with nature, awareness and appreciation retreat. This breeds apathy toward environmental concerns, and, inevitably, further degradation of the common habitat.
>
> So it goes, on and on, the extinction of experience sucking the life from the land, the intimacy from our connections. (146–47)

Robert Michael Pyle is one of our strongest advocates for urban wildness. Like David Orr (1994), he knows that architecture and—by only a slight extension—urban design constitute a very powerful form of education. Where children play and explore on a daily basis teaches them more about the cultural meaning of nature than they learn from the formal classroom or Earth Day activities.

Urban children need wild places, and such places—like the High Line Canal—can be reclaimed and restored. Urban wildlands, even secondhand ones, provide the chance to interact with the kind of wildness remembered by Bass's swamp boy and described by John Hanson Mitchell. Without such urban wild places, the critical task of inculcating wildness grows more and more difficult and, as Pyle argues, this promotes a steady downward spiral of environmental degradation.

ONLY CONNECT

So there we were: eight teachers and 180 freshmen in a class that simply was not working nearly as well as we had hoped. The sense of impending loss that comes with the prospect of a class, any class, drifting loose from its moorings was compounded by the special characteristics of this situation. This class was an integral part of a large-scale, somewhat controversial, experimental program then in its formative stages. Using linked classes, peer mentoring and tutoring, collaborative learning, and dedicated campus space—with classrooms, computer facilities, and lounge areas—we were trying to increase retention and academic success for our largely commuter student body. This meant that we felt more than the usual pressure to succeed, but it also meant that we had more day-to-day informal access to our students than is usually the case on a campus like ours. We talked to them at length, and we redesigned the course. We sent our students out on campus to write about where the trees were, about what kind of trees they were, how healthy they were, and why. We encouraged them to write about campus fountains, squirrels, and, yes, even starlings. Then, they turned to the larger city—the parks and cemeteries, the Houston Astrodome, the new domed butterfly garden attached to the Museum of Natural Science, the famous one-hundred-foot Transco Water Wall affixed to the glitziest shopping mall in consumer-rich Houston, the miles of freeways leading out to ever more distant and isolated suburbs, and the toxic waste dump in one student's neighborhood.

All of this helped move the notion of environment from abstraction to a tangible concern. Nature that had seemed at first to start at the city limits or even farther away came to be seen as a daily presence; it was reconstructed as something of both immediate and durable importance to our students' lives. Building on this new sense of involvement, the class slowly worked its way back into the original reading list. This time the connections came more easily. Thoreau's notion of wildness—the students now saw—could help improve their corner of the world as well as to preserve Yosemite National Park. It came to hold more interest and appeal.

Many of the students started to grow beyond a desire to move up and out to Greatwood and its gated cousins and to think about living in communities that are a deeper, wilder shade of green. This class experience educated the teachers as well. We learned something about trying to teach environmental literature in our own very urban place, about how to make those absolutely crucial pedagogical and personal connections between a threatened wilderness that cries out for preservation and an urban park that needs native plant restoration, wild butterflies, and some wild space. We learned what urban nature writers like Rick Bass, John Hanson Mitchell, and Robert Michael Pyle seek to teach us: In contemporary America, we must connect the remote wilderness preservation so important to us with the cities where most of us now live. Because a good part of our urban commuter student population does not have a family tradition of summer backpacking trips or camping expeditions, ecocomposition and environmental literature need to emphasize that its concerns with wildness encompass the city as well as the country, Brazos Bend and Greatwood as well as the Arctic National Wildlife Refuge and the Brooks Range.

One brief follow-up to this class speaks to the connections that can arise when we attempt to inculcate wildness in urban ecocomposition and literature classes. Several years later, when many of those first freshmen were successfully into their junior year, I taught an advanced class on "Literature and the Environment." We began with *Walden* and *Rural Hours,* moved on to such contemporaries as Ana Castillo and Barbara Kingsolver, and finished with an emphasis on the urban nature writing that I had finally realized needed to be included in city classes on environmental literature. A young Hispanic American woman from the earlier ecocomposition section signed up for this class as well. In that freshman class, she had written a memorable paper about a toxic waste dump in her parents' neighborhood, and this time she chose to write about Henry David Thoreau and Ana Castillo. These were good papers that in intriguing ways built on what she had learned. On the night of the final exam, a group of us were standing around talking and sharing some recent experiences and our summer plans. It emerged as we talked that she—together with her sister and two cousins from Houston—had made a Spring Break trip to visit family members who lived in Boston. Her final snapshot from this trip stays with me most strongly: It pictured the four of them, arms around each other, standing on the shore of Walden Pond.[4]

NOTES

1. Despite the fact that over eighty percent of us now live in urban areas, nature writing about urban and suburban life is not a topic often addressed in the growing body of academic ecocriticism. This is partially because, given the ways in which nature is usually constructed in contemporary American culture, inculcating wildness has its own oxymoronic overtones. Wildness, some part of us still wants to assume, is natural; it does not need to be protected, nurtured, taught, or learned, and—most importantly—it stops at the city-limits sign. One significant exception to this rule is the Fall 1996 issue of *Terra Nova* on the "Wild City." Also of interest is the Autumn 1994 issue of *Orion Magazine,* with its special section entitled "A Dream of Cities."

2. The notion of urban retreat, which appears in an article entitled "Urban Escapes" by Jeff Wallach in *Sierra Magazine,* is an interesting one that will need further attention as we move ahead with our study of urban nature.

3. A list of other significant writers would have to include at least Michael Pollan. His witty book *Second Nature,* on the tyranny of the American lawn and the importance of gardens, is an engaging look at how American culture has gotten to where it is today, with some intriguing suggestions about where we should go from here. This list would also include Charles Siebert, whose book *Wickerby* is a beautiful effort to dissolve those conceptual dichotomies between city and country, man and nature, that work to cloud our view of urban nature. Finally, we must not forget *The Inland Island,* a beautifully written, earlier book by Josephine Johnson about an urban retreat composed of thirty-seven acres of land near Cincinnati, Ohio.

4. My thanks to colleagues John McNamara, Shannon Borg, Stephen Browning, Nancy Ford, Michelle Miller, Kerry Neville, and John Michael Riveria, whose creativity and attention to urban nature made this class work.

WORKS CITED

Bass, Rick. *In the Loyal Mountains.* New York: Houghton Mifflin, 1995.
——. *The Watch.* New York: Norton, 1989.

Johnson, Josephine. *The Inland Island.* Columbus: Ohio State UP, 1969.

Mitchell, John Hanson. *Ceremonial Time: Fifteen Thousand Years on One Square Mile.* New York: Doubleday Anchor, 1984.

——. *A Field Guide to Your Own Back Yard.* New York: Norton, 1985.

——. *Living at the End of Time.* New York: Houghton Mifflin, 1990.

Orion Magazine 13.4 (Autumn 1994).

Orr, David. *Earth in Mind: On Education, Environment, and the Human Prospect.* Washington, D.C.: Island Press, 1994.

Pollan, Michael. *Second Nature.* New York: Atlantic Monthly Press, 1991.

Pyle, Robert Michael. *The Thunder Tree: Lessons from an Urban Wildland.* New York: Houghton Mifflin, 1993.

Siebert, Charles. *Wickerby.* New York: Crown, 1998.

Terra Nova: Nature and Culture 1.4 (Fall 1996).

Wallach, Jeff. "Urban Escapes." *Sierra Magazine* May/June 1997: 41–46, 77.

3

CITY PARKS

6

WRITERS AND DILETTANTES
Central Park and the Literary Origins of Antebellum Urban Nature
Adam W. Sweeting

This chapter is informed by a simple, although unusual, claim: Central Park and other large nineteenth-century urban parks were works of literature as much as they were works of architecture. If we look at the campaign to build the park in the context of mid-nineteenth-century belles lettres, a narrative not told in traditional accounts of urban parks emerges. It is a story of power whereby comfortable New Yorkers used their literary connections and the organs of the city's publishing establishment to fashion a new street-scape. The park also told a sentimental tale wherein the concerns of city life were temporarily put aside while one walked through an idyl of greenery. The two tales—of power and sentimentality—are of course related. When we read them with care, with an understanding of the literary concerns of the day, we come to understand the origins of created green spaces in our cities. Central Park, then, emerges as a crucial document in the literature of urban nature.

The literary tale told by Central Park was perhaps best exemplified in the life and work of the many authors who campaigned for its construction. Although they represented only one faction in the movement to build a large New York park, writers helped galvanize public support for the project. When, for example, city and state officials finally agreed on a location and method of funding for the park in 1856, they asked several writers to serve on the consulting board that was charged with hiring a staff and soliciting designs. They chose well. The writers tapped for the board—Washington

Irving, William Cullen Bryant, George Bancroft, and Charles F. Briggs—were drawn from the highest echelons of the city's literary establishment. Irving had long reigned as America's literary lion, and although he lived only another year, his presence on the board provided a level of prestige that few others could have offered. Bryant, the city's leading newspaper man and a poet of note, combined the rough-and-tumble world of urban journalism with the lightness of his verse. Bancroft, a Massachusetts native like Bryant, was an important historian of early America. Finally, Briggs, a leading voice in the literary movement known as Young America, published novels, engaged in literary criticism, and coedited a journal with Edgar Allan Poe. The writers on the board in turn tapped one of their own, the editor and author Frederick Law Olmsted, to serve as construction superintendent. The distinguished group lent cultural authority to a project that was both controversial and unprecedented. After a decade of debate, litigation, and delay, city leaders needed to assure restive New Yorkers that this new undertaking would neither drain the municipal treasury nor unduly benefit the well-to-do. These authors helped in that endeavor.

The connection between literature and park-building highlights a type of environmental activism not usually associated with antebellum writers, particularly the genteel coterie considered in this chapter. With the important exception of Thoreau, few writers of the period urged communities to set aside open space. However, the New York–based writers actively used the public presses to cajole their neighbors into constructing metropolitan oases of green. Their activism never attained the poignancy and intensity of Edward Abbey's or Rick Bass's modern mixture of literature and environmental agitation. But if we wish to understand the origins of recent literary environmental agitation, the combination of writing and park-building represented by Olmsted and his contemporaries is a good place to start.

Antebellum urban nature advocates possessed an environmental consciousness quite distinct from the voices most often associated with that era's nature writers and chroniclers of city life. Lacking the resplendent vocabulary of Emerson and Thoreau, literary park advocates instead relied on the domesticated Romanticism of writers such as the now-forgotten George Curtis. In place of the dark urbanism of Poe, one finds the polite urbanity of Bryant. When we look at the life and work of several key park advocates (Bryant and Curtis among them), we encounter a literature and history of

Central Park drawing equally from these traditions. When they spoke of nature, park advocates referred to a man-centered cosmos in which the natural realm functioned as a beneficent, orderly presence.

A list of the literary voices active in the movement to build urban parks reads like a "Who's Who" of metropolitan literary life. In addition to the distinguished litterateurs on the consulting board, writers associated with either the planning or building of Central Park or similar spaces in other cities included Donald Grant Mitchell, George Curtis, Horace Bushnell, Andrew Jackson Downing, and, of course, Frederick Law Olmsted, who prior to turning to landscape gardening enjoyed a distinguished career as a journalist and author. Drawn primarily from the intersection of newspaper and magazine journalism, Olmsted and the others helped establish New York as the center of the nation's publishing industry. As essayists, sketch writers, and editors, they embraced a multitude of styles and genres. However, at least two things united them: their interest in the appearance of the urban environment and their taming of the language of Romanticism. Essentially conservative in their political views, they embraced the priorities of New York's cultured elite, many of whom felt threatened by the city's rapid growth. As a result, their views concerning the disposition of urban space were informed by an impulse that attempted to corral and contain the energies of New York's working classes. These views had both direct and indirect influence on the ultimate appearance of Central Park.

THE ENVIRONMENTAL NEED FOR THE PARK

The proper allocation of space became a pressing issue as the nineteenth century reached its midpoint. When proposals to build a large park first circulated in the mid-1840s, the developed sections of Manhattan contained precious little open space. Rivers surrounded the island city, but industry had transformed the waterfront into an unsightly and foul-smelling collection of factories, saloons, and piers. Although the 1811 official plan of the city called for 450 acres of "squares" or "places," by 1838 only 120 acres had been appropriately landscaped. Housing and businesses had gobbled up areas originally designated as parkland, leaving a few small squares and promenades—many of them crumbling badly—as the only readily available parkland (Spann 161–62).

The absence of open space seemed particularly glaring because of the unprecedented cultural and demographic changes that characterized mid-century New York. Older residents in the 1830s and 1840s, many of whom remembered Manhattan's agricultural past, found themselves in a crowded and unhealthy metropolis. Between 1840 and 1860 the city experienced a population increase of 160 percent, a growth spurt that transformed a moderate-sized New World community into a major urban center of nearly one million inhabitants (Spann 430). The city also expanded physically as development—aided by the easy building lots created by the city's gridded street pattern—pushed further and further uptown. The rapid growth had disastrous results for the local environment. For example, potable water grew ever more scarce as streets were paved over formerly clear streams. The closing of the Collect Pond in 1817, a move pushed by real estate pressures, forced Manhattanites to turn to increasingly fetid sources of drinking water. It was not uncommon for a spring or pool to serve simultaneously as sewer, storm drainage, and drinking supply. One popular well located in the Trinity Church Burial Ground tapped water beneath layers of dead bodies, which produced a liquid that was foul and unsafe. Only upon completing the Croton Aqueduct system in 1842 could the city provide safe water to its inhabitants (White 39). Still, outbreaks of cholera, influenza, typhoid, and other infectious diseases continued to terrorize residents, even after the introduction of Croton water. During the 1849 cholera epidemic, one resident of every one hundred perished, a statistic that improved only slightly during the next outbreak in 1854. Street sanitation also posed problems for a city overrun by people, horses, and swine. Carcasses and blood flowing from the more than two hundred slaughter houses created an ever-present problem of waste disposal, as did the tons of ash produced by the city's heavy reliance on coal. In the absence of reliable sewers, not only was New York at mid-century the nation's largest metropolis, it was also the dirtiest (Spann 133–34).

Writers quickly grasped the spatial and environmental implications of the new metropolis. A literature of environmental reform shocked many residents into a heightened awareness of their surroundings. This was particularly evident in the frequent descriptions of the notorious Five Points District, most notably in Charles Dickens's 1842 *American Notes* (Bergman 115). When Dickens visited the neighborhood just north of City Hall, Five

Points stood as an emblem of urban decay, a place where the decrepit state of the buildings matched that of the residents: "Debauchery has made the very houses prematurely old. Open the door of one of these cramped hutches full of Negroes . . . [and] from every corner some figure crawls half awakened, as if the judgement hour were near at hand, and every obscene grave were giving up its dead" (Dickens 88–89). Other writers followed Dickens's lead. In the privacy of his diary Richard Henry Dana Jr., the Boston-reared author of *Two Years Before the Mast,* described the "dark filthy, violent & degraded regions" of Five Points (Homberger 47–49). Similarly, the novelist and *New York Tribune* columnist George G. Foster described Five Points as "the very rotting skeleton of civilization" (Bergman 39). Foster, one of the first journalists to regularly cover the seamier aspects of urban life, struck a balance between titillation and disgust when describing neighborhoods such as Five Points. Like Dickens, Foster linked architectural disarray to moral degradation: The physical "aspect of the place is a striking indication of its character and purposes. . . . Nearly every house and cellar is a groggery below and a brothel above" (23). Wherever physical chaos prevailed, these authors suggested, moral chaos could also be found.

Of course, no one could guarantee that a large park would even partially alleviate the problems of Five Points and other poor neighborhoods. Nor was there anything approaching universal support for the project, even after both the Democratic and Whig candidates for mayor ran on a pro-park platform in the 1851 election. Opposition came from many quarters. Certainly, the 1,600 residents cleared from the park site objected to the forced removal from their homes. Others, including advocates for the poor, believed that the city simply had other pressing needs and could not afford to spend money on such an unprecedented project (Rosenzweig and Blackmur 42, 60). Concerns over how to finance the park troubled many in the business community. Although some favored using general tax revenues, others sought to assess property owners adjacent to the proposed park. Indeed, the *Journal of Commerce,* a leading voice in opposition to the park, denounced the "scoundrels and speculators" whose properties soared in value as a result of the project (18 June 1853).[1]

New York's geography provided park opponents with additional reasons why a park might not be necessary. Citing the proximity of West Point, Newport, and the Hamptons, the *Journal of Commerce* argued that fresh air and open space could easily be obtained. "With all the facilities of intercommunication now existing," claimed one editorial, "there is no need to turn half the island into a permanent forest" (5 June 1851). Moreover, Manhattan's miles of riverfront were "far better for the purpose of air and salubrity than so much park, or any other description of land or water" (13 June 1851). Indeed, the *Journal* argued that "a continuous park, with its unwholesome dampness in the summer, and decaying foliage in the autumn" (18 June 1853) would lessen, rather than improve, public health—a position supported by the centuries-old tradition of draining swamps and damp ground.

A general suspicion of open space informed much of the anti-park rhetoric. Outbreaks of working-class violence on city streets shocked many residents, particularly after the Astor Place riots of 1849 and an 1850 strike by tailors (Wilentz 358–59, 378). In the wake of such disturbances, the *Journal of Commerce* argued that the park would require an "army of policemen" to protect the public from "vagabonds, robbers, gamblers, and fornicators" (7 July 1853). In light of these threats to public order, the *Journal*'s editors feared that additional open space would provide further avenues for lower-class violence.

Literary park supporters had suspicions of their own. Several accounts sympathetic to the plight of the urban poor assumed that lower economic classes would not know how to behave themselves in parklike settings. In 1835, the diarist George Templeton Strong expressed the view of many when he described the behavior of a Sunday crowd in City Hall Park, then the city's largest public space: "The Park presented a shameful spectacle: the booths lighted up, the people as drunk as dogs, and such a popping of squibs, rockets, pistols, etc as I never heard. I'm not much given to moralizing, but it did not look much like Sunday evening in a Christian country" (27).

The novelist and abolitionist Lydia Maria Child responded similarly during an excursion to Hoboken, a rural New Jersey retreat that overlooked the Hudson River. The "city intrudes her vices into this beautiful sanctuary of nature" (28), she wrote in *Letters from New York*. With the numerous barrooms and bowling alleys that crowded its streets, Hoboken had become little more than a "resort for the idle and profligate" (28). Coney Island, yet another common retreat from the city, was notorious for its large number of prostitutes, which led George G. Foster to warn his readers of the "rowdies and other improper characters" (89) who frequented the vicinity.

Despite these fears, writers who campaigned for a park believed open city space offered the opportunity for both moral and aesthetic uplift. It was to this spirit of genteel reform that most writers subscribed when they participated in the effort to build a park. Authors such as Bryant, Olmsted, and Downing looked to European cities as physical embodiments of the genteel, and they turned to these models in an effort to introduce the behavioral and spatial preferences of the well-to-do. Specifically, they urged that English ideals of the Picturesque be grafted onto America's urban fabric. However, whereas Foster—and to lesser extent Dickens—presented the degraded conditions of Five Points as an inevitable cause of moral degradation, Downing, Bryant, and Olmsted inverted this deterministic logic to argue that polite and open surroundings would expose the poor to the proper way to behave. In both cases, the urban environment was thought to directly affect urban character.

WILLIAM CULLEN BRYANT

William Cullen Bryant most obviously represented the combination of park advocacy, writing, and environmental consciousness that I am considering. Although we usually remember Bryant for his youthful nature poetry, he was in fact a committed urbanite. As an editor and man-about-town, Bryant knew Manhattan like few others of his generation. Even upon building a suburban retreat at Roslyn, Long Island, after 18 years in the city, Bryant remained an important presence in metropolitan affairs (Bryant and Voss 189–93). While continuing to write verse throughout his long life, major poems such as "Thanatopsis" and "To a Waterfowl" were behind Bryant when he abandoned his law practice in the Berkshires in 1825 to try his hand at urban journalism. In 1829, Bryant assumed the editor's position at *The New-York Evening Post,* which he held for more than four decades. Under his stewardship, the *Evening Post* emerged as a major voice for urban reform, at various times calling for sanitary improvements and the professionalization of police and fire departments. Among Bryant's most significant projects was his call for the construction of a large urban park, a campaign that he first brought to public attention in 1844 (Brown 261–82).

Despite private fears that large parks encouraged disorderly behavior, Bryant nonetheless viewed such spaces as the most efficient way to improve the moral health of the poor. His first recorded discussion of the subject occurs in private letters written during an 1835 journey through Italy. Italians, Bryant believed, had created open spaces that allowed for relatively relaxed interactions between economic and social classes. Responding to an earlier letter from the Reverend William Ware, who had asked the editor to describe the notable aspects of "Sunday in Catholic countries," Bryant favorably compared the behavior of Italians to that of his countrymen. He was fascinated by the apparent joy with which the people, who, after attending mass, "proceed to some of the public walks and gardens and amuse themselves by walking about, observing the crowd and greeting their acquaintances." While some simply enjoyed the fresh air, others listened to "concerts" played by "philharmonic societies." American Sundays, on the other hand, suffered from the "good deal of gambling and drinking" that occurred in "obscure corners." Indeed, he found "more drunkenness in Hoboken Sundays than all of Italy," a claim that resembles Lydia Maria Child's remarks concerning that New Jersey retreat (*Letters* 469–70). The gentle and respectful behavior that Bryant noticed in Italian parks (which he recalled in a series of letters written during an 1845 trip through England) eventually inspired the editor to call for similar environments in his home city. However, the inspiration had roots in Bryant's long-standing interest in the welfare of the poor. Although he later joined the Republican Party, throughout the 1830s and 1840s Bryant used the *Evening Post* to support the loco foco faction of the Democratic Party, a group dedicated to building a broad coalition of workers (Brown 235–39). Yet without healthful recreational environments, Bryant feared that the very same workers whose rights he championed would devote their spare hours to barrooms. The Italian parks solved this dilemma: without promoting distasteful behavior they provided for the needs of the urban poor (*Letters* 469–70).

A July 1844 editorial in the *Evening Post*—one that is often cited as the opening salvo in the campaign to build a New York park—brought Bryant's previously private musings on the subject into public discussion. The editorial, simply titled "A New Public Park," began by recognizing the annual departure of wealthy New Yorkers during the summer months. Bryant noted that some residents left "the town for shady retreats in the country," while "others refresh themselves with short excursions to Hoboken and New Brighton." Of course, for many residents limited finances prevented easy removal from the city, even to such nearby places as New Jersey or Brooklyn. The misery of sweltering New Yorkers, Bryant suggested, could be alleviated if municipal authorities "give our vast population an extensive ground for shade and recreation in these sultry afternoons." He identified a 160-acre tract running along the East River from Sixty-Eighth to Seventy-Seventh Street. With its river view and breezes, the site seemed ideal for an urban park: "The swift tides of the East River sweep its rocky shores, and the fresh breezes of the bay come in . . . over the restless waters." There could not be "a finer situation for the public garden of a great city."

Bryant's proposals raised two seemingly contradictory aims. The first was consistent with his reputation as a lover of nature, and many commentators have looked to Bryant's early poetry as evidence that his view of parks was nostalgic, a backward glance to a rural past. There is an element of truth to this view. Concerned that commercial development was "devouring inch by inch the coast" of Manhattan, Bryant urged that the remaining open space be "rescued." However, Bryant also saw cultivated greenery as an essential urban accouterment, a necessary component of his envisioned "great city." While European cities "have their extensive public grounds and parks," New York offered its residents little in the way of grand public spaces. Across the East River in Brooklyn, a similar vocabulary was employed by advocates who saw parks as essential to urban growth. Walt Whitman used the pages of the *Brooklyn Eagle* to campaign for the construction of Fort Greene Park, a thirty-eight-acre tract that he saw as vital to assuring economic and spiritual health of the then-still separate city. Thus, although Bryant and Whitman hoped that the imagery of their respective new parks would be rural—and Bryant in fact drew on his rural childhood for inspiration—both saw city greenery as a way to make the metropolitan area more urbane (Bluestone 537).

ANDREW JACKSON DOWNING

Andrew Jackson Downing offered a second important literary voice to the campaign to build a large public park. We do not often think of Downing as an urban reformer. He lived and died in rural Newburgh, New York, and devoted much of his professional life to writing about and designing rural retreats. Still, Downing displayed occasional interest in city spaces and wrote a series of influential essays calling for the construction of a large park in New York. Although he is today usually referred to as a landscape gardener or a horticulturist (he was both), Downing's contemporaries knew him best as the author of books on domestic architecture and as the editor of *The Horticulturist,* a monthly journal celebrating rural life. Indeed, Downing enjoyed greater commercial success than any American architectural writer before or since (Sweeting 1–13).

Despite his professional interests in physical spaces, Downing was essentially concerned with the state of the human soul, and it was this element of his work that led him to advocate for urban parks. Indeed, the belief that environment influenced behavior runs throughout his books and journal articles. In a *Horticulturist* essay, for example, he argued that "horticulture and its kindred arts tend strongly to fix the habits and elevate the character of the whole population." The proper decoration of one's surroundings would improve one's moral health. Likewise, cities, towns, and villages that allowed themselves to fall into physical disarray risked a corresponding spiritual decline. America's "GRACELESS VILLAGES," he believed, required "apostles of taste" to prevent such a state. Downing was particularly concerned that communities plant trees along their thoroughfares. A community "whose streets are bare of trees," he claimed, "ought to be looked upon as in a condition not less pitiable than a community without a schoolmaster or a teacher of religion" (*Rural Essays* 230–31).

Downing's most important contributions to the park movement appeared in the *Horticulturist.* In an October 1848 editorial written in the form of a dialogue between an editor and a traveler recently returned from Europe, he presented his views on the necessity of urban open space. Concerned that the traveler might have lost his patience for American institutions after witnessing the beauties of the Old World, the editor asks his friend to describe the perceived advantages of European life. The traveler reassures the editor of his patriotism, but adds that one pleasant aspect of European civilization he found lacking in America are "public parks open to all classes of people, provided by public cost [and] maintained at public expense." Parks, the traveler asserts, are essential building blocks for a humane society, even more so than "picture galleries" and "libraries." While these latter spaces are "intellectual luxuries," and therefore more private, an urban park allows "Man's social nature" to shine (Sweeting 15–38).

Downing drew his greatest inspiration from English landscaped estates and parks, an influence that subsequently affected the appearance of Central Park. Despite efforts to introduce the aristocratic heritage of landscape gardening to Americans of moderate means, he remained a committed Anglophile and admirer of England's landholding elite, particularly their vast estates. The modes of landscaping that Downing advocated, and those that Olmsted eventually employed in Central Park, were developed by gardeners serving the wealthiest British landowners. Downing's preferred landscaping styles—the Beautiful and the Picturesque—arose in England during the eighteenth century in reaction to the formal conventions of continental gardens. The Beautiful, the earlier of the two styles, emphasized smooth, gently rolling lawns of green punctuated here and there by glistening water and round-headed trees. The Picturesque was a slightly rougher form, one that relied on shadows and dense, intricate thickets to create a vaguely romantic landscape of mystery. Both forms aspired to appear natural, the former by recreating a prelapsarian terrain, the latter by paying closer attention to the varieties of light and flora.

Downing assumed that the apparent naturalism of British estates would improve his countrymen's spiritual health when introduced to American cities. Echoing Bryant, he praised parks for creating "salubrious and wholesome breathing spaces" that functioned as "the pleasant drawing-rooms of the whole population." The imaginary traveler from Downing's October 1848 *Horticulturist* essay asserts that parks are "better preachers of temperance than temperance societies"; no organization was a "better refiner of national manners." In July of the following year, Downing again addressed the need for a park, underscoring in this second essay the contrast between the hoped-for polite behaviors possible in parks and the popular urban entertainments that he and other reformers feared. If "hundreds of thousands will pay to see stuffed boa constrictors and un-human Belgian giants," he argued, then surely "a much higher number would visit a public garden" or park. Like Bryant, Downing mistrusted existing urban entertainments such as P. T. Barnum's American Museum because they encouraged sordidness. Urbanized forms of nature such as parks, on the other hand, encouraged more polite behaviors.

George W. Curtis

Downing's friend and biographer George Curtis shared the horticulturist's interest in landscape, literature, and parks. Such interests came early to Curtis, who as a teenager spent two years at the Transcendentalist community at Brook Farm in Massachusetts. In between his farming duties, the young Curtis studied German, music, and chemistry under the tutelage of the community's several fine scholars (Milne 12–33). In 1844, Curtis abandoned communal life for a two-year stay in Concord, where he worked as a farmer's helper while cultivating friendships with Emerson, Hawthorne, and Thoreau. In 1845, Curtis traveled to Newburgh, New York, to meet Downing, beginning what proved be a warm friendship. Following Downing's death in an 1852 steamship explosion, Curtis wrote a laudatory biography that served as the introduction to a posthumous collection of Downing's essays. Like Bryant, Curtis was a writer greatly interested in the artistic representation of space. He enjoyed a decades-long friendship with the landscape painter Christopher Cranch and was perhaps the most sensitive commentator on that artist's work. He also contributed several essays to the 1851 collection *Homes of American Authors,* a volume that celebrated the building decisions of leading American writers.

Aside from his outspoken support for abolition, Curtis's literary career kept him safely within the confines of New York's literary establishment. He earned his national reputation with a series of travel books detailing trips through Europe and the Middle East in the late 1840s. Travel writing and scenic descriptions proved lucrative for Curtis and helped him establish his powerful place in New York's large community of editors, journalists, and essayists. In 1851, he contributed sketches of visits to fashionable New York and New England vacation spots to the *New York Tribune,* most of which he subsequently collected and published in a popular volume. From 1853 to 1857 Curtis served as editor of *Putnam's Monthly Magazine,* a journal that in its short life published such leading voices in American letters as Emerson, Melville, Longfellow, and Stowe. From 1855 to 1857, in a literary partnership that was to have enormous impact on the environment of New York, Curtis shared editorial duties at *Putnam's* with Frederick Law Olmsted, the eventual designer of Central Park. In 1855, Curtis assumed a second important editorial post at *Harper's New Monthly Magazine,* for which he penned a series of essays entitled "From the Editor's Chair" (Milne). From this post, Curtis employed his breezy prose style to comment on a broad spectrum of literary and political subjects, not least of which was Central Park.

Curtis printed his boldest statements on parks in the June 1855 edition of *Harper's*. His column could not have come at a more opportune time, because it looked at that moment like the campaign to build a park might be permanently stalled. Opponents to the park had filed suit challenging the funding mechanism and the value of lands to be taken by eminent domain. Curtis blasted the political establishment for the delay: "Jealousy, spite, and meanness control public movements so that the intelligent and humane recoil from the contact of politics." In language that echoed Bryant, Curtis bemoaned the absence of open space in New York. The city, he wrote, has "none of those charming rural retreats . . . which atone to those who cannot escape into the real country." He also displayed little patience for those who claimed that open space would lead to disreputable behavior: Is "the immense majority of the population so rowdy that there is no hope for the success of decency over debauchery?" A park, Curtis added, will not become a public nuisance; "it will abate" such problems (124–25).

In the very next issue of *Harper's*, Curtis quickly dispelled any doubt that he viewed the proposed park as a way to preserve rural values. Here he argued that rural life offered little more than drudgery that was equally deadening to the mind and the body. Odes to the joys of country life, he felt, are generally written "by men who have chosen the city, and have not the slightest intention" of permanently removing themselves from town. Curtis saw America's professed love of the countryside as nothing but a hoax. Unfortunately, "few people are brave enough to confess that they do not like" rural living. The city, he claimed, is the place for "talent and ambition" as well as the "triumphs of literature, of art, and of general affairs" (July 1855 271–72). These remarks, coming so soon after Curtis's call for a public park, leave little doubt that the proposed urban oasis was to be a great urban spectacle, not a glance toward a vanishing (and unmissed) rural past.

Curtis's mixture of belles lettres and environmental reform typified the approach of the literary park advocates. The park was part of a broader campaign of reforms that included improvements in sanitation, the professionalization of municipal services, and beautification of the streetscape. With the important exception of Curtis, writers involved in the park campaign paid lip service to the country's rural past, but they recognized that the center of American life was rapidly relocating to cities. However, the city the literary reformers desired was a place where proper control had to be established; it was a conglomeration of people who needed to be protected from themselves. Central Park, then, must be seen as an essentially middle-class gesture, one that coincided with the aspirations of that class. Other than Bryant's early support for the radical wing of the Democratic Party, there was little talk among the writers of altering the economic relations between the poor and the rich. Polite literature provided the cultural cover necessary to bring the poor outdoors without upsetting established economic relations.

Frederick Law Olmsted

No writer did more to solidify the connection between genteel literature and urban environmental reform than Frederick Law Olmsted. Olmsted the architect has received a good deal of scholarly attention, but the literary milieu from which he emerged has not. Before turning his attention to landscape gardening, Olmsted was best known as a literary man. Indeed, his professional and personal connections with authors led to his initial employment as superintendent of the park. Without these connections to Downing, Curtis, and other writers, Olmsted would never have come to design Central Park, let alone the many other parks upon which his reputation rests.

Olmsted's early career was not auspicious. Relying on his father's support until he was thirty-five, the future designer dabbled in one career after another, including a disastrous stint at sea (Hall 15–35). He apparently found his calling in the late 1840s when he established a "model farm" on Staten Island, where he attempted to prove that a farm could be run scientifically, efficiently, and profitably. In 1846 he met Downing, who opened the pages of *The Horticulturist* to Olmsted's reviews of agricultural books. By appearing in such a well-known journal, these essays helped establish Olmsted's reputation as an expert on environmental and agricultural subjects.

Olmsted first achieved a national reputation upon the 1852 publication of *Walks and Talks of an American Farmer in England*. The two-volume work provided readers with a compendium of scenic description, analysis of farming techniques, and sociology of rural England. Its popular success brought Olmsted into the inner circles of literary life, a career development that hastened his abandonment of the model farm. The following year, he made a similar journey through the American South, this time as a correspondent of the *New York Daily Times,* to which he sent a series of letters detailing his observations on the economy, geography, and racial relations in the South. The letters angered many northern abolitionists, who believed that Olmsted was too quick to condemn northern labor practices and overly anxious to find pleasant things to say about slave holders. When in 1856 Olmsted put the sketches in book form, entitled *Journey in the Seaboard Slave States,* he revised his earlier views and adopted a more aggressive form of abolitionism, although his critique of slavery highlighted the economic inefficiencies of the system rather than the moral implications of bonded servitude. Despite, or perhaps because of, the controversy, Olmsted's work on slavery solidified his journalistic credentials and his place in the city's literary life (Roper 82–83).

Such were Olmsted's aspirations that in 1855, just two years before submitting his design for Central Park, he hoped to "take and keep a position as a recognized litterateur, a man of influence in literary manners" (Hall 47). Socially, he achieved his wish; as an active member of the Press Club, Olmsted dined with the likes of Thackeray and hosted luncheons for visiting or departing men of letters. His influence grew professionally as well when he joined the editorial staff of *Putnam's.* Although George Curtis apparently wielded most of the editorial power, Olmsted functioned as an emissary to its contributors and the public. Over an eighteen-month period, he visited with and solicited contributions from Emerson, Longfellow, and Stowe (Roper 110–13). Unfortunately, financial mismanagement caused the magazine to fold less than two years after Olmsted joined its staff. However, during his brief tenure, the future designer sat near the top of New York's literary hierarchy.

Olmsted's literary connections served him well during the critical period after the collapse of *Putnam's.* Out of work and apparently without prospects in New York, Olmsted returned to Connecticut in 1857 to work on a new volume of travel sketches. When word reached him that the position of construction superintendent was open, he pulled out all the stops to relentlessly pursue the job. Figuring that his experience as a farmer, agricultural writer, and student of English landscapes provided the necessary insight into managing a large landscaping project, Olmsted turned to his literary network to help him secure the post. His application was signed by leading figures in the city's literary community, including Bryant. Irving signed another letter to assure the newly empaneled board of commissioners, which had replaced the consulting board on which he previously sat, that despite his friend's literary accomplishments, Olmsted still had the pluck and managerial wisdom to supervise the construction of the park (Roper 128–29). Later, when the first design for the park proved unsatisfactory, Olmsted's literary connections again served him well. Calvert Vaux, formerly the architectural partner of Andrew Jackson Downing, convinced Olmsted to join him in submitting a plan in the competition for a new park design. It was a fortuitous partnership, because their winning plan, known as the Greensward Plan, established Olmsted and Vaux as master American landscapers. Irving was proved correct: Olmsted did possess the talent to supervise (and later design) such a project. However, without the community of literati that had supported him for years, that talent would never have emerged.

Physically, the Greensward Plan embodied the belletristic literature that Olmsted and his literary colleagues had previously confined to the page. Bright open spaces contrasted with intricate thickets and trails, which combined the smoothness of the English lawn with vaguely mysterious woods. Romantic mystery complemented Enlightenment cheer. The surfaces of the park allowed for both gentle hills and jutting rocks, a topography that Irving had described in his better-known tales. Also, the vistas, at once expansive and enclosed, allowed visitors to be part of an urban throng without the distractions of noise, odor, and troublesome behavior that so bothered the park advocates. The Greensward Plan was a regreening of the streetscape that did not turn its back on the metropolis.

The question remains, however, of what Olmsted, Downing, and their fellow literati hoped to gain first by calling for and then actually building an urban park. It is too easy and not entirely accurate to say that they hoped simply to maintain a rural order in an increasingly urbanized country. Central Park was not rural, although it drew on rural iconography. Nor is it true that the park just represented the concerns of a nervous elite who saw it as a way to drag the poor out of the taverns and into the open, although Downing's hopes that a park could serve as an open-air temperance society does sound like so much upper-class do-goodism.

However, if we keep the biographies and literary careers of the park advocates in mind, we come to another possible interpretation, one based in the history of American letters: Irving was a sketch writer, lawyer, and editor; Bryant, a poet and newspaper man; Olmsted, an author, occasional abolitionist, and landscape architect; and Downing, an architect, nursery owner, landscaper, and best-selling author. Many held political positions as well. Irving served as consulate to Spain. Bryant and Curtis were influential figures in the early years of the Republican Party and both were mentioned for national office. Only Downing among the literary park figures eschewed electoral politics, although his designs and writings were laced with political implications. The writers discussed in this chapter were, in short, gentlemen dabblers who perfected a conservative approach to the practice of literature. Bryant, Downing, and the others did not push American literature into new and challenging directions so much as they domesticated the language of English Romanticism and made it accessible to an American readership. They consolidated the fears and aspirations of an emerging middle class. Their approach to landscape was similarly divided: They hoped to preserve natural beauty while also stimulating urban growth. In landscape and letters, they tried to have it both ways. They wanted to preserve the old while seeing in the new. Central Park, then, represented a physical embodiment of these cultural tensions. Like its proponents, the park offered a hesitant look forward and a halting look backward.

NOTE

1. All citations from the *Journal of Commerce* are from page one editorials.

WORKS CITED

Bergman, Hans. *God in the Street: New York Writing from the Penny Press to Melville.* Philadelphia: Temple UP, 1995.

Bluestone, Daniel. "From Promenade to Park: The Gregarious Origins of Brooklyn's Park Movement." *American Quarterly* 39 (1987): 520–50.

Brown, Charles H. *William Cullen Bryant*. New York: Charles Scribner's Sons, 1971.

Bryant, William Cullen. *The Letters of William Cullen Bryant*. Ed. William Cullen Bryant II and Thomas G. Voss. Vol. 1. New York: Fordham UP, 1975. 6 vols. 1975–92.

Bryant, William Cullen II, and Thomas G. Voss. "A Place in the Country." *The Letters of William Cullen Bryant*. Ed. Bryant and Voss. Vol. 2. New York: Fordham UP, 1977. 189–93. 6 vols. 1975–92.

Child, Lydia Maria. *Letters from New York*. New York, 1843.

Curtis, George. *Harper's New Monthly Magazine*. New York, 1855.

Dickens, Charles. *American Notes: A Journey*. New York: International Publishing Corp., 1985.

Downing, Andrew Jackson. "Public Cemeteries and Public Gardens." *The Horticulturist* 4 July 1849: 9–12.

——. *Rural Essays*. New York, 1855.

——. "A Talk About Public Parks." *The Horticulturist*. 3 October 1848: 153–58.

Foster, George. *New York in Slices*. New York, 1849.

Hall, Lee. *Olmsted's America: An "Unpractical" Man and His Vision of Civilization*. Boston: Bullfinch Press, 1995.

Homberger, Eric. *Scenes from the Life of a City: Corruption and Conscience in Old New York*. New Haven, Conn.: Yale UP, 1994.

Milne, Gordon. *George William Curtis and the Genteel Tradition*. Bloomington: U of Indiana P, 1956.

Olmsted, Frederick Law. *Journey in the Seaboard Slave States*. New York, 1856.

——. *Walks and Talks of an American Farmer in England*. New York, 1851.

Roper, Laura Wood. *FLO: A Biography of Frederick Law Olmsted*. Baltimore, Md.: Johns Hopkins UP, 1973.

Rosenzweig, Roy, and Elizabeth Blackmur. *The Park and the People: A History of Central Park*. Ithaca, N.Y.: Cornell UP, 1992.

Spann, Edward K. *The New Metropolis: New York City, 1840–1857*. New York: Columbia UP, 1981.

Strong, George Templeton. *Diary*. Ed. Alan Nevins and M. H. Thomas. New York: Macmillan, 1952.

Sweeting, Adam W. *Reading Houses and Building Books: Andrew Jackson Downing and the Architecture of Popular Antebellum Literature, 1835–1855*. Hanover, N.H.: UP of New England, 1996.

White, Norval. *New York: A Physical History*. New York: Atheneum, 1987.

Wilentz, Sean. *Chants Democratic: New York City and the Rise of the American Working Class, 1778–1850*. New York: Oxford UP, 1984.

7

POSTINDUSTRIAL PARK OR BOURGEOIS PLAYGROUND?

Preservation and Urban Restructuring at Seattle's Gas Works Park

Richard Heyman

POSTINDUSTRIAL PARK

When Seattle's Gas Works Park opened on the northern shore of Lake Union in 1975 on the promontory previously known as Brown's Point, it was the world's first industrial-site-conversion park (figs. 7.1 and 7.2). On the former location of Seattle Gas Light Company's Lake Station Gasification Plant, this public park, which incorporates pieces of preserved industrial machinery with open green space, has since won numerous design awards and become the prototype for adaptive-use parks in deindustrializing cities across the country and abroad. Indeed, it seems to have fulfilled the 1971 prediction made by Eric DeLony of the National Park Service's Historic American Engineering Record: "The Lake Station Gas Works Park will not only be a unique first in the United States, if not the world, but will set an important precedent for the future preservation of industrial structures through an imaginative plan for adaptive use." The *Design and Environment* Award for Excellence citation (1975) praised "The successful conversion of a gas utility station into a fascinating exhibition of obsolete industrial hardware." Craig Campbell sounded a common note, repeated again and again in many professional and popular journals, when he wrote in *Landscape Architecture* that "The new 'Iron Gothic' park will remind Seattle of a noxious chapter in its past" (339). This high-profile park

Figure 7.1. Preserved industrial equipment at Gas Works Park, 1998. Photograph by the author.

is usually understood within a local history narrative that places the park and its industrial culture in a previous era that has virtually disappeared in the course of Seattle's march into the future, but for landscape architect Richard Haag's "Iron Gothic" monuments. As the Friends of Gas Works Park's home page maintains, "Gas Works Parks tells a story of Seattle and its people."

Far from being a simple expression of the evolution of a contemporary "postindustrial" or "postmodern" society, however, Gas Works Park articulates the spatial and conceptual reshaping of the urban landscape that has accompanied economic restructuring since the onset of a global capitalist crisis in the early 1970s, thus helping to produce a "postindustrial" discourse. Anthony King has argued that "we need to see the social production of buildings as well as their 'adaptive reuse' within this global context" (127). Also, just as "much of the social construction of mental illness in the nineteenth century depended on its architectural and physical-spatial representation" (King 130), we need to see Gas Works Park in the context of global economics and the social production of "postindustrialism." As Edward Soja argues, "Deindustrialization has been a critical fulcrum around

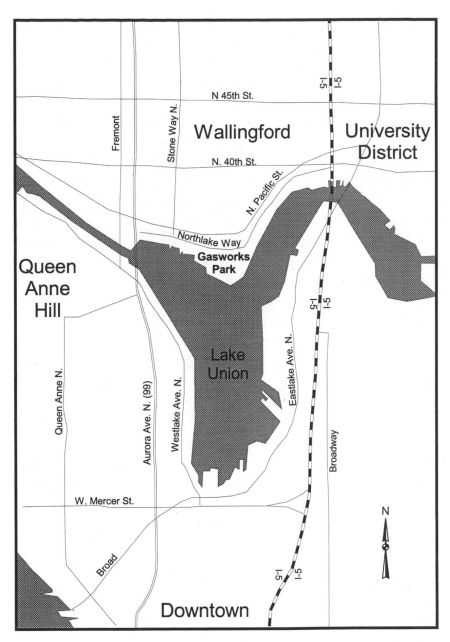

Figure 7.2. Map of Seattle, Washington. Lake Union is in the center, with Gas Works Park on the northern shore. Wallingford is to the north, downtown to the south, Queen Anne Hill to the west, and the University District to the northeast. Map prepared by W. Scott Moore, University of Washington Libraries. Data provided by Wessex. Used with permission.

which many other aspects of social and spatial restructuring revolve" (204). It was on the grounds of the Gas Works that Seattle made *its* social and spatial turn to a "postindustrial city." Gas Works Park was both produced by and helped to produce the economic, social, and spatial restructuring of Seattle in the 1970s.

Despite what designer Richard Haag and others say about the "historical" value of the preserved industrial hardware on the site, the rusting generators, scrubbers, and compressors tell us more about the present phase of capitalism than the Fordist era that begat them. As Evan Watkins argues in his book *Throwaways,* "obsolescence involves conditions of both cultural and economic production *in the present,* not what has survived, uselessly, from the past, as obsolescence stories would have it. . . . [It is] produced by and indispensable to present social organization" (7, original emphasis). Gas Works Park is not a memorial to an industrial urban past, but a mechanism for producing a present that attempts to erase the urban social structure of both that past and the present through a reorientation, a spatial restructuring, and a reconceptualization of the urban landscape. The park belongs to a contemporary movement that Soja calls "a naive and simplistic 'rush to the post'—to a postindustrialism . . . that insists on a finalizing end to an era, as if the past can be peeled away and discarded" (170).

Even this formulation failed to account for the ways in which the preservation of sites like the Gas Works actually produce that very "past," which is not so much discarded as entombed. Preservation theorist David Lowenthal maintains that "Preservation can fairly be charged with segregating the past. Consciousness of the past as a separate realm arouses the urge to save it; doing so then further sunders it from the present" (404–5). Lowenthal locates "the impulse to preserve" in a "destructive and disruptive change . . . in our own time" (396) that he believes began in the early 1970s.[1] Rapid changes made to the built environment since the restructuring of the 1970s first devalorized many American urban industrial sites and then dismantled them in a process similar to the more familiar gentrification of housing stock, as Neil Smith points out:

> Thus, although the media emphasis is on recent gentrification and the rehabilitation of working-class residences, there has also been a considerable transformation of old industrial areas of the city. This did not

simply begin with the conversion of old warehouses into chic loft apartments [see Zukin]; much more significant was the early urban renewal activity which, although certainly a process of slum clearance, was also the clearance of 'obsolete' (meaning also devalorized) industrial buildings (factories, warehouses, wharves, etc.) where many of the slum dwellers had once worked. (25)

As the "last operational oil gas plant in the United States and one of the few in the world still standing" in the early 1970s (Richard 10), Seattle's Gas Works seemed perfectly poised for the kind of gentrified preservation and adaptive reuse Smith describes. Lowenthal views this process in the context of local history: "Nothing so quickens preservation sympathies as the fear of imminent extinction, whether of a building, a bird, or a folkway" (399). However, in a global context, the preservation of the Gas Works actually produced the very sense of "extinction" in the service of constructing a "postindustrial" landscape. It became part of an emerging narrative popularized by Daniel Bell's influential 1973 book, *The Coming of Post-Industrial Society.*

Ironically, despite Lowenthal's insistence that "the past is a foreign country," he fails to develop the link between the rise of preservation in Europe and North America and the ongoing restructuring of the global economy. He argues that the past can be conceived as a foreign country because preservation "forms the temporal distinction which helped engender it to begin with. It is the express function of museums to sequester relics so as to save and display them. But survivals adapted to new uses are equally set apart from present-day things, their anachronisms highlighted, their antiqueness emphasized, the obsolescence of their original use underscored. Whether museumized or readapted, the preserved past is strongly differentiated from the everyday milieu" (405).

In the context of industrial preservation and reuse, the dual character of this differentiation, both temporal and spatial, places the "industrial" simultaneously in the past and reproduces common imperialist notions that identify that past with the "foreign," which is seen as occupying earlier stages of a universal development narrative. In the case of a "postindustrial" narrative such as Bell's, an industrial-site-conversion park like Gas Works Park produces an obsolescence that differentiates industrial-production sites as belonging to the past and, more specifically, to a past that is occupied by the "foreign"—in this case, the "developing" nations of the "Third World." For Smith, the differentiation Lowenthal identifies is linked to the new accumulation strategies of the restructured economy. Smith sketches the history of geographical differentiation beginning with the nineteenth century, when economic growth "was accomplished in part through absolute geographical expansion," and contrasts this development with a present in which "as far as its spatial basis is concerned, economic expansion takes place . . . not through absolute geographical expansion but through the internal differentiation of geographical space" (18). Although in earlier periods of capitalism expansion proceeded through an international division of labor by a differentiation between the First World industrial core and a Third World periphery of raw materials, contemporary economic expansion moves through a globalized spatial logic in which a postindustrial core and an industrial periphery exist side by side in the same nation and city—a new international division of labor. Mike Davis shows how Los Angeles has become a "burgeoning city of Third World immigrants" ("Urban" 84), on the one hand, and an "archipelago" of "pleasure domes," on the other (*City* 227)—a process in which "redevelopment massively reproduced spatial apartheid" (*City* 230). This new "internal differentiation" depends on both the temporal and spatial distinctions that Lowenthal finds are produced, in part, by preservation. The process of preservation is part of the social production of the contemporary, a process that depends upon a new spatial organization. It is within the changing global history of this link between economic and geographical expansion that we can trace the local history of Gas Works Park. The park's creation was part of a social restructuring that found justification through a postindustrial narrative, a reshaping of the landscape in which the concept of "the urban" was redefined away from "the industrial" through discursive and economic processes that produced a new international division of labor.

PARK TO INDUSTRIAL PLANT, INDUSTRIAL PLANT TO PARK

Prior to 1906, inhabitants of Seattle regularly used Brown's Point for picnicking and other leisure activities.[2] Situated at the bottom of a wooded

Figure 7.3. Seattle Gas Light Company's Lake Station Gasification Plant, 1910, looking east from Queen Anne Hill. Photograph courtesy of Special Collections Division, University of Washington Libraries, negative no. Webster & Stevens 16636.

hillside that was to become the residential neighborhood of Wallingford and across the lake from a city that began rapidly expanding toward the end of the nineteenth century, Brown's Point was a convenient spot for day-long getaways from an increasingly noisy, increasingly urban life. As Seattle began industrializing, spurred on by the gold rushes of the 1890s, so did Lake Union's character change; it started becoming a "working lake." Industry required access to an ample supply of both raw materials and fresh water for its production processes. As a promontory surrounded by a fresh water lake on three sides and close to the city center—and with hopes of soon connecting to Puget Sound by canal—Brown's Point was a prime location for a factory.

In 1906, the Seattle Gas Light Company purchased the site and erected a gasification plant there to manufacture illuminating or "town" gas, which was used to supply the gas lamps and heaters of the city's rapidly propagating businesses and residences (figs. 7.3 and 7.4). Production of manufactured gas through the carbonization of coal (later crude oil was used) required the thermal "cracking" of large hydrocarbon chains into smaller molecules that were lighter than air. This gas then had to be "scrubbed" or purified of tar,

Figure 7.4. Aerial view of Seattle, 1924, looking north across downtown and Lake Union. Smoke from the Gas Works can be seen rising on the far side of the lake. The Smith Tower is the tall building in the foreground. Photograph courtesy of Special Collections Division, University of Washington Libraries, negative no. uw4116.

lampblack or carbon dust, various oils, hydrogen sulfide, and other dangerous by-products before it was safe for use. The process was filthy, required an immense amount of water to "quench" the impurities, and produced noxious fumes and clouds of smoke that deposited ash and tar on local neighborhoods. The manufactured gas was then compressed for distribution and pumped out through hundreds of miles of pipes to communities all around the Seattle area.

At its inception, the belching plant was on the outskirts of the city. However, as the century marched on, pulling the city further into the industrial economy, people marched north and houses went up on the hills above the gas works. Due to the incessant complaints from residents of Wallingford, in 1934 the Gas Light Company was forced to install pollution-reducing devices. However, increasing production countered decreased emissions, and smoke increased through the war years. Houses in Walling-

Figure 7.5. The derelict Gas Works in the early 1970s. The shed that Richard Haag used as an office is the white building in the lower right portion of the site. Photograph courtesy of Special Collections Division, University of Washington Libraries, negative no. uw4796.

ford were built facing north in attempts to minimize contact with the offensive plant, and the neighborhood was oriented away from the urban "working lake" and the industries lining its shores (Richard 31–32).

By 1956, cheap, "clean" natural gas had entirely replaced the expensive and odious process of manufacturing gas, and the Gas Works was closed. The plant remained standing and became a favorite topic of complaint for Seattlites: an industrial "eyesore," part of the discourse of "urban blight" taking shape (fig. 7.5). In 1962, Myrtle Edwards, Seattle city council member and chair of the parks committee, proposed acquiring the lakeside property for development into a traditional Victorian-style, landscaped urban park, a return to the pre-1906 days when Brown's Point was an escape from the city. She negotiated the purchase of the site from the Gas Light Company for $1.3 million. The deal required the gas company to remove all equipment and clear the site by the 1973 transfer date. By 1968 voters were squarely behind Edwards's efforts to remove this symbol of urban blight and create a sanctuary from modern life; they approved the Forward Thrust Bond Issue, which allocated $1.75 million for the "acquisition and development [of the site] into an urban park" ("Fact Sheet"). Myrtle Edwards died

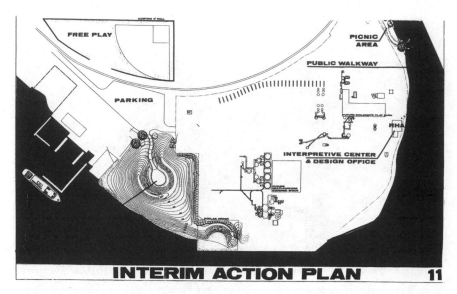

Figure 7.6. Drawing submitted as part of Richard Haag's Interim Action Plan for Myrtle Edwards Park. From Gas Works Park Case Study, Library of Architecture and Urban Planning, University of Washington.

shortly afterward in a car accident, and it was agreed that the park would be named in her memory.

In 1970, the Seattle Department of Parks awarded the commission of a master plan for the Myrtle Edwards Park to landscape architect Richard Haag. Haag converted a small shed on the 20.5-acre lot into an office and used it as the staging ground for an intensive study of the site. In 1971, to the horror of the city council and the public, Haag submitted a master plan that called for the "selective preservation" of structures from the gas works (fig. 7.6). For the year and a half following the disclosure of his radical plan, Haag mounted a vigorous offensive to convince the city council and the public of the viability and merits of his vision. He described his own conversion this way: "I started hanging around there and I suddenly realized that the city's intention to raze the site was all wrong. . . . So I decided to launch a campaign to save the gas works" (Goldberger 1). Haag's campaign took a three-pronged approach, focusing, as he stated in his master plan, on the "geographic location, historic significance and esthetic resources" of the site. He argued that "the site's most commanding asset is the reflected panorama of Seattle's skyline as seen across the length of Lake Union.

Imbued with a sense of flight and catalyzed by intense marine activity, this overview presents a day/night metamorphosis of space and light unequaled anywhere in Seattle; a full scale, natural 'light show.' " (9)

Haag wanted to create an urban park where users would be drawn into the city experience, not escape it, as Wallingford had tried to do by "turn[ing] its back on the view of the city skyline and a choice southern aspect" (8). Haag maintained that a Victorian "greensward" park was anachronistic because "the traditional escape from the city into the sylvan settings of remote areas has changed for many people into a seeking of a more active encounter. . . . The experience most needed in Seattle's park system is a highly active urban park" (2). Furthermore, Haag argued, the "timeless grandeur" of the industrial equipment was of historic and aesthetic importance. To demonstrate this he held a highly publicized series of presentations that juxtaposed slides of modernist art and sculpture with images of the gas works' "iron gothic forms," along with sketches of children playing on the obsolete machinery (fig. 7.7). Haag's aestheticization of the gas works effectively produced an obsolescence narrative that succeeded in winning unanimous approval for his master plan from the city council with the support of the public. Myrtle Edwards's family, however, was not convinced; in the end they refused to allow an active urban "postindustrial" park to bear her name. The Gas Works Park was born and was finally opened to the public in 1975.

The passive, escapist Victorian park envisioned by Myrtle Edwards and embraced by the public in 1968 belonged to the manufacturing-dominated urban landscape and social structure of industrial capitalism, embodied in the factory, that existed in the United States prior to the crisis and restructuring of the early 1970s. However, Haag's 1971 plan for Gas Works Park was part of the restructured urban landscape of the contemporary social structure of capitalism, embodied in the corporate office tower. The two park concepts encapsulate two different social and economic structures inscribed in the landscape and represent two different spatial orientations: one had its back turned on a grimy "working lake" and city of industry and externally differentiated space, whereas the other looked inward and embraced an aestheticized city figured in the burgeoning skyline of office buildings—it internally differentiated space. What changed between 1968 and 1971 was the very meaning of the notion "urban."

SMALL CHILDREN'S   **PLAY BARN**

Figure 7.7. Drawing submitted as part of Richard Haag's Master Plan for Myrtle Edwards Park. From Gas Works Park Case Study, Library of Architecture and Urban Planning, University of Washington.

According to the Employment Security Department of Washington State, between 1968 and 1971 Seattle (King County) lost nearly thirty-four thousand jobs overall, a decrease of about 9 percent, while the manufacturing sector lost almost fifty-seven thousand, or 41 percent, of its jobs. The service sector, however, gained twenty-five hundred jobs, an increase of about 5 percent. Astonishingly, government employment jumped from under one thousand in 1968 to over thirty-six thousand in just three years, an increase of 395 percent (table 7.1). In terms of the percentage of total jobs countywide, only these three sectors show significant change over the last fifty years and only these showed more than a change of one percentage point between 1968 and 1971. Manufacturing jobs dropped from 35 percent of the work force—a level it had maintained from 1956, the year the Gas Works closed—to 23 percent in 1971; 22 percent in 1975, when the park

Table 7.1. Number of Jobs by Sector, King County, Washington

SECTOR	1968	1971	CHANGE
Forestry and fishing	1,317	1,369	+52
Mining and quarrying	312	233	−79
Construction	25,211	18,534	−6,677
Manufacturing	140,325	83,482	−56,843
Transportation, communication, and utilities	32,939	31,787	−1,152
Wholesale and retail trade	114,347	106,993	−7,354
Finance, insurance, and real estate	31,568	31,967	+399
Services	52,798	55,343	+2,545
Government	886	36,019	+35,133
Total	399,703	365,728	−33,975

Source: Washington State Employment Security Department.

opened; and less than 15 percent today. The service sector increased its share of jobs by 2 percent between 1968 and 1971, the same increase it showed in the previous twelve years from the closing of the Gas Works. It captured another 4 percent of the workforce in the four years the park was under construction and has continued to increase to a current 27.8 percent of the total jobs in King County. Government employment, which in 1956 was not even listed by the Washington State Employment Security Department and which had an insignificant 0.2 percent of the work force in 1968, jumped to nearly 10 percent in 1971. Today it accounts for 13.7 percent of all jobs in the county, just one percentage point behind manufacturing. In fact, manufacturing occupies roughly the same relative position today that services did in 1947, the year the state began its statistical measurements, whereas the service sector accounts for nearly the same percentage of jobs today that manufacturing held in 1947 (fig. 7.8). That is, the economic structure of Seattle has done a complete about-face in the last fifty years. The pivotal point in time came between the Forward Thrust Bond Issue of 1968 and Haag's master plan of 1971.

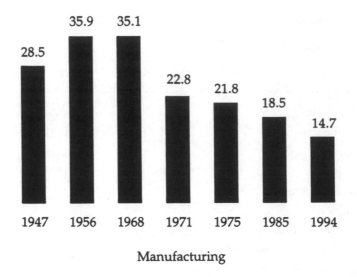

Manufacturing

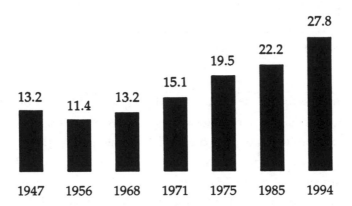

Services (include. engineering, accounting, and management)

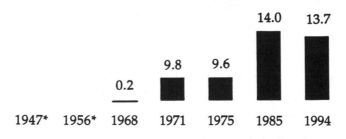

Government (*not classified in 1947 or 1956)

Figure 7.8. Percentage of total jobs by sector, King County, 1947–94. Source: Washington State Employment Security Department. Prepared by the author.

The astonishingly rapid deindustrialization and social restructuring of Seattle between 1968 and 1971 accompanied a spatial reshaping of the urban landscape, which manifested itself in the exploding skyline of downtown. The city was no longer the "urban jungle" that it had been under industrial capitalism. The "return to the city" had begun, and the collection of office towers downtown was the material sign of that shift written onto the landscape. The Gas Works went from being the space of industrial urban rejection to the premiere site for the aestheticization of the new urban landscape of a service-oriented office culture and the valorization of a local "postindustrial" narrative. It was the space on which Seattle's economy pivoted between 1968 and 1971. Historic preservation of the Gas Works accomplished much of the groundwork necessary for the social production of contemporary Seattle.

"Urban Pioneers" and Urban Blight

Haag's successful campaign to "save the gas works" was part of a movement that Neil Smith connects to the changing link between economic and geographical expansion:

> Anti-urbanism has been a dominant theme in American culture. In a pattern analogous to the original experience of wilderness, the last 20 years have seen a shift from fear to romanticism and a progression of urban imagery from wilderness to frontier. . . . Thus the term "urban pioneer" is as arrogant as the original notion of the "pioneer" in that it conveys the impression of a city that is not yet socially inhabited; like the Native Americans, the contemporary urban working class is seen as less than social, simply part of the physical environment. (16)

Many writings on Gas Works Park see Richard Haag in just such a role, treat him with an appropriate reverential tone, and use the term "pioneer" to characterize him (Richard 13). In fact, Haag seems to see himself in just such a historic line. He claims, "I haunted the buildings and let the spirit of place enjoin me. I began seeing what I liked then I liked what I saw—new eyes for old. Permanent oil slicks became plains with outcroppings of concrete, industrial middens were drumlins, the towers were ferro-forests and their brooding presence became the most sacred of symbols" (Richard 15).

Haag's use of "wilderness" metaphors effectively removes the Gas Works from both the realm of the social and the present; it recycles older frontier ideas about westward expansion, but turns them back on the urban. This discourse is widespread. Kevin Lynch, another preservation theorist, wrote in 1972 that "urban and rural wastelands already serve as a new wilderness" (192). Writing for *Architectural Record* in 1993, Charles Linn celebrates the process of reclaiming "parks from wasteland" (108). Smith's formulation helps us see the "pioneer" narrative shared by Haag and other commentators in the context of the dual movement of industrial-site preservation that places industrial production in a realm that is both in the "past" and "foreign"; that is, it sets up a narrative of underdevelopment that facilitates urban redevelopment and "renaissance," which leads to the creation of Bell's "post-industrial society."

"URBAN RENAISSANCE" OR BOURGEOIS PLAYGROUND?

A discourse emerged around Haag's master plan that reveled in the spectacle of the corporate office tower as the expression of a contemporary "postindustrial" era while consigning the industrial to the "past." The possibility for a Gas Works Park rose out of that shift. The park became the primary space for reinforcing the changing aesthetic of the urban, with its "choice southern aspect" the primary viewing point for the new urban orientation and spatialization caused by the "return to the city" or the new "urban renaissance." Roman Cybriwsky et al. have identified the "downtown-focused service orientation characteristic of the 'postindustrial' city" (94) that has emerged since the beginning of urban and economic restructuring in the 1970s. Smith explains how this increased concentration of "central decision making in the form of corporate or governmental headquarters" has come into being: "Together with the expansion of this sector *per se* and the cyclical movement of capital into the built environment, this spatial response to temporal and financial irregularity helps to explain the recent office boom in urban centers. . . . In the advanced capitalist city it is the *financial* and administrative dictates which perpetuate the tendency toward centralization. This helps to explain why . . . the restructuring of the urban core takes on the corporate/professional character that it does" (29; original empha-

Figure 7.9. Northeast view from the Smith Tower, 1957. Lake Union and Wallingford are visible in the distance. Photograph courtesy of Special Collections Division, University of Washington Libraries, negative no. Hamilton 3086.

sis). The preservation and conversion of the Gas Works into a park that had as its "primary asset" a view of the emerging office-oriented urban core helped create the kind of internal differentiation of space on which the continuing economic expansion and restructuring relied (figs. 7.9 and 7.10).

With its emphasis on the spectacle of office buildings, Gas Works Park helps reinforce the new urban orientation, in which its own "obsolete" nature is not so much the basis for a memorial to the past, but the grounds for the emergence of a "postindustrial" narrative. This vision is emphasized on the home page of the Friends of Gas Works Park, which opens on a photograph of downtown Seattle as seen from the park, with no pictures of the park itself. The stated mission of the Friends of Gas Works Park is twofold: "To celebrate our industrial past" and to gather support for "the installation of a camera obscura" in one of the preserved generator towers. The link between the production of—or insistence on—an "industrial past" and the spectacle of the downtown skyline is striking in the context of global restructuring. The joining of these two strands of preservation, the temporal and spatial differentiation, places our vision not on "our industrial past," but elsewhere, on the tableau of the city (soon to be "pictured" with a camera obscura).

Figure 7.10. Northeast view from the Smith Tower, 1982. Compare to figure 7.9. Photograph courtesy of Special Collections Division, University of Washington Libraries, negative no. Hamilton 4175.

Writing about urban preservation projects—specifically the South Street Seaport in New York, but also the Faneuil Hall / Quincy Market project in Boston, Harbor Place in Baltimore, Fisherman's Wharf in San Francisco, and Riverwalk in New Orleans—M. Christine Boyer explains the function of these sites in creating a spectacle of the "present" city around them:

> City tableaux are the places where a society turns back upon itself to view the spectacle of its own performance. . . . The spectacle, moreover, is a visual delight intended to immobilize our attention in the act of "just looking." In the scenographic tableaux of our contemporary cities, whether a historic district, a contextually zoned district, or a carefully managed theme park, the act of "just looking" and enjoying the pure visibility of the show absorbs the spectator's view. . . . These tableaux separate pleasure from necessity, escape from reality. They widen the gap between the city on display and the city beyond our view. (191–92)

Through the internal differentiation of space, the production of "postindustrialism" directs our gaze on the "renewed" urban office core while placing industrial production out of view, in the "foreign" past. This movement bolsters the "development" narrative in which the First and Third Worlds, which increasingly live side by side, exist in different time periods and are defined by the economic sectors that dominate them. As a result, the global dispersal of industrial production into the traditional "periphery" and the peripheralization of parts of the traditional "core" creates a new international division of labor and a new social organization for a world unified in the accumulation of capital, but differentiated spatially and temporally. Similarly, Bell's book, which crystallized the concept, focuses exclusively on the U.S. economy and ignores the wider, global changes taking place. In local history narratives, such as the one surrounding Gas Works Park, the structural links between the two worlds are erased and the "contemporary" can only be seen as "postindustrial."

Many critics have noticed this "dual" character of the new international division of labor. William Greider explains this process of polarization by pointing out that

> The most alarming aspect of how globalization degrades law is in the conditions for work. The new information technology has been popularized as the dawn of a "postindustrial age," but that blithe vision ignores what is actually happening to industrial workers. In the primitive legal climate of poorer nations, industry has found it can revive the worst forms of nineteenth-century exploitation, abuses outlawed long ago in the advanced economies, including extreme physical dangers to workers and the use of children as expendable cheap labor. Indeed, the powerful strands of the global market also undermine legal protections for workers in some advanced economies. Sweatshops are back in the United States, visible from Los Angeles to New York and across the rural South. (34)

In identifying the "blithe vision" of "postindustrialism," however, Greider maintains the temporal distinction in the conditions of production and misses the *in*visibility inherent in the focus on the "contemporary." Various contributors to John Mollenkopf and Manuel Castells's *Dual City* explore the issue by describing the process that I have been outlining as an increasing "polarization" between the professional/managerial class and the working class in what they call a "changing ethnic/racial division of labor." As they demonstrate, industrial production is increasingly shifting to women and people of color around the world. The "postindustrial"

Figure 7.11. Aerial view of Seattle in the early 1980s, looking north across downtown. Lake Union can be seen in the upper right. The Smith Tower is barely distinguishable in front of the new skyscrapers. Compare to figure 7.4. Photograph courtesy of Special Collections Division, University of Washington Libraries, negative no. Hamilton 81-17.

ideology ignores the structural—and therefore contemporaneous—links between these people of the internally differentiated "Third World" and those in the "information society." In her contribution to *Dual City*, "The Informal Economy," Saskia Sassen examines the rise of sweatshops and finds that "what are perceived as backward sectors of the economy may not be remnants from an earlier phase of industrialization but may well represent a downgrading of work involving *growing* sectors of the economy" (82, my emphasis). Sassen concludes that "the growth of the informal economy in New York City represents not a regression from or an anomaly in an otherwise advanced capitalist economy, but a fundamental aspect of the postindustrial city" (94). Viewed in a global perspective, through the lens of the new international division of labor rather than through a local development narrative, industrial production must be seen as part of the present.

Thus, the effect of the "postindustrial" ideology, the "blithe vision" Greider describes, is an attempt to create what Smith calls "a bourgeois playground" (32) by erasing the structural and contemporaneous connections between the differentiated "core" and "periphery." Through the dual nature of preservation, Gas Works Park directs our gaze at its "choice southern aspect" in service of the production of the "contemporary" urban skyline of downtown Seattle while placing industrial production out of sight, in the "foreign" "past" of the contemporary "Third World." The emergence of a "postindustrial" narrative was facilitated by the Gas Works, while at the same time it made possible a Gas Works Park (fig. 7.11).

THE RETURN OF THE PAST: SOME INDUSTRIAL REMINDERS

In a very material way, the construction of corporate office buildings helped produce Gas Works Park through attempted erasure of the past. When the city received the site from the Gas Light Company in 1973, the ground was saturated by oil and chemicals and littered with industrial waste. Some soil was removed, and the waste—mostly carbon dust called lampblack, along with discarded arsenic—was pushed into a pile on the southwestern portion of the site. Clean dirt from the excavation for the construction of the Safeco Building in the university district—the only office tower north of the Lake Washington Ship Canal—was used as a new top layer for much of the park and comprises the majority of dirt in the Great Mound, known colloquially as Kite Hill. Haag's biggest concern was getting grass and other top-cover to grow in the polluted park; little thought was given to health risks.

However, in 1984 Gas Works Park had to be shut down for five months while the Environmental Protection Agency (EPA) conducted tests of the soil and ground water. PCBs, DDT, lead, and other carcinogens and toxins were found seeping into Lake Union from the park. Similar substances were discovered in the park itself. Although levels are low enough to allow the EPA to declare the park "safe," signs still warn users to avoid direct contact with the soil.[3] This "return of the past" constitutes the truly "historic" significance of Gas Works Park. In fact, I would maintain that only in 1984, when the toxic nature of industrial capitalism became undeniable, did the Gas Works become a truly "postindustrial" park. The discovery of toxins in the soil of the park provides us with a powerful reminder of the persistence of industrial labor into the present and its structural connection to the park's spectacular view of downtown. The oozing chemicals force us to see that "postindustrialism" comprises not only the "pleasure domes" of a "bourgeois playground," but the spaces of peripheralized "Third World" labor as well. Only by seeing Gas Works Park in a global economic context can we make sense of Seattle's spatial reorientation, which was signaled by Wallingford's turn toward the former "working lake" to capitalize on the spectacle of office buildings visible on its "choice southern aspect."

Although we tend to see preserved sites as "historic," we must also keep in mind the extent to which they are what Kevin Lynch calls "device[s] for explaining the advancing present" (226). In preserving sites such as Gas Works, we must also heed Lowenthal's reminder that "Relics are mute; they require interpretation" (243). We need to move beyond the local history narrative and celebration of Haag's urban "pioneering genius" and focus on what Michael Frisch calls "a shared authority"—the recognition that sites such as Gas Works Park are the products of many "authors": the industrial laborers who worked on the site from 1906 to 1956 during the Gas Works' operation as well as industrial workers in less visible, peripheralized locations around the globe. In this way, Gas Works Park can better fulfill Dolores Hayden's ideal of "landscape as public history"—it can resist the pressure of development narratives that figure the working class as "less than social, simply part of the physical environment" (Smith 16) that can be peeled away and discarded in the promotion of a new "postindustrial" ideology.

Lest this seems an easy task, Frisch warns that "we cannot expect cultural authority to be shared willingly by those who exercise it, rendering the sharing of other forms of authority increasingly problematic" (xxiii). The fight to see the history of preserved sites not exclusively in local terms, but as the intersection of local and global processes of which they have always been a part, will not be easy. However, a commitment to social history must seek to acknowledge all the "authors" of a site, both local and international. The authors of Gas Works Park include not only Richard Haag and workers from "our industrial past," but industrial workers in the "postindustrial" present at home and abroad.[4]

NOTES

1. For more on the genealogy of the "impulse to preserve," see Lowenthal 387–96.
2. For the history of the site, I have relied on Richard's *Seattle's Gas Works Park,*

Haag's *Report,* the Seattle Department of Parks and Recreation's "Fact Sheet," and the *Gas Works Park Case Study* at the Library of Architecture and Urban Planning at the University of Washington.

3. For the story of the park's pollution problems, see Jones's "In 1962" and "Park Designer" and Jones and Kenick's "Park."

4. I would like to thank Katharyne Mitchell, Gail Dubrow, and Matt Sparke for their guidance during the development of this project. The librarians in the Library of Architecture and Urban Planning and in the Special Collections Division at the University of Washington provided invaluable assistance in locating documents and photos. Participants in the University of Washington's 1996 Americanist Conference, Princeton University's 1996 Tales of the City Conference, and the 1997 ASLE Conference at the University of Montana were patient with me while I worked out these ideas and stopped me from entering many dark alleyways.

WORKS CITED

Bell, Daniel. *The Coming of Post-Industrial Society.* New York: Basic Books, 1973.

Boyer, M. Christine. "Cities for Sale: Merchandising History at South Street Seaport." *Variations on a Theme Park.* Ed. Michael Sorkin. New York: Hill and Wang, 1992. 181–204.

Campbell, Craig C. "Seattle's Gas Plant Park." *Landscape Architecture* (July 1973): 338–48.

Cybriwsky, Roman A., David Ley, and John Western. "The Political and Social Construction of Revitalized Neighborhoods: Society Hill, Philadelphia, and False Creek, Vancouver." *Gentrification of the City.* Eds. Neil Smith and Peter Williams. Boston: Allen & Unwin, 1986. 92–120.

Davis, Mike. *City of Quartz.* New York: Vintage, 1990.

——. "Urban Renaissance and the Spirit of Postmodernism." *Postmodernism and Its Discontents.* Ed. E. Ann Kaplan. London: Verso, 1988. 79–87.

DeLony, Eric. Letter to Victor Steinbrueck. 15 April 1971. *Gas Works Park Case Study.* Library of Architecture and Urban Planning, University of Washington.

Employment Security Department of Washington State. *Employment and Payrolls in Washington State by Area and by Industry.* Olympia: Employment Security Department of Washington State, 1947–94.

"Fact Sheet." *Seattle Washington Gas Works Park Fact Sheet.* Seattle: Department of Parks and Recreation, 1975.

Friends of Gas Works Park Page. http://www.astro.washington.edu/waddell/FoGWP.html. Seattle: Friends of Gas Works Park, 1997.

Frisch, Michael. *A Shared Authority.* Albany: State U of New York P, 1990.

"Gas Works Park." *Design and Environment Projects.* Washington D.C.: R. C. Publications, 1976. 44–45.

Gas Works Park Case Study. Library of Architecture and Urban Planning, University of Washington.

Goldberger, Paul. "Gas Works is Centerpiece of Seattle Park." *New York Times* 30 August 1975: 1.

Greider, William. *One World, Ready or Not: The Manic Logic of Global Capitalism.* New York: Simon & Schuster: 1997.

Haag, Richard. *A Report Substantiating the Master Plan for Myrtle Edwards Park.* Seattle: Department of Parks and Recreation, 1970.

Hayden, Dolores. *Power of Place: Urban Landscapes as Public History.* Cambridge, Mass.: MIT Press, 1995.

Jones, Lansing. "In 1962, Gas Works Park Was a 'Fantastic Deal.' " *Seattle Times / Seattle Post-Intelligencer* 29 April 1984: A26.

——. "Park Designer Defends Pollution Plan." *Seattle Times* 16 April 1984: 1+.

Jones, Lansing, and Lisa Kenick. "Park Was Built on Foul Mound of Chemical Soup." *Seattle Times* 22 April 1984: B1.

King, Anthony D. "Building Institutionally Significant Histories: On Understanding the Adaptive Reuse of Buildings." *Changing Places: Remaking Industrial Buildings.* Eds. Lynda H. Schneekloth, Marcia F. Feuerstein, and Barbara A. Campagna. Freedonia, N.Y.: White Pine Press, 1992. 124–36.

Linn, Charles D. "Paradise Lost and Found." *Architectural Record* 181 (1993): 108.

Lowenthal, David. *The Past Is a Foreign Country.* New York: Cambridge UP, 1985.

Lynch, Kevin. *What Time Is This Place?* Cambridge, Mass.: MIT Press, 1972.

Mollenkopf, John, and Manuel Castells, eds. *Dual City: Restructuring New York.* New York: Russel Sage Foundation, 1991.

Richard, Michael. *Seattle's Gas Works Park.* Seattle: Michael Richard, 1983.

Smith, Neil. "Gentrification, the Frontier, and the Restructuring of Urban Space." *Gentrification of the City.* Eds. Neil Smith and Peter Williams. Boston: Allen & Unwin, 1986. 15–34.

Soja, Edward. *Postmodern Geographies.* London: Verso, 1989.

Watkins, Evan. *Throwaways: Work Culture and Consumer Education.* Stanford, Calif.: Stanford UP, 1993.

Zukin, Sharon. *Loft Living.* New Brunswick, N.J.: Rutgers UP, 1982.

4

URBAN ``WILDERNESS''

8

BOYZ IN THE WOODS
Urban Wilderness in American Cinema
Andrew Light

This chapter tracks the malicious representation in recent American cinema of the city as an urban wilderness of the "classical" sort. I begin by revisiting and summarizing arguments I have made earlier about the meaning of classical wilderness (Light "Metaphorical," "Urban") and then identify its use in two sets of films about the city. First, I look at the film *Falling Down,* which portrays the wild city from the perspective of whites seemingly trapped in the urban environment. In this film, our acceptance of the breakdown of the antihero (an unemployed defense worker) is parasitic on a depiction of Los Angeles as an urban wilderness. Second, and more hopeful, are the responses to the trope of an "urban wilderness" in portrayals of the inner city by African American film makers like Spike Lee, John Singleton, and the Hughs brothers. The point of this analysis will be to provide a normative critique of the filmic description of racial minorities as the savage inhabitants of an urban wilderness—a continuation of the general legacy of the depiction of racial others and nature itself as uncivilized and thus unworthy of equal moral consideration.

CLASSICAL WILDERNESS DEFINED

According to the classical view of wilderness, human society is the standard by which the world is measured and, hence, conquest of the nonhuman areas—the wild—signals a form of human achievement, "a victory over the dark forces and a measure of social progress" (Short 6). By contrast, the Romantic view of wilderness depicts it as that form of nature that has remained close to its "pristine" state, meaning that it has not been "corrupted" by human intervention.[1] Although contemporary Americans tend to be at least neutral to wild nature, even pseudo-Romantics, the idea of an unknown evil at the edge of civilization still haunts us. The question is: Where does that evil reside in our society?

The classical view foregrounds what I call a *cognitive dimension* of wilderness, a notion of wilderness as a place that is always marked as the realm of the savage, who is thought to be cognitively, or mentally, distinct from the civilized human. The savage is always marked as the thing that we civilized people are not. We are superior to the savage simply in not being the savage, and part of what makes us not savage is that we think we have possession of reason or control over our passions. The savage, according to the classical view, is completely subject to his passions. In fact, he is driven by them to the point where he cannot escape the wilderness because leaving would require more than merely a physical escape; if the savage leaves wild nature, he is still wild because of the "cognitive" wilderness within. Thus, the cognitive dimension of wilderness refers to the misperceived wildness within the beings who are part of wild nature; it is not the mere physical surroundings, but the supposed claim of those surroundings on the mental states of its inhabitants, that truly matters. To be able to mark off the wild from civilization does not therefore require any specialized knowledge of wild places with respect to their physicality, but only a strong sense of the difference between us and them—between we civilized, rational agents and those uncivilized, passion-filled savages.

The classical view, with this important cognitive presupposition, was the dominant view of wilderness that traveled from the Old World to the New World and shaped the early European American perceptions of Native Americans. So uncontested was this assumption of a cognitive distinction between civilized and uncivilized peoples that early American thinkers developed radically different views of the potential for civilizing various kinds of savages without ever questioning the grounds for their debate. While some believed that the African "savage" could be made to be civilized (with appropriate "guidance") outside of his wild jungles, they held that the Native American was beyond hope. Others, like Thomas Jefferson, argued that the formula was reversed.[2]

One way of understanding the extremity of this view is to recognize that the classical wilderness becomes a stand-in for a state of spiritual despair. Wilderness is represented as a kind of hell. For the early Puritans, the wilderness was a projection of their deepest fears of what they would become in this new land if they were not careful. As John Rennie Short notes, "the [classical] Wilderness becomes an environmental metaphor for the dark side of the human psyche" (9). If one entered wilderness without "taming" it, one risked succumbing to one's potential for evil.

Let me try to be more precise about this characterization of the classical view of wilderness. It can be summarized as emerging out of three related and often overlapping theses:

1. Separation. Because the wilderness is bad, evil, cruel, etcetera, it must be separated from humans—it must be marked off as distinct and kept out of civilized spaces.
2. Savagery. The inhabitants of the wilderness are nonhuman beasts and are to be accordingly demonized and vilified.
3. Superiority. In contrast, civilization (and its inhabitants) may be celebrated for its superiority over wilderness as a haven of virtue.

I will continue to refer to these theses to demonstrate the existence of a classical wilderness ideology in contemporary American films.

Of course, the idea of the classical wilderness is constantly going through revision. Therefore, the relative existence of these characteristics, as applied to certain spaces and texts, may indicate a kind of wilderness in transition. For example, one could speculate that as European Americans completed a concentrated effort to eliminate Native Americans in the 1800s, the relevance of thesis 2 diminished for a time (because there were many fewer Indians to vilify), while the wilderness still existed as a place inferior to white civilization (thesis 3). It could also be argued that the process of westward expansion was a gradual move from thesis 1 to 3, that is, a gradual move from fear of the wilderness to triumph over it. Still, the stimulation for conquering wilderness as evidence of our superiority was our fear as expressed in theses 1 and 2.

Certainly the classical account of wilderness is a cultural construction with an identifiable history.[3] Importantly though, my claim is not that everything is a cultural construction, or even that all expressions referring to parts or processes of nature are cultural constructions. In my view, for example, the actual process of photosynthesis is not a cultural construction. However, wilderness, or as I prefer to think about it given this genealogical account, "wild nature," is somehow different in kind than photosynthesis. Although wild nature certainly does contain a dimension that is scary and harsh, the experience of which helped to form the classical ideal, it can also be other things. It could also be a source of special transcendence, as some Romantics claimed. But the reality of the wild must lie somewhere between these two poles of terror and bliss: Wild nature is savage and beneficent, but certainly not exclusively either all of the time.

If classical wilderness was something more like a metaphor, then what kind of representation was it? Particularly in the case of North America, the classical conception of wilderness as applied to wild nature imbued an ideological overlay on the land. What was being referred to was not wild nature at all. Because of this absence of a physical reference, classical wilderness is a metaphor that primarily describes a view of how certain people project themselves into, and in opposition to, the world around them. Therefore, for the classical conception of wilderness, the cognitive metaphorical dimension is the most important, and perhaps the only coherent, aspect of the term.

I think that this perspective is needed to make sense of the evolution of classical wilderness from its status in the early American colonial period to its use today. As Europeans Americans came to think that nature was no longer an evil place, the classical ideal still persisted in some rather unusual areas. The metaphorical legacy of classical wilderness is the claim that urban areas are a sort of wilderness. The primary vehicle of this transformation is the shift of the cognitive dimension of wilderness to a focus on cities. Even though the evil physical space picked out by the term was either never really there or is at least no longer there (because, after all, it has been "conquered"), what is "out there" still, projected as the cognitive wilderness, is a sense of fear of a "savage space" and its "savage inhabitants."

This metaphorical transformation of urban space into a kind of wilderness, through a new construction on old themes, is an interesting subversion of the original physical subject of classical wilderness that retains the overall cognitive meaning of the idea. As long as the idea is still around and recognizable, why not put it to good use? The problem is that today we are coming back to a redescription of urban areas as a kind of classical wilderness using the original cognitive content present in the three theses that I suggested earlier. However, instead of utilizing these themes for the purpose of beneficial reform, as authors like Upton Sinclair did in *The Jungle,* the three theses are appropriated today for one of the more insidious purposes of classical wilderness: vilification of urban inhabitants and urban spaces in the same way that aboriginals and natural spaces were demonized in the past.

Los Angeles as Urban Chaos

In the sense just described, Los Angeles is one of the premiere urban wilderness areas in the United States today. We may even think of Los Angeles as something of a "wilderness preserve," maintaining a rigid separation between white suburbanites and inner-city racial minorities trapped in "concrete jungles." Although many films have evoked a sense of the city as a dangerous place full of corrupted inhabitants, one of the most fascinating uses of the metaphor of urban wilderness is provided by the 1992 Hollywood release *Falling Down,* directed by Joel Schumacher and written by Ebbe Roe Smith. In this urban fable, we follow the last day in the life of an out-of-work, Los Angeles–area defense worker (played by Michael Douglas). The character goes through a series of crises as he traverses the landscape of a predominantly Hispanic area of Los Angeles, which transforms him from an easily angered, but as yet nonviolent, average Joe into a gun-toting killer of the supposed scum of the city. Divided neatly into ten episodes, Douglas takes on the persona of a warped contemporary Odysseus trying vainly to find his way home from an urban war zone. By entering the city, he becomes tainted (which is consistent with some of the Puritans' worries in their version of thesis 1). As Douglas's character loses his everyday attire, changes into a black military outfit, and becomes a warped image of the new white hope of the inner city, we can tell that he, like Conrad's Mister Kurtz, has been corrupted by his journey into the heart of darkness. The three theses of urban wilderness are prevalent throughout this transformation.

THESIS 1: SEPARATION

If *Falling Down* is about anything, it is about the separation of inner-city Los Angeles from its civilized surroundings. As Mike Davis has argued, Los Angeles is a city transformed by a process of "Ulsterization," deeply divided along seemingly intransigent lines ("Who" 32). The opening scenes of *Falling Down* clearly rely on the acceptance of this separation. The first scene shows Michael Douglas's character sitting in his car, stuck in a traffic jam on a highway somewhere in East Los Angeles. Pressure builds in the scene as he stares at a child seemingly out of a Third World relief poster staring back at him from another car. The heat of the day is pervasive; his air conditioning does not work; his window will not roll down. With an extremely short military style hair cut and a cheap white shirt and tie, he looks like an annoyed missionary in sub-Saharan Africa. We have no idea who this man is, although he is presumably middle class and definitely in a spot that none of the film's assumed middle-class audience would like to find themselves. Finally he breaks. Douglas's unnamed everyman abandons his car and walks into a shrubbed embankment by the freeway. Our only clue to his identity is a personalized license plate reading "D-FENS." Although we later learn that his name is Bill Foster, even the credits list him by the name on the license plate.

D-fens is an out-of-work engineer who made a career in Southern California's once-booming aerospace defense industry. A victim of the end of the Cold War, he was fired from his job over a month ago. Somewhere along the way to unemployment, he lost his wife and child in a divorce and has since been living with his mother. Today is his daughter's birthday, and he is determined to make his way across town to Venice to give her a present, over his wife's objections and against a restraining order. A product of the military-industrial complex, he was a believer in his profession and his country. As his mother explains later to the police, under the misperception that her son is still going to work every day, "He's building important things to protect us from the Communists."

It is telling that our antihero is a defense worker. Now that America's greatest enemy has been defeated, his country no longer needs him. Consistent with the rise in white racist militias and crypto-nationalists following the fall of the Berlin wall, new enemies are needed to occupy the minds of middle America. The Right capitalized on this search for new enemies by turning our attention inward. In this climate, D-fens sees the inner city as enemy territory, and his journey through it gives him a purpose for the first time since losing his job. At the end of this day, D-fens—who has presumably lived his whole life in the area—expresses surprise at what he has found in his journey through the city, as if he had never been there before. In response to his wife's plea that he is sick and needs help, after he finally catches up with her in Venice and holds her hostage at gunpoint, D-fens retorts, "Sick? You wanna see sick. You ever walk around this town? *That's* sick." His bizarre adventures have generated a hatred for the city he once took for granted. At last, he has read his environment, and his reading is colored by the ideology of the classical wilderness.

However, the thesis of separation comes out sharpest in two persistent themes of the film: (1) the inner city is just as dangerous, violent, and chaotic as the most uninformed outsider would imagine; and (2) the separation of one part of the city from another is justified and rational. The first theme is pervasive, especially early in the film soon after D-fens leaves his car on the highway. At his first stop, a dingy Korean-owned convenience store in a Hispanic neighborhood, we see D-fens surrounded by the decaying, graffiti-covered barrio. The overwhelming yellow and brown tone of the cinematography (shot by Andrzej Barkowiak) evokes a clear sense that the place is incredibly ugly, smelly, and generally vile. Although surely such areas are impoverished, the mise-en-scene suggests that they are homogeneously unappealing. There is no room for any urban aesthetic value here until D-fens finds his way through the barrio to a rich neighborhood and later in the colors of the Venice pier.

Still, many spaces can be given an undesirable description. The wilderness metaphor comes across more discernibly in the recognition that because the inner city is dangerous, white Los Angeles residents must separate themselves from it. There are at least two ways in which the propriety of separation is portrayed in the film. The first is D-fens's own recognition of the territoriality of his adventure. The second is the external observations made by the police of why this man is in this place.

After leaving the Korean store, D-fens walks to a vacant lot in the Hispanic neighborhood. He has taken a baseball bat from the Korean store owner, which he used to smash things in the store during a rant about how the owner was overcharging his customers. He sits on the concrete remains of a staircase to a house no longer in the abandoned lot. There he is approached by two young Hispanic men, who are visibly marked as gang bangers. The two men immediately tell D-fens that he has to leave the lot. He is sitting on private property, they claim, identifiable by a crude gang symbol painted on the concrete block. The camera perspective here is telling. As the young men threaten D-fens, they begin to circle him. In an earlier establishment shot, we had seen that the abandoned lot is open and affords a broad view above the smoggy Los Angeles cityscape. But as the young men circle D-fens, the camera moves to a continuing tracking shot closing in on the circle from the outside. From this perspective, the open scene becomes a cramped, trapped space, and the young men and D-fens seem caught within a closing circle rather than on a vista overlooking the city. As in a "nature" film, D-fens appears in the position of prey trapped by circling wolves.

Finally, fed up with this threat, D-fens condescendingly assesses the situation: "This is a gangland thing. I've walked into your territorial dispute. I've wandered into your pissing ground or whatever it is!" Although he knows that he has crossed the line, that he is now in forbidden territory, D-fens has decided that here he will begin to take a stand. Like the Medieval monks who burned European forests to exorcise them of the devil, D-fens decides to begin cleaning house in the hood. Shouting about how he does not care about this "piece of shit hill," D-fens begins beating the young Hispanic men with his baseball bat. Clearly evoking his desire now to cross back into his home territory and leave the wilderness, D-fens shouts at one of his victims, "I'm going home, clear a path you motherfucker, I'm going home!"

The recognition of D-fens's status as an outsider is repeated explicitly at least twice in the film. Once in a public park, D-fens is approached by a panhandler who lamely tries to con D-fens out of money. As the superior representative of civilized society, D-fens easily sees through the pitch and rebuffs the man. As D-fens walks away from the scene, the panhandler shouts that D-fens has no right to be in *his* park. D-fens laughs and continues on his journey. Later, after leaving the barrio, D-fens must cross through a rich neighborhood in West Los Angeles to finish his journey to Venice. He takes a shortcut through a private golf course and upsets two old men who are trying to finish their game. When one of them begins yelling at him to get off of the course (a mark of territoriality), D-fens becomes the conscience of the working class, arguing that this space should be open for kids and families and not reserved for old men with money. Armed with weapons taken from his earlier would-be assailants, D-fens shoots the golfer's motorized cart and it rolls into a lake. The angry golfer begins to have a heart attack and pleads for someone to get his heart medicine out of the cart. D-fens stands over the dying man, amused and gloating. Although this last portrayal of territoriality is in a more affluent area, the sense of savagery is no less acute. One could argue that just as Upton Sinclair recognized the wild overtones of a kind of social Darwinism at work in the attitudes of owning classes, here the urban wilderness encountered by D-fens contains similar hazards.

The separation theme is also evident when the film's hero, Detective Pendergrast (played by Robert Duvall), realizes that a white man is responsible for reports of violence in the barrio. Pendergrast's theory is dismissed out-of-hand by his fellow officers. Why would a white man be in these neighborhoods? The film parades a series of ethnic detectives in front of Pendergrast—Hispanic, African American, and Asian. Each of them dismisses the idea that the assailant on the Korean grocer, the object of a drive-by shooting, and the man firing at phone booths and fast food restaurants in the barrio could all be the same white person. Pendergrast voices this dismay himself, finally shouting "Yeah, what would a white guy be doing in *gangland?*" The separation of the city is so common and accepted that it prevents the police from believing that a "normal" citizen could possibly be in this area.

The film reifies the assumption that there is nothing wrong with the separation of one part of the city from another. It is almost as if the classical wilderness of the inner city is an object of preservation, similar to an area set aside by the U.S. Wilderness Act. Rather than a pseudo-Romantic view that the wilderness should be set aside because its good qualities deserve protection, the representation of the separation of Los Angeles seems implicitly to argue that we should encircle the inner city because it is beyond salvation. There is no Sinclairian reform instinct here. "We" would not even think of allowing "them" into our areas, so we ought to just control this wild place and keep it separate as best we can and for as long as possible.

THESIS 2: SAVAGERY

Why must this separation be maintained? Because the savagery of the inner city corrupts those who find their way in. This is clearly the message of *Falling Down*. The title alone evokes a descent into the chaos of the wild city along with its obvious reference to the descent into the violence that D-fens finds himself committing in ever-escalating circumstances. Aside from the uniform depiction of inner-city inhabitants—particularly nonwhites—as violent, irrational savages, the suggestion of corruption from exposure to this environment is the most evocative of the effects of wilderness on the civilized, according to the classical metaphor.

D-fens knows he has crossed the border and recognizes that he will have to vigorously defend himself to make it from East Los Angeles to Venice. Still, he may not yet realize how violent he will become to make it to civilization. It is clear by the end that he makes no conscious decision to become a gun-wielding fanatic; he becomes one through his journey. When a break comes in the violence and he is able to reflect on what he has become, D-fens realizes that he is no longer a member of civilized, rational, polite society.

When D-fens wanders into an army-surplus store to replace his worn-out shoes with a telling pair of combat boots, the neo-Nazi store owner recognizes D-fens's clothes as those of the suspect in several shootings that have been broadcast over a police scanner kept in the store. Nick the Nazi openly embraces D-fens as a comrade-in-arms. From the account he learned on the scanner, Nick has decided that D-fens has been "kicking ass" in the city and so must sympathize with his neo-Nazi affiliations. In a bizarre parody of show-and-tell, Nick takes D-fens into a back room to show him his private collection. There Nick pulls out a stash of war surplus equipment, culminating in a can of Zyklon-B. Clearly amused with himself, Nick the Nazi remarks, "I wonder how many kikes this little can took out?" When D-fens asks why he is getting this treatment, Nick explains, "I know you. We're the same, you and me. We're the same." This is certainly a plausible interpretation given D-fens's actions thus far, and it accounts for an outburst of nationalistic comments made by D-fens in the Korean grocery store at the beginning of the film. However, D-fens denies the comparison: "I am not a vigilante; I'm just trying to get home for my little girl's birthday. . . . I'm an American, and you're a sick asshole!" Duly insulted, Nick decides to handcuff D-fens and take him into the police. D-fens responds by first stabbing Nick and then shooting him several times.

What can we make of this scene? Clearly, we are not supposed to equate D-fens with Nick nor explain D-fens's actions so far as an appeal to such extremist views. D-fens is depicted as just an average, middle-class person with average, middle-class, conservative politics. He is not a sophisticated racist like Nick. So why has he suddenly become so violent? The obvious choice of the film is simply that D-fens is suffering from stress and some sort of mental breakdown. However, it would be ludicrous to discount the environment through which he is traveling and the supposed effects of this landscape on his change in perspective, whereby it becomes permissible to break even the most mundane conventions of the society at large. The landscape itself, as it is portrayed in the film, provides the most convincing explanation for D-fens's savage turn. Certainly D-fens had to be on the edge to begin with, but no more so than many people today. In fact, this is a large part of D-fens's appeal: He is the quintessential '90s down-on-his-luck everyman. It is no accident that D-fens is wandering through the inner city and that the city releases his passions. Consistent with the early Puritan view that all people have a barely contained dark side, the wilderness of the city has only brought out the worst in D-fens, like it has corrupted those who are its everyday residents. One could have made a similar film where a character like D-fens had a similar breakdown in a suburban New Jersey bedroom community and then started shooting his middle-class neighbors. However, *Falling Down* is not just a film about the internal collapse of one man, it is a film in which the journey through the urban environment is itself the trigger of D-fens's savagery. It is the urban wild that corrupts him and it is this corruption that he carries back into the civilized sections of the city.

In this sense, the scene with Nick marks a transitional moment in the film. When D-fens leaves the Nazi's store, he clearly feels that he has crossed a line, that he has been completely transformed into a product of the inner city where guns can be used to settle any dispute. D-fens has made his first kill and now is part of the inner-city tribe. He leaves the store dressed all in black, a dark warrior in the wild terrain. If there is any doubt he has made a significant change, D-fens calls his wife from Nick's store before leaving to tell the audience that he has recognized his own corruption. He remarks to her that he is "past the point of no return" now, which he explains as "the point in a journey where it is longer to go back to the beginning than it is to continue to the end."

Although this observation may seem to romanticize his situation— which is not at all inconsistent with a reading of the filmmaker's perspective on this character—D-fens later takes one step back from his transformation to see what he has become. Running from the police, D-fens comes over a security wall into the backyard of a Westwood mansion. There he encounters a family having a barbecue and swimming in a pool. We learn quickly that these are not the owners of the house, but the caretaker and his family. D-fens hears police sirens, grabs the caretaker's young daughter, runs for the house, and waves his gun at the family to come along. While hiding in an alcove of the house, the family waits nervously for this strange man to make his next move. Convinced that D-fens will kill his daughter, the caretaker offers himself as a hostage and begs that his family be let go. At this moment, D-fens breaks down for the first time in the film. Realizing that the caretaker thinks he will harm the girl, D-fens explains that he is supposed to be with his own daughter, "having a barbecue like you guys." D-fens is confronted here not by East Los Angeles gangsters, neo-Nazis, or wealthy capitalists, but middle-class people like himself. D-fens acknowledges at this point that he has become something other than what he should be, that the city has remolded him. He realizes that the caretaker and his family must see him as a savage, an outsider. Although he does not fully understand his transformation—at the end of the film he remarks to Pendergrast, "I'm the bad guy? How did that happen?"—in this particular scene D-fens appears to be granted a moment of clarity to absorb and be horrified at his transformation. He is now the savage. By empathizing with him, we in the audience are supposed to realize how we could similarly be transformed by the wilderness.

THESIS 3: SUPERIORITY

Even during his descent into savagery, D-fens tries to maintain his superiority and the superiority of rational, middle America. At several moments in the narrative, D-fens rants about how he thinks the world should be. For example, even as he shoots up a fast-food restaurant because they will not serve him breakfast three minutes after the transition to the lunch menu, the film endorses D-fens's complaint that such establishments should be more flexible in their service. The press materials that accompanied the film were filled with reminders that D-fens stands as a representative of the correct middle American perspective on the world. Michael Douglas sees the focus of the film as one of the "loss of our middle class." Joel Schumacher suggests that the film is about a society that "seems to give people today a general sense of having been cheated or shortchanged." But again, the force behind such themes is provided by the inner-city environment in which D-fens is placed. This is not a film about the general loss of the middle class and middle-class sensibility in the suburbs; this film contrasts such a sensibility with an inner-city other.

At the beginning of the film, in the scene where D-fens smashes up the Korean grocery store, it is supposed to be over his outrage at the prices being charged by this foreigner. It all starts when the owner, Mr. Lee, refuses to give D-fens change for a pay phone unless he buys something. D-fens brings a Coke to the cash register and is told that the price is eighty-five cents. This price gouging leads to a sustained outburst by D-fens about how grateful the Korean should be for everything that America has done for his country. D-fens mocks the man for his accent and inability to speak English. After terrorizing Mr. Lee and destroying much of the store's merchandise with a baseball bat (grabbed from the hands of the owner), D-fens formally says "Pleasure frequenting your establishment," as he exits the scene. The contrast here is noteworthy. D-fens holds the upper hand as the nostalgic representative of a time when the simple amenities of life were reasonably priced. The problem appears to be that foreigners have come in and somehow caused inflation. D-fens not only knows how this man should be running his business, but, more importantly, he controls the language of the exchange as a representative of a superior culture.

All together, the three identifying theses of the urban wilderness that are at work in *Falling Down,* like much of the discourse of what passes for urban policy in Los Angeles, have very distressing social implications. Films like *Falling Down* encourage a dismissive attitude toward the real problems of urban life. Before the 1992 Los Angeles riots, Mike Davis chronicled the growing Balkanization of Los Angles in *City of Quartz.* Throughout the book, one sees the imagery of the three theses of urban wilderness:

> The carefully manicured lawns of LA's Westside sprout forests of ominous little signs warning: "Armed Response." . . . Downtown, a publicly-subsidized "urban renaissance" has raised the nation's largest corporate citadel, segregated from the poor neighborhoods around it by monumental architectural glaciers. . . . In the Westlake and San

Fernando areas the LA police department barricade streets and seal off poor neighborhoods as part of their "war on drugs." In Watts . . . [a recolonization] of the inner-city retail markets: a panopticon shopping mall surrounded by staked metal fences and a substation of the L.A.P.D. in a central surveillance tower. (223)

Even though works like Davis's helped to reinvigorate critical discussions of the legacy of disastrous post-Watts urban policies, we should not find it surprising that the overwhelming response to the Rodney King riots was to continue to view the inner city in the context of theses 1–3, rather than to begin to publicly address the sources and reinforcements of the demonization of the inner city. Police abuses (including several questionable shootings by the Los Angeles Police Department) continued against inner-city residents. Youth gangs have been solidified in the public mind as the savage enemy within the city, which is consistent with a distanced identification of urban wilderness. Separation efforts were redoubled in an attempt to protect threatened white suburbs at the insistence of the post-King-riot Webster Commission. Successful arguments were made in the California State Legislature to justify increased spending for imprisoning urban "savages," while aid to rebuild the city remains at a standstill. A consensus in the business community seems to be forming that the region as a whole is slipping backward into what Davis calls a "neo-Disney, plastic Stone Age" ("Who" 47).[4]

Even if it is true that the city is the new inheritor of classical wilderness, worries about the effects of this shift on the inhabitants can be easily ignored. A simple "law-and-order" stance is all that is needed to argue that just as the idea of the classical wilderness was in part motivated by real dangers "out there," characterization of an urban wilderness is justified due to the actual (soberly perceived) dangers of life in American inner cities. Still, there is good reason to believe that such savage hating causes harm beyond its representational effects. Acknowledging a danger is one thing, but unnecessarily dehumanizing the source of a real or only perceived threat is quite another. Without the designation of the inner city as an alien savage place, is it not plausible that a more reasoned discussion of its problems could be accomplished? Films like *Falling Down* may reflect the real attitudes of middle America toward its inner cities. Its damage may be realized too late.[5]

Boyz in the Woods

What are the alternatives to the imagery of urban wilderness in depictions of the city? One largely implicit body of work can be found in the new African American urban cinema of auteur filmmakers like Spike Lee, John Singleton, and Allen and Albert Hughs. In different ways, each filmmaker responds to overly simplified and demonized portrayals of urban life without romanticizing the real problems of the inner city. All of these filmmakers realize that the city can be a dangerous place, although certainly most dangerous for its own residents rather than as a threat to white outsiders. Just as any depiction of wilderness must acknowledge the real threats that in part inspired the classical view, a sober portrayal of the inner city must realistically describe its dangers. Although Lee has the most developed body of work, I want to focus here on the first films of John Singleton and the Hughs brothers, which, unlike Lee's New York–based films, are set in the Los Angeles of *Falling Down*. Although not directly aimed at responding to portrayals of the inner city as a savage space, both the Hughs brothers' *Menace II Society* and Singleton's *Boyz in the Hood* contain implicit and explicit rejections of the imagery of urban wilderness.

Menace II Society begins with historical footage of the 1965 Watts riots, which clearly attempts to historicize the violence of Los Angeles today. A voice-over from the film's protagonist, Caine (played by Tyrin Turner), explains, "when the riots stopped, the drugs started." The film follows Caine, a minor drug dealer, in his attempt to extricate himself from his surroundings. Unlike the main character of *Boyz in the Hood,* the college-bound Trey, Caine begins the film fairly satisfied with his surroundings. However, after he sees his cousin killed in a carjacking, Caine begins to doubt the sustainability of his environment and to rethink his expressed nonchalance about the possibility of his own death. Caine begins to contemplate a move out of the city and eventually commits to move to Atlanta with an imprisoned friend's wife and child. Rarely does the explicit imagery of the three theses of urban wilderness come up, although the mise-en-scene of the film is one of extreme violence, albeit violence that has been historically oriented.

Two scenes are especially interesting in this regard. In one, the father of a friend of Caine (played by Charles Dutton) urges him to leave the city.

Trying to make a point about how dangerous things have become he says, "Being a black man in America isn't easy. The hunt is on and *you're the prey.*" Because this scene is immediately followed by one of extreme police brutality, the comment does not seem to be one that reifies thesis 2; rather it reminds us that the savages may not be the inner-city residents, but instead the police as strong arms of a white government. Similarly, one of the most threatening characters in *Boyz in the Hood* is a black police officer whose uniform seems to have made him an irrational and indiscriminate hater of inner-city youth. However, clearly, even to suggest that Caine and his friends are prey plays off the characterization of inner-city inhabitants as animals. The city must in part be a classical wilderness to turn the tables and see the police as a threat and to motivate a social concern for the young black inhabitants of the city. The danger, however, with the Dutton character's comment is how easily it resonates with animalistic representations of African American men. For example, in Robert Gooding-Williams's account of the rhetorical strategies of the defense attorneys in the first Rodney King trial, the language of classical wilderness is rife:

> After inviting jurors to see events from the point of view of the police officers, the defense attorneys elicited testimony from King's assailants that depicted King as a *bear,* and as emitting *bearlike groans.* In the eyes of the police and then again in the eyes of the jurors, King's black body became that of a *wild "hulk-like" and "wounded" animal, whose every gesture threatened the existence of civilized society.* Not surprisingly, the defense attorneys portrayed the white bodies which assailed King *as guardians against the wild, and as embodying a "thin blue line" that separates civil society from the dangerous chaos of the essence of the wild.* (166; my emphases)[6]

Perhaps anticipating such negative associations, the Hughs brothers insert a scene that clearly rejects the imagery of thesis 2. Toward the end of the film, when Caine is visiting an old street mentor in jail (the husband of the woman he plans to accompany to Atlanta), Caine reveals that he did not want to visit his old friend before because he did not want to see him in a "cage." His friend quickly retorts, "You think I'm some kind of animal?" Caine says "No." Such a quick reply may not be enough to clearly reject the pernicious use of the imagery of urban wilderness, but this film, like others made by the Hughs brothers, stands as a strong response to the one-dimensional portrayal of inner-city life found in films like *Falling Down*.

Boyz in the Hood opens with a historicizing moment too, although one more personalized than in *Menace*. It begins with a view of the protagonist, Trey Styles (the adult character is played by Cuba Gooding Jr.), as a small child seeing his first shooting site on the way to school one morning. Trey appears to be a very bright, if somewhat argumentative, child. After Trey gets in a fight at school, his mother decides to send him to live with his father, Furious (played by Lawrence Fishburne). After a few scenes showing Trey as a child, the film jumps seven years to focus on him as an adult and highlights his interaction with two neighbors, the brothers Dough Boy (rapper Ice Cube) and Ricky (Morris Chestnut). Ricky is a rising football star on his way to a college career at USC; Dough Boy has been in and out of prisons and seems to be very similar to Caine from *Menace*—both thoughtful and violent. Trey is the most reflective of the three, and, although ambivalent at the moment, we learn by the end of the film that he will be attending Morehouse College in Atlanta.

Themes very similar to those found in *Menace* play through this film, particularly the violence of inner-city neighborhoods and the drive to leave the city. One unique scene occurs toward the end of the film when Furious takes Trey and Ricky to Compton to give them a lesson on gentrification. Even though we have seen these characters in extremely hostile environments, both Trey and Ricky are afraid to be in Compton. As though he is responding to the uniformly negative imagery of films like *Falling Down,* Furious tells the boys, "it's the '90s, we can't afford to be afraid of our own people anymore." He goes on to give a sophisticated critique of the claim that South-central Los Angeles has become run down at the hands of its black residents and them alone. He asks us to consider how it is that crack has made its way into the inner city and why gun and liquor stores are on every street corner. "Because they want us to kill ourselves," explains Furious. In this one scene, the film asks us to reconsider all the stereotypes that cause us to fear the city and its inhabitants and to examine the ways in which we simplify issues of violence in our urban centers. In a similar scene at the very end of the film, after Ricky has been killed in a drive-by shooting,

Dough Boy tells Trey that he has just seen a television show about how we "live in a violent world." Reflecting on the show, Dough Boy suggests, "They don't know, don't show, or don't care what's going on in the hood." Of course, we know that "they" do show what goes on in the hood, but only from afar and through a lens that demonizes the inner city and those who reside there rather than contributing to a solution to the problem of urban violence.

It is important to recognize that both of these films focus on the African American experience of the inner city from an African American perspective. *Falling Down,* by contrast, is very much a voyeuristic film, dropping an agitated white man into East Los Angeles just to see what happens. *Menace* and *Boyz* are representations of the inner city's perception of itself and its own problems rather than the white perception of the city. Although each film draws a line between different kinds of characters, with some seeming able to rise above their situation in a self-critical gesture and others mired in failure, neither film resorts to an external critique from a white audience or appeals to white prejudices in its depiction of inner-city violence. The focus of both films is black-on-black crime. To drive this message home, public-service spots at the beginnings of the videotape editions of both films feature commentary about internal violence in the black community.

It is also important to note that the problem of inner-city violence portrayed in *Menace* and *Boyz* is more explicit than anything Spike Lee has yet produced. One can compare this portrayal to the use of the turn-of-the-century social reform image of the city as wilderness, both of which serve as a call for urban improvement and social justice. Importantly, the imagery of the urban wilderness that is most clearly rejected in both films is the idea of savagery (thesis 2). Both films strive to show that inner-city residents cannot be easily demonized or homogeneously vilified as savages. The violent images and themes of drive-by shootings and gang activity are overshadowed by scenes of police brutality and harassment. The feel of the two films may be consistent with the highly tense atmosphere of *Falling Down,* at least in focusing on the violent aspects of city life. However, the former two films are both *about* the very real problems of violence in Los Angeles today, rather than taking pleasure in the portrayal of violence. Nonetheless, although I do not have space to fully develop the idea here, a problem that these portrayals share with a film like *Falling Down* is their implicit appeal to the terms of classical wilderness. After all, it was the availability of this metaphor from its use by authors like Sinclair that made it possible to use the pernicious representations of the city found in *Falling Down*. What makes the portrayal of the city as a wild, savage place plausible to us is at least in part our cultural memory that the city can legitimately be described as a jungle. This is not to say that *Menace* and *Boyz* should be rejected as powerful social films. It is only to say that we must work harder to get out from under the ideology of classical wilderness because it shapes and distorts our understanding of the city and detracts from a comprehension of the truly complicated diversity of urban life.[7]

NOTES

1. For a history of this argument see Nash and Sax.

2. See Takaki for an extended discussion of different early American theories of the relative savagery of various nonwhite races.

3. See Oelschlaeger for an excellent genealogy of the idea of wilderness, especially his account of wilderness in the Western middle ages. See Cronon for the best current version of the claim that wilderness represents a cultural construction.

4. Davis's current research gives us reason to suspect that nature itself has also become demonized in Los Angeles. In "Los Angeles after the Storm," he argues that residents of that city, victims of many "natural" disasters over the past few years, are beginning to think of their home as an "apocalypse theme park" (222).

5. I attempted some preliminary conclusions on the effects of the urban wilderness imagery on inner-city residents (Light "Urban"). However, a full analysis awaits more rigorous psychological and sociological research.

6. Gooding-Williams in part drew the record of the trial from the *Los Angeles Times* of 3 April 1992, 21 April 1992, and 22 April 1992.

7. Another possibility would be to try to subvert the traditional paradigms of wilderness rather than simply rejecting them. Although I think that such a move is certainly plausible, I feel that the most positive and helpful portrayals of urban life more often come from films that entirely reject this wilderness imagery. In a manuscript I have in progress (tentatively titled *Reel Politics*), I discuss John Sayles's *City of Hope* as just such a film. Nonetheless, the subversion thesis has much to say for it. See Andrew Feenberg's work for more on this possibility in relation to questions of the politics of technology and technological systems in general.

WORKS CITED

Cronon, William. "The Trouble with Wilderness." *Uncommon Ground: Rethinking the Human Place in Nature.* Ed. William Cronon. New York: W. W. Norton, 1996. 1–35.

Davis, Mike. *City of Quartz.* New York: Vintage Books, 1992.

——. "Los Angeles after the Storm: The Dialectic of Ordinary Disasters." *Antipode* 27.3 (1995): 221–41.

——. "Who Killed Los Angeles? Part Two: The Verdict is Given." *New Left Review* 199 (1993): 29–54.

Feenberg, Andrew. *Alternative Modernity: The Technical Turn in Philosophy and Social Theory.* Los Angeles: U of California P, 1995.

Gooding-Williams, Robert. "Look, A Negro!" *Reading Rodney King / Reading Urban Uprising.* Ed. Robert Gooding-Williams. New York: Routledge, 1993. 157–77.

Light, Andrew. "The Metaphorical Drift of Classical Wilderness." *Geography Research Forum* 15 (1995): 14–32.

——. "Urban Wilderness." *Wild Ideas.* Ed. David Rothenberg. Minneapolis: U of Minnesota P, 1995. 195–211.

Nash, Roderick. *Wilderness and the American Mind.* New Haven, Conn.: Yale UP, 1982.

Oelschlaeger, Max. *The Idea of Wilderness: From Prehistory to the Age of Ecology.* New Haven, Conn.: Yale UP, 1991.

Sax, Joseph. *Mountains without Handrails: Reflections on the National Parks.* Ann Arbor: U of Michigan P, 1980.

Short, John Rennie. *Imagined Country: Environment, Culture and Society.* New York: Routledge, 1991.

Takaki, Ronald. *Iron Cages.* Oxford: Oxford UP, 1988.

9

CENTRAL HIGH AND THE SUBURBAN LANDSCAPE

The Ecology of White Flight

David W. Teague

In the United States, we badmouth the suburbs and distrust them—for good reason—but we keep moving there. The suburbs are often treated with condescension and disdain by urbanites, yet approximately seventy-two percent of new single-family dwelling construction starts on previously undeveloped property within forty miles of an urban center—in new suburbs (National Association of Realtors 15). Especially in the South, some of the faster-growing suburbs are expanding as much as one hundred percent every decade (Faulkner County Special Census 1996).

The suburb is an ambiguous place. It provokes an accordingly ambivalent set of responses in Americans. These responses—myriad, diverse, and even contradictory—are difficult to assess because they are rarely present in any one venue at any one time.[1] However, the nexus of associations represented by contemporary suburban fiction in the United States—the literary map with which, over the past thirty years, American writers have overlain suburban landscapes—does begin to organize and codify generalized responses. Thus, I begin with a brief survey of recent fictional treatments of the suburbs.

STORYBOOK AND OTHER TOWNS

For all their shortcomings, suburbs in this country remain landscapes of promise and are ideal in many ways—the American version of pastoral. As late-twentieth-century examples of Leo Marx's "society of the middle land-scape" (226), the consummate hybrid of the urban and the wild green worlds, suburbs are represented as places of hope. In Rick Moody's *Purple America,* the suburbs provide the *"ideal rural paradise"* (20; original emphasis) where a Manhattanite family, the Raitliffes, has migrated to experience the pristine environment of the Connecticut shore. There, the family "took in the patio, the pool, and the vista: not a hundred yards away, the shoals of Long Island Sound. The physics of those gentle waves against this peninsula, the very respiration of nature. How those waves comforted" (21).

Although it is true that the young Raitliffe son, Hex, misses the world he has left behind in Manhattan, where "the hills, shrubs, open fields, and statuary of Frederick Law Olmsted's Central Park" had been his "rightful home," where, even if "the kids were always trying to steal his muffler and taunt him with it, he was a little feudal lord in a dream of old New York," it is also true that Hex and his family value life in the Connecticut suburbs more than they valued life in the city (19). Connecticut seems to them like a more "natural" place to live, serene and comfortable.

This is a common theme in the literature of the suburbs: physical, psychological, and even spiritual comfort. Because, despite all else, life in suburbia is perceived as easeful. To the extent that when all other responses to the landscape have been exhausted, a nostalgia for the soothing order of the place remains, as in the case of the collective first-person narrator of Jeffrey Eugenides's *The Virgin Suicides.* This narrator, a "we" who watches five sisters kill themselves one by one, still describes the suburban landscape in idyllic terms, even after the suicides and the disillusionment they en-gender among the residents of their unnamed suburb of Detroit. The first of the suicides among the young women of the Lisbon family occurs in June, which is "fish-fly season, when each year our town is covered by the flotsam of those ephemeral insects. Rising in clouds . . . they blacken windows, coat cars and streetlamps, plaster the municipal docks and festoon the rigging of sailboats" (4). The streets, trees, and lawns provide a distinct, if somewhat guilty, pleasure for those of us (like this collective narrator) who live in suburbs or who once did and secretly entertain the notion, from time to time, of returning, if only vicariously, in the pages of a novel.

The pleasure most of us take in suburban landscapes is guilty because suburban landscapes are problematic, built at great cost to many for the benefit of a few. There is always a dark side to life in suburban spaces, as John Updike, to give a distinguished example, has been insisting for the past forty years. In his Rabbit Angstrom series, Updike gets at the psychic cost of decentralized, insular, single-family life: It leads to a thin culture. Updike's suburban landscape as it appears in the final book of his trilogy, *Rabbit is Rich,* is one of highway-strip shopping malls, car lots, high gasoline prices, and blank-eyed consumers. His fictional Pennsylvania Route 111, upon which sits Rabbit Angstrom's Toyota dealership, is a place without a soul:

> Usually on a Saturday Route 111 is buzzing with shoppers pillaging the malls hacked from the former fields of corn, rye, tomatoes, cabbages, and strawberries. Across the highway, the four concrete lanes, and the median divider of aluminum battered by many forgotten accidents, stands a low building faced in dark clinker brick that in the years since Harry watched its shell being slapped together of plywood, has been a succession of unsuccessful restaurants and now serves as the Chuck Wagon, specializing in barbecued take-outs. . . . Beyond its lot littered with flattened take-out cartons, a lone tree, a dusty maple, drinks from a stream that has become a mere ditch. This shapely old maple from its distance seems always to be making to Harry an appeal he must ignore. (7)

This is the "appeal" that most suburb dwellers must ignore to preserve their contentment. It is the appeal of a lost landscape and the lost ways of life that once thrived on that landscape. These lost ways of life generally would have involved human beings interacting personally, rather than passing one another in automobiles at seventy-five miles per hour on four-lane state highways off of which they pull to purchase fast-food on the way to the auto dealership or the discount store. As Updike suggests, the culture of the suburbs exacts an extreme toll on those who participate in it.

In his fictional treatment of suburban life on the West Coast, Raymond Carver has demonstrated that this toll is often paid at the cost of extreme loneliness. When suburb dwellers experience catastrophic loss, as they often do in Carver's fiction, there is no one to whom they can turn. In "A Small Good Thing," for instance, the death of a child is not only in itself a nearly insurmountable life crisis for Ann and Howard Weiss, but it is made more devastating by the fact that the two have absolutely no one, outside of themselves, to help them through their tragedy. The geography of their place works against them—the insularity of their suburban household is broken only by a series of pathologically cruel telephone calls from a baker in a strip mall who is upset that the Weiss's have not claimed the birthday cake he baked for their son shortly before he died.

This isolation—distance both physical and psychological—has its effects on the places as well as the inhabitants. Suburban landscapes are diseased places in much American fiction. In *Rabbit is Rich,* Updike outlines the sort of environmental and economic costs hidden in low-density, suburban living. Rabbit Angstrom is a car dealer who is well aware of these costs because they provide his living. "Running out of gas," Rabbit Angstrom thinks as he stands behind the summer-dusty windows of the "Springer Motors display room watching the traffic go by on Route 111, traffic somehow thin and scared compared to what it used to be. The fucking world is running out of gas" (4). The response of the people who live in one place, work in another, shop in a third, and eat in a fourth is simply to buy new cars from Rabbit Angstrom.

The suburbs is a landscape that requires travel. Richard Ford and Russell Banks have explored its geography and provided some conclusions about why: In the United States, one must migrate to find a tolerable life. Often, one must migrate daily. Frank Bascombe, the narrator of Ford's *Independence Day* and a realtor (who is therefore an authority on the suburban landscape of New Jersey), holds no illusions about what his job is as he describes it to an acquaintance, Mr. Tanks:

> My view is, if I sell you a house in a town where life's tolerable, then I've done you a big favor. And if I try and I don't succeed, then you've got a view you like better (assuming you can afford it). Plus, I don't cotton to the idea of raising the drawbridge, which Mr. Tanks probably has experienced. I mean to guarantee the same rights and freedoms to all. And if that means merchandising New Jersey dirt like dog-nuts so we all get our one sweet piece, then so be it. We'll all be dead in forty years anyway. (206)

Bascombe assumes the "drawbridge" to towns where life is tolerable has been raised to exclude his friend, Mr. Tanks, because Mr. Tanks is black. In fact, Bascombe regularly does his own part in keeping the drawbridge raised by showing houses selectively to customers based on their races.

Russell Banks writes of slightly less affluent Americans in a trailer community in Florida (trailer parks are often suburban landscapes, too). He lays out the lines in somewhat more stark language in *Continental Drift* because the lower the economic level, the more bluntly suburban strife appears to manifest itself. Bob Dubois, having been given a handgun by his brother to carry to work in a convenience store, asks Eddie what he is supposed to do with it. Eddie answers, "I don't give a flying fuck what you do with it, so long's you keep it with you when you're at the store. The niggers know you got a gun in the store, believe me, they know, they get the word out. Leastwise the niggers in this town do, because they all know each other. Then on Friday night when they're out looking for easy cash, they'll keep on moving down the line" (69–70). There is no sentimentality about the quiet lives lived in small suburban American towns here, only theories about how the lives are kept quiet.

In Banks's novel, the suburbs and the "suburbs of suburbs," as he calls them, contain a "glut of McDonald's and Burger Kings, Kentucky Fried Chickens and Pizza Huts, a long straight tunnel of franchises broken intermittently by storefront loan companies and paved lots crammed with glistening Corvettes, T-Birds, Camaros and Trans Ams" (61). They reflect little but their "builders' and landowners' greed" (62) and the social strife that comes out of it. The idyllic world to which Rick Moody's *Purple America* characters had escaped in the late 1950s has, by the late 1980s, begun to show through its cracks the oppressive structures upon which it has been built.

However, in other novels, the suburban quiet takes on a life of its own, becomes a value in and of itself, apart from the violence—social, cultural, and actual—that gives birth to it. The quiet inspires Frank Bascombe to lyrical flights as he describes his small hometown: "In Haddam, summer floats over tree-softened streets like a sweet lotion balm from a careless, languorous god, and the world falls in tune with its own mysterious anthems" (Ford 4). Also, the suburb is a landscape as truly inspired as it is empty. It could have been—could still be, so the dream goes—a life of grace and happiness in the new American pastoral landscape. However, the dream has proven empty, which is the point at which fiction fails me in this inquiry. In this instance, fiction does not seem to explore adequately the how or the why of the emptiness that infects the landscape in which so many of us live. So I turn to a case study of a suburban landscape with which I am intimately familiar.

A City on the Plain

Conway, Arkansas, is located twenty-five miles northwest of Little Rock on Interstate 40. There are four exits serving Conway and approximately eighteen serving Little Rock. The interstate, which is two lanes in each direction once outside the Little Rock city limits, was "completed" (a somewhat nebulous term, I have discovered, because the interstate is still not officially "complete")—so I will say, "was in approximately its current state" by the mid-1960s. Traffic moved along it smoothly for twenty years. It was not until the mid-1980s—at about the time that Rabbit Angstrom was looking out at fictional Pennsylvania Route 111, rubbing his hands over the potential gas-burning customers he saw clogging the road in front of his car lot—that the first backups began along Interstate 40 between Little Rock and Conway. At first, these backups occurred during the morning and evening rush hours, but now they happen regularly on this "rural" stretch of road, according to Conway's city planner, Bill Polk.

Large numbers of Americans work in urban centers like Little Rock and, increasingly, live in suburbs like Conway. This phenomenon is nothing new. Most of us are familiar with the stereotypical, white, middle-class couple, one or both of whom commutes to overwhelmingly white (sometimes 100 percent white) middle-class subdivisions built along major state and federal highways. These are the people who populate the fiction I have discussed. The population of Conway, my home town and the place where I have commenced my inquiry into suburban ecosystems, has increased 120 percent since 1970. Its minority population has increased less than 30 percent (Faulkner County Historical Society 43). The numbers for urban Little Rock are, within a few percentage points, almost exactly reversed (Emfinger). This is a phenomenon widely, if somewhat inelegantly, known as "white flight." It is by no means a new story, and the culture and politics of white-flight suburbanization have been well and widely studied (see Frey 1977, 1979), so I will not go into those questions here. What I will explore are the hidden costs of the exodus to the suburbs, the costs chronicled by Updike, Eugenides, Banks, and others—that is, the human and environmental costs. I will examine a particular, small environment with which I was once very intimate, in the hope that it will shed light on some larger ones.

The part of Conway, Arkansas, I begin with is my former backyard, which I first encountered in 1970, the year I moved into the house in which I grew up. That was also the year I began attending public school in a building that had, until two years before, been the "black" school building in town—Pine Street School. My backyard was a relatively large one—two and a half acres. It was actually platted out in the early 1920s along a state highway, well before today's half-acre lots and subdivision-roadway arcs, loops, and cul-de-sacs became the standard. According to the observations I made of that small "ecosystem" and recorded in spiral notebooks through the mid-1970s, it supported twelve species of trees, fifteen species of grass, eleven species of birds, and two species of fish (my back yard adjoined a creek, and, in fact, much of the property served as a flood plain for this creek). There were also squirrels, several possum families, moles, voles, and insects that I collected by the box, but never catalogued, totaling over one hundred different species. Last year, when I began doing research for this chapter, I checked with a biologist at a local college, Matthew Moran, who estimated that I had probably, in every case except the trees, underestimated the biodiversity of the place by between fifty and ninety percent.

My parents sold the home five years ago to developers and moved further out of town to live in a new subdivision. Their new house sits on half an acre of land, which also floods in the rain. There are no trees on the new lot, and I have only seen three kinds of birds there on my visits. It chiefly supports the mid-South's typical, well-manicured, Chem-Lawned mono-culture of zoysia grass.

However, my old backyard—the flood plain that once supported all of those birds, trees, and animals—now sports a one-acre asphalt parking lot, near the rear of which sits a daycare center and along one edge of which a developer has sandwiched in a couple of $100 thousand houses behind six-foot wooden-slat fences. In each of these houses lives a couple that works in Little Rock and commutes home in the traffic on Interstate 40 every work-day. Last March, when I was visiting Conway, it rained hard one afternoon between about 4:00 and 8:00 P.M. As I had seen happen several times in my life, the creek at the edge of the newly developed property, Tucker Creek, rose. Within the next hour it covered the property of the daycare center and damaged the yards of the new houses. Indeed, it came within six inches of one of the houses. I know by experience that before too long an even bigger storm will come, as it inevitably does in Arkansas, and Tucker Creek will enter the front doors of one or both of the new houses. It is worth asking why people are willing to buy houses and build businesses in such an unstable environment, because this scenario does not really represent an ideal state of affairs either for the current human inhabitants or the displaced nonhuman ones. The answer, I think, is one Rick Moody has already supplied: To live in such a place is to live in the *ideal rural landscape*—apart from localized flooding—with a daycare center next door.

This state of affairs bears examination on several fronts. First, it bears examination because this two-and-a-half-acre plot of ground in Conway, Arkansas, represents what is happening on huge acreages across the United States. As we are learning today, suburbanization is one of the chief environmental problems facing both the human and nonhuman populations of the United States, with its deleterious environmental effects, particularly in terms of resource depletion—people who live in suburbs, for instance, do a lot of driving and burn a lot of gas. Suburbs also accelerate other kinds of pollution, most notably fertilizer and pesticide run-off from supergreen lawns. Suburbs precipitate species and habitat loss. Suburbs are places of low human-population density and, therefore, of inefficient land-use policies.

The expansion of American suburbs is increasingly perceived, and rightly so, as a sort of geographical and ecological miscalculation that might be reversed if we begin to count environmental and ecological costs. It is a problem that might properly be addressed using the rhetoric of environmental conservation, an increasingly persuasive rhetoric in our country. By seriously and publicly evaluating the cost-benefit ratio of lost resources versus the comfort and convenience of suburban life, we might rethink the values that lead us to flee to the suburbs. Such an environmentally aware re-evaluation might prove to be an effective strategy, but it seems unlikely that the reasons to stop going to the suburbs will, at any time in the near future, be as compelling to most Americans as the reasons to continue fleeing there.

Last spring, I spent a day asking two questions to the people who had begun to populate and use my old backyard—the people who lived in the houses in and around it and the people who left children at the daycare center. The first question was, "Where do you work?" If the answer was "I work in Little Rock," as it was in forty-eight percent of the cases, my second question was, "Why do you live in Conway?" The answer to that question was, in seventy percent of the cases, "the schools." Not the Conway schools—the Little Rock schools. I also got answers like "crime" and "better neighborhoods," which are terms closely related in the nexus of urban signifiers to "schools." However, mostly it was simply and plainly "schools."

In contexts like this one, "school" is a code word (Emfinger). It has been ever since Orval Faubus fought the final battle of the Civil War in 1957 against the 101st Airborne Division of the United States Army. The word brings us into the territory Banks and Ford address in their suburban fictions. When associated with migration patterns in cities, "school" has been a signifier. Through the period of desegregation, through busing, through the end of busing, through the end of desegregation, on into the present era of school vouchers, neighborhood schools, and into the future, "school" has been, is, and will be a signifier for a failure of egalitarian, democratic ideals. "School" has always been a primary concern of the middle-class, mostly white, families who have abandoned the country's urban areas.

"School" was an interesting proposition in Conway, Arkansas, in 1970. I spent my first year of school (kindergarten) at Pine Street School in Conway. Pine Street had a nice, nearly new, barely used building. It was a little large in scale for kindergarten students because it had been built in the early 1960s as a high school. By 1970, only two of the classrooms were in use, the two in which our kindergarten, an experimental exercise run by the State College of Arkansas across town, met. The school itself had shut down—a victim of integration.

In 1968, when city officials set out to integrate the schools in Conway, they very equitably approached the task from both directions. They invited black students to go to school in the white neighborhood and invited white students to go to school in the black neighborhood, at Pine Street School. On the first day at Pine Street, nobody showed up but the teachers. The school in the white neighborhood was a more desirable place to be. There was more money behind it, so the building itself was more attractive. The teachers were better trained. Sitting as it was on the edge of town in a solidly middle-class tax base, it was in nearly every respect a better educational institution (Meriwether). Everybody, from whatever socioeconomic or ethnic background, sent their children there, and it is hard to blame them for their choice.

It is still hard to blame people for such choices, which is the paradox of the suburbs. On most scales of evaluation, life is better there, in spite of the fact—or because of it—that insularity becomes a "family value" there. A nearly complete withdrawal from larger systems, both cultural and ecological, becomes possible. "Public schools" give way to "neighborhood schools," which give way to "home schools." Then wooden-slat fences go up around the home schools (Lasker).

The phenomenon of white flight has been addressed as a racial question, as a question of cultural intolerance, as a failure of will, and sometimes as an economic, educational, or even moral question. Such is also the case for the growing "crack" neighborhoods in Little Rock, which suburban residents of Conway demonize—places defined primarily by the drug their presumably felonious inhabitants are thought to prefer (Simmons). Still, the problem is not an intractable one. The fact is that ideologically motivated migration and suburbanization are both practically and conceptually the same question. The "cultural" dimension of white flight is inseparable from the "ecological" dimension of suburbanization, as Carver and Updike have observed. The same solipsistic ideology that drives a family to be terrified of sending its children to mingle with children of other ethnicities at Little Rock's Central High School also drives the family to demand the sort of insularity and autonomy that characterize suburban life. The illusion is that nuclear families may be "liberated" from their contexts, both cultural and environmental, that residents of the suburbs are excused from their obligations as citizens of the United States and as occupants of its landscape. However, the illusion is, in fiction and otherwise, increasingly untenable.

Suburbs are a self-perpetuating cultural practice, one that must be cut through all at once, like the gordian knot. Because the libertarian, self-centered thinking that drives Americans to value life in the suburbs effectively takes them out of the cultural systems of the United States, it also tends to take them out of the ecosystems of the United States. The question of suburbanization in this country is a question of environmental justice in the largest sense, one that will not be answered until those of us who populate these places learn to think of ourselves as citizens of a community larger than ourselves, learn to weigh the costs of isolating ourselves from the world around us—both human and nonhuman—learn to forego the guilty pleasure of retreating to a house in the middle of a green half acre and locking the door behind us.

NOTE

1. There is no dearth of scholarship concerning U.S. suburbs. Studies such as William Dobriner's *The Suburban Community* (1958) or Robert Wood's *Suburbia: Its People and Their Politics* (1958) laid the groundwork for contemporary discussions of the growth patterns, social organization, lifestyles, and political disposition of suburban communities. More contemporary works such as John Stilgoe's *Borderland: Origins of the American Suburbs* (1988) and Richard Harris's *Unplanned Suburbs: Toronto's American Tragedy 1900 to 1950* (1996) provide case studies in suburban scholarship. Mark Baldassare's *Trouble in Paradise* (1986) examines growth controversies, housing crises, fiscal strain, and governmental conflict associated with established suburban communities.

WORKS CITED

Baldassare, Mark. *Trouble in Paradise*. New York: Columbia UP, 1986.

Banks, Russell. *Continental Drift*. New York: Harper and Row, 1985.

Carver, Raymond. *Cathedral*. New York: Alfred A. Knopf, 1983.

Dobriner, William. *The Suburban Community*. New York: Putnam's, 1958.

Emfinger, Dina. Personal Interview. 10 March 1997.

Eugenides, Jeffrey. *The Virgin Suicides*. New York: Warner Books, 1993.

Faulkner County Historical Society. *Faulkner County: Its Land and People*. Conway, Ark.: River Road Press, 1996.

Ford, Richard. *Independence Day*. New York: Alfred A. Knopf, 1995.

Frey, William H. *Black In-Migration, White Flight and the Changing Economic Base of the City*. Madison: U of Wisconsin P, 1979.

——. *White Flight and Central-City Loss: Application of an Analytic Migration Framework*. Madison: U of Wisconsin P, 1977.

Harris, Richard. *Unplanned Suburbs: Toronto's American Tragedy, 1900 to 1950*. Baltimore, Md.: Johns Hopkins UP, 1996.

Lasker, Greg. Personal Interview. 9 January 1997.

Marx, Leo. *The Machine in the Garden*. New York: Oxford UP, 1964.

Meriwether, Robert. Personal Interview. 5 January 1997.

Moody, Rick. *Purple America*. Boston: Little, Brown and Co., 1997.

Moran, Matthew. Personal Interview. 15 May 1998.

National Association of Realtors. *Housing Trends, 1998*. Chicago, Ill.: National Association of Realtors, 1998.

Polk, Bill. Personal Interview. 18 May 1998.

Simmons, June. Personal Interview. 6 March 1997.

Stilgoe, John. *Borderland: Origins of the American Suburb*. New Haven, Conn.: Yale UP, 1988.

Updike, John. *Rabbit Is Rich*. New York: Alfred A. Knopf, 1981.

Wood, Robert. *Suburbia: Its People and Their Politics*. Boston: Houghton Mifflin, 1958.

10

MANUFACTURING THE GHETTO
Anti-urbanism and the Spatialization of Race
Michael Bennett

If ecocriticism has not been quick to address urban issues, as David Teague and I suggest in the introduction to this volume, then the same could be said of environmentalism in general. Lately, however, the environmental justice movement has become one of the largest and most active social movements in the United States, largely by addressing the concerns of urbanites and people of color that had been overlooked by mainstream environmental organizations. Only after grassroot movements developed to confront the biohazards and ecological challenges faced by inner-city poor and minority communities did national environmentalist organizations begin to devote resources to combatting environmental racism.[1] In a relatively short period, the growth of the environmental justice movement has transformed the landscape of the ecological movement, changing "the pastoral face of green politics" (Ross 103). In the process, socioeconomic and political concerns—with regard to such inner-city problems as housing, health care, and workplace safety—have been added to the usual concerns of clean air and water and maintaining wildlands. As a result, the green movement has extended well beyond its former base among the mostly white, upper-middle to upper classes and encompassed a much more diverse group of citizens concerned about the spaces in which they live.

This challenge to mainstream environmentalism could provide an equally important corrective for the deficiencies of mainstream ecocriticism. If a cognate of the environmental justice movement could be translated into the domain of ecological cultural criticism, ecocriticism would become a more diverse and productive force for confronting the full range of issues existing at the intersection of ecology and culture in the United States, including the nature of cities. Much as Black Aesthetics grew out of and then in tandem with the Black Power movement, an urban ecocriticism attuned to the spatialization of race needs to develop in partnership with the environmental justice movement. In fact, unless the political and cultural arms of the environmental movement come together to confront the ecological devastation being wreaked upon inner cities and the ideologies that underlie this assault, then the racist public policy that has been feeding the expansion of American ghettos will continue apace.

Manufacturing the Ghetto

The hopes for racial equality most profoundly addressed in the United States during the 1960s were never translated into a spatial reality. Instead, since World War II, "central-city residence, race, joblessness, and poverty have become inextricably intertwined" in American ghettos (Sugrue 3). For the purposes of this essay, I will use the terms inner city and ghetto interchangeably, accepting Cater and Jones's definition of the latter term as "a territory rigidly segregated from white neighbourhoods and a permanent base rather than a springboard for the dispersal of inhabitants . . . a quantitatively and qualitatively distinct category, implying severity, persistence, greater territorial extent and, most importantly, enforcement" (145). The element of enforcement, or policing, of ghetto borders is in accord with the concept of the ghetto as an "internal colony"—a concept that makes a fundamental connection between the processes of international capital and domestic economic planning and public policy. In this context, Cater and Jones continue, "the ghetto may be interpreted as the 'Third World within,' a space existing in the same economic relationship to the surrounding white city as does the colony to the metropolis" (148).

Carmichael and Hamilton provided a classic description of the internal colonial model as it was articulated through the Black Power movement: "The political power exercised over [black] communities [by white society] goes hand in glove with the economic deprivation experienced by the black citizens. Historically, colonies have existed for the sole purpose of enriching, in one form or another, the 'colonizer'; the consequence is to maintain the economic dependency of the 'colonized'" (17). It's difficult not to recognize the echo of these words in the current situation confronted by those in the environmental justice movement. In recent years, the hyper-segregation that prompted the Black Power movement to develop the model of internal colonization has been on the increase as these inner-city "colonies" are ever more separated from the surrounding white suburbs.

One of the major critiques of the internal-colonization model has been that it fails to credit the residents of inner-city neighborhoods for their achievements in resisting the stereotypes of the dominant culture and in formulating creative alternatives. Manning Marable notes that black community activists across the nation have carried on campaigns working for local empowerment and against the many manifestations of racism, following in the tradition of "the early N.A.A.C.P., the National Negro Congress of the Depression years, the Southern Christian Leadership Conference of the fifties or the Student Nonviolent Coordinating Committee and the League of Revolutionary Black Workers of the sixties" (21). Although none of the recent campaigns have had the national structure of these precursors, they have had an impact from coast to coast. In Portland, Oregon, community groups have kept the pressure on to preserve and expand the urban-planning initiatives and growth-management strategies that have made their city one of the country's most livable places (Walljasper). In New York City, Steven Gregory documents the vibrant political culture of one inner-city black neighborhood and challenges the monolithic perception of "ghetto" inhabitants as dysfunctional victims.

However, the fact remains that only the most extraordinarily fortunate individuals can triumph over the overwhelming social barriers constructed by the spatialization of race. The Community Justice Center notes that each year over seventy-five percent of the new inhabitants of the New York State prison system come from just seven neighborhoods in New York City. Popular wisdom tells us that there are hundreds of stories in the naked city, but they are all bracketed by the socioeconomic isolation and resulting poverty and crime mapped by the spatialization of race. Colonies, internal and external, can have vital cultures, but the opportunities therein are still circumscribed by the colonizer.

Anti-urbanism

The collapse of an urban policy in the United States capable of responding to this growing internal colonization has found ideological cover in a general sentiment of anti-urbanism that has come to pervade the American landscape, which justifies and expands the assault on inner cities. This anti-urban ideology, which has underwritten the resegregation of the United States, is evident in popular culture from relatively highbrow films like Ridley Scott's *Bladerunner* to the resolutely anti-urban *Escape from New York* and *Falling Down* to the city-as-hell imagery of the seemingly endless series of *Batman* films, to say nothing of the mushrooming "true crime" shows on television. Lest we underestimate the impact of these anti-urban images, Stephen Haymes argues that "cultural images and historical images have as much influence on the spatial form of the city as do economics" (3). Peter McLaren and Henry Giroux point out in their introduction to Haymes's work that the "racializing of urban space from the standpoint of white supremacist ideologies that privatize and pathologize black bodies . . . discursively constitute black urban populations through jungle metaphors and racist myths surrounding the exotic black subject" (xi). Massey and Denton note that the political and ideological constructs that accomplished the spatial isolation of black Americans were achieved by "a conjunction of racist attitudes, private behaviors, and institutional practices that disenfranchised blacks from urban housing markets and led to the creation of the ghetto" (83). They explain how segregation produces and promotes the features of inner-city life that are used to justify prejudice against the inhabitants of these areas: "By building physical decay, crime, and social disorder into the residential structure of black communities, segregation creates a harsh and extremely disadvantaged environment to which ghetto blacks must adapt. In concentrating poverty, moreover, segregation also concentrates conditions such as drug use, joblessness, welfare dependency, teenage childbearing, and unwed parenthood, producing a social context where these conditions are not only common but the norm" (13). Rather than seeing these behaviors as the result of the decline of inner cities, many whites see black "pathology" as the *cause* of such decline.

This is precisely the juncture at which the environmental justice movement is most at odds with traditional environmentalism and ecocriticism. Quick to condemn the cities for their ecocrimes, many ecological thinkers remain blithely ignorant of the consequences such rhetoric has for the inhabitants of these beleaguered areas. Such anti-urbanism provides an alibi for the cyclical process of disinvestment and gentrification by building "a symbolic construction of 'white places' as civilized, rational, and orderly and 'black places' as uncivilized, irrational, and disorderly," which allows for "police occupation and the removal of black people from their public spaces" (Haymes 21).

Many ecocritics have participated in the anti-urban ideology that underlies such policy through their almost exclusive focus on nonurban environments as privileged spaces—the domain of nature a priori conceptualized as cut off from human contact. In fact, the glorification of wild nature at the expense of urban ecosystems can, purposefully or inadvertently, feed into the assault on American cities that has been underway at least since the 1970s. Andrew Ross argues that anti-urbanism and back-to-nature movements "can be tied directly to the economic cycles of investment and disinvestment in city centers" (100), that is, the spaces that tend to be devalued or dismissed by ecocritics.

THE SPATIALIZATION OF RACE

The spatialization of race has enabled this anti-urban ideology, at work in much ecocriticism and American culture generally, to have real social force in the shape of retrograde urban policies—of a magnitude that calls forth military metaphors of the "assault" on cities, urban "warfare," and the "casualties" of the ghetto. Although these policies have caused some "collateral damage" to white inhabitants of urban areas, the overwhelming majority of those affected are minorities. The environmental justice movement has demonstrated that the increasing spatialization of racism means that people of color can be targeted with counterproductive or negligent public policy on the basis of where they reside, without policymakers having to mention race per se. As Massey and Denton have argued in *American Apartheid,* "This lack of overt racism, however, did not mean that prejudice and discrimination had ended; although racist attitudes and behaviors went underground, they did not disappear" (84). One might argue that it was precisely because racism went underground—or, more accurately, *into* the ground through the spatialization of race—that it became invisible and in some ways more pernicious. In contemporary cultural discourse and public policy, "the urban has become a metaphor for race, for black people" (Haymes 104), and we are now confronted with the very real social and cultural effects of this semantic slippage from "black" to "urban."

The always fluid boundaries of racial ideology have shifted such that in postwar America "blackness and whiteness assumed a spatial definition," what Thomas Sugrue has called a "racial geography " (9, 121). That is, many of the racist distinctions between black and white citizens were displaced onto supposedly more neutral observations of the differences between black and white neighborhoods. The adjectives formerly applied to African Americans by the now-repudiated old racism—violent, immoral, subhuman—were, by the calculus of the newest racism, transmuted onto the ghetto. A new generation of whites who had been taught not to believe, or at least vocalize, racist stereotypes simply transposed those stereotypes onto the deteriorating inner city, whose inhabitants just happened to be overwhelmingly people of color. As Sugrue argues, deteriorating neighborhoods became "signs of individual moral deficiencies, not manifestations of structural inequalities" (9). Racial ideology continued to function, as always, as a way of displacing social responsibility onto individual failures, but this time with a geographic metaphorics.

This form of racism did not come from nowhere; it is because of the racist ideologies and structures built into our culture over time that the stealth racism of anti-urbanism is able to flourish. Still, Cross and Keith explain how this the spatialization of race is something unique in the history of racial prejudice:

> In racist discourse, race has conventionally signified sets of pejorative associations of both individualized attributes (e.g., sexuality, criminality) and collective attributes (e.g., family structure, cultural pathologies), all of which do service in ideologies of racial subordination. But this range of signification is so deeply entrenched in western late capitalist culture that it can now be taken for granted in racist discourse: the significations do not have to be so clearly articulated, but can be con-

noted by the mere hint of racial content. This is more than just the elevation of the cultural over the biological which characterized the 'new' racism. ("Racism" 15)

Thus, this newest form of racism replaces direct references to race, whether biological or cultural, with spatialized terms like "urban" and "ghetto." Linguistically, these terms have followed the usual developmental pattern from metaphors (in which one must recognize that such terms are mere "figures of speech" connoting certain racial groups) to metonymic substitutions for race (in which the fiction of the racial connection is erased and the terms come to automatically denote "nonwhite"). This linguistic phenomena has been catalyzed by a regressive political agenda that such language serves; the terms evoke images of shiftless minorities in the general public imagination because the constant bombardment of conservative ideology has pounded them into our lexicon of cultural literacy.

This prejudice is a distorted reading of certain historical facts: African Americans and other people of color have become increasingly located in inner cities.[2] In the case of African Americans, as the proportion of poor African Americans living in inner cities rose from thirty-eight percent in 1959 to eighty percent in 1991, the concentration of poverty in the United States also moved to the inner cities—where over sixty percent of American poverty is now located, as opposed to less than one-third in the 1960s (Kasarda). Over eighty-five percent of the inhabitants of these impoverished inner cities are now people of color (Jargowsky). In other words, low-income people of color, especially African Americans and nonwhite Hispanics, are increasingly isolated in inner-city pockets of poverty. As Massey and Denton argue, this concentration of poverty, particularly within black neighborhoods, is subject to a multiplier effect: "racial segregation acts to concentrate poor blacks in a small number of neighborhoods, raising the poverty rate to which they are exposed and lowering the corresponding rate for whites. By itself, racial segregation concentrates poverty in *black* neighborhoods, but the addition of class segregation concentrates poverty primarily in *poor black* neighborhoods" (123–24; original emphases). Therefore, any downturn in the American economy has a much greater impact on poor, black, inner-city neighborhoods than on other areas.

Thus, the last thirty years or so have told an almost uninterrupted story of urban decline. A vicious circle has been created whereby white urban residents who can afford to do so flee to the suburbs to escape life in the financially strapped cities, which decreases the tax base for these cities and feeds a greater exodus from the increasingly desperate urban poverty that results. An equally vicious circle has kept people of color from leaving decaying inner cities. As Thomas Sugrue argues, "the combination of de-industrialization, white flight, and hardening ghettoization" fed the "increasing joblessness, and the decaying infrastructure of inner-city neighborhoods," which reinforced white stereotypes of black behavior by placing the blame for neighborhood decline on the poor people who live there (8). This blame-the-victim mentality has been perpetuated by various elements in American culture, the popular press, and the academy. Neil Smith illustrates one of the major reasons why it is easier to pin the cause of ghettoization on inner-city residents themselves than it is to confront the forces that act upon them: "You can't see the decision to disinvest from a house; what you *can* see is a black family moving in next door one year. You can't see a landlord having earlier made the decision not to invest but rather to let the house decay so that it becomes cheap housing. So the fundamental issue is the movement of capital" (Smith 113). In other words, the planned movement of capital out of ghetto areas is invisible and so the predominantly minority inhabitants of these neighborhoods are left holding the bag.

The invisibility of capital flight has made it easier to point to the visible effects of the spatialization of race while ignoring the causes. One way to confront this development is to reveal the mechanisms of the anti-urban ideology that make the urban "wilderness" a visible sign covering the hidden forces manufacturing the ghetto.[3] Another strategy, which is pursued in this essay, is to reveal the invisible forces working to deprive inner-city residents of safe and healthy environments by exploring the real social effects of these forces.

THE VISIBLE EFFECTS OF INVISIBLE FORCES

The governmental assault on urban areas has been well documented. During the Reagan-Bush years, the percentage of city budgets derived from the federal government declined almost threefold, from 14.3 percent to 5 percent (Dreier). The federal government has undertaken a series of policy initiatives that have undermined inner-city neighborhoods, which include redlining in mortgage appraisals; terminating urban-development action grants and most public-housing initiatives; building highways that destroyed housing and sealed off most people of color from the suburbanizing white middle class; and, in general, colluding "to transform much public housing into stigmatized, segregated, underfunded ghettos" (Katz 82–83). In short, "federal government policies have supported and encouraged suburbanization, metropolitan deconcentration, corporate and job flight, and disinvestment patterns that have contributed to the decline of U.S. cities" (Eitzen and Zinn 128). Through these policies, the government has transformed many black communities into pockets of unremitting poverty. This assault on the inner city has made visible the ways in which the combined effects of anti-urbanism and the spatialization of race have been built into current public policy, which leaves a majority of African Americans in communities deprived of adequate education, employment, health care, housing, and overall social capital.

Despite the intimate association between desegregation and education established by the *Brown v. Board of Education* decision, education has been a prime target of the newest racism's dismantling of inner-city services through isolating children of color from their white suburban counterparts. The isolation of black students from white students has actually increased over the last two decades, especially in metropolitan areas where students of color are concentrated: Three-fourths of the students are nonwhite in the largest urban school districts and two-thirds of black students attend schools that have a majority of nonwhite students (Galster "More").

In short, American schools are more separate and unequal than ever before. School desegregation has virtually been abandoned, along with busing and other remedies for educational inequality. The geographic discrimination in the financing of public schools in urban versus suburban school districts has been well documented (e.g., Galster, Kozol, Schiller). As the gap between urban and suburban financial resources increase, so too does inequity in schooling because public schools are financed primarily by property taxes and the suburbs have a much larger tax base. In Los Angeles, the decline of inner-city schools, coupled with the unavailability of employment opportunities and support services, has resulted in a situation where "Black males from Southcentral are now three times more likely to end up in prison than at the University of California" (Davis 307). This is the outcome not just of blatant discrimination, but of the "social ecology of American cities," which has "compounded the educational obstacles confronting poor and inner-city minority students by concentrating them in schools that discourage learning and achievement and that precipitate dropping out . . . the reorganization of social space has intensified the educational problems of urban schoolchildren" (Kantor and Brenzel 384, 401).

Any attempt to address this horrific imbalance must respond to the spatialization of race. Boger puts it bluntly: "No education solution that fails to reduce the concentration of poor children in inner-city schools can be effective in providing meaningful educational opportunities" (28). Sadly, such attempts will have to be carried on outside of the judicial system. A series of Supreme Court rulings since *Brown v. Board of Education* have limited the effectiveness of mandated school integration: *Keyes v. School Dist. N. 1* (1972) held that the mere existence of racial segregation was not a cause for judicial intervention absent proof of intentional discrimination by government officials, and *Milliken v. Bradley* (1974) made it difficult, if not impossible, for desegregation plans to reach beyond city limits to the suburbs. The latter case has engendered much analysis of how the suburban-urban imbalance in educational opportunities has deprived inner-city children of color of access to the benefits of desegregated schooling in any meaningful sense (e.g., Kantor and Brenzel, Katznelson and Weir). The requirements to prove intentional racial discrimination laid out in the former case have vitiated any judicial solution to institutional racism that is not necessarily the result of malevolent individuals but of structural and geographic racism. Thus, attempts to cope with the effects of the spatialization of race and anti-urbanism in the areas of education, employment, health care—or in any sphere, for that matter—are all beyond the purview of judicial solutions (barring an unlikely abandonment of these earlier decisions by the present Supreme Court).

In terms of employment, numerous commentators—including Wilson, Aronowitz and DiFazio, and Bluestone and Harrison—have noted that African American workers have largely been left behind over the last few decades by the United States' transition from an industrial and manufacturing economy to an information and service economy. The deindustrialization of the U.S. economy has caused a mismatch between African American education/training and the postindustrial labor market. At the same time, African Americans have quite literally been left behind as the newly available jobs are moved to the suburbs and the employment opportunities in inner-city areas shrink precipitously, which ties black unemployment to residential segregation. In other words, there has been "a spatial mismatch on top of the skills mismatch" (Galster "Polarization" 209) between the African American job pool and the jobs available. This spatial mismatch theory was analyzed in Rosenbaum and Popkin's contribution to the Brookings Institution collection *The Urban Underclass,* although other contributors to that volume (e.g., Kirshenman and Neckerman) suggested that overt employer discrimination remained an important factor. What is clear is that the suburbanization of employment opportunities did not happen accidentally; it was the planned result of racialized governmental policy. Industrial and tax policies encouraged the shift of jobs from urban to suburban areas (Sugrue). At the same time, residential segregation, which was sanctioned by law until well into the latter half of this century and continued by custom to this day, prevented African Americans from following these jobs to the suburbs.

In Los Angeles, for instance, an investigating committee of the California Legislature found that the South-central neighborhoods in which the city's African American population is concentrated experienced a fifty percent increase in unemployment between the early 1970s and mid 1980s, while community purchasing power declined by a third (Davis). Davis notes that the unemployment rate among black youth in Los Angeles County approached fifty percent as the 1980s drew to a close; as a result, the increasing "juvenation of poverty" (306)—the doubling of poverty among children statewide and the concentration of this effect in inner cities (to poverty rates approaching forty percent in Los Angeles County)—led to an increase in the black-market drug industry and youth crime. Thus, racist public policy led to behaviors that increase racial stereotypes about black youth while ignoring the impetus for antisocial behavior. These stereotypes ignore the fact that inner-city youth have been victimized by social disinvestment policies that have ensured residential segregation through the redistribution of tax resources upward.

Just as the inner-city communities inhabited by African Americans, young and old, have been disproportionately affected by unemployment,

Boger notes that "racial disparities in health care coverage have an important geographical dimension as well" (29) and that the percentage of inner-city residents lacking health insurance is double the national average. Also, even those residents who are able to pay for health care or secure insurance are unlikely to find adequate medical facilities in their neighborhoods. Ivie reports that physicians in private practice and for-profit hospitals shun poor minority communities, which means that "public hospitals are the primary providers of care for inner-city poor minorities" (305). However, these hospitals are overcrowded, underfunded, and closing at a fairly rapid rate, partly as a result of counterproductive federal intervention like the budget-cutting prescriptions of the Omnibus Budget Reconciliation Act of 1981 (Institute of Medicine). Sage documents that there was a significant correlation between hospital closures and the percentage of African Americans in the communities served.

At the same time, the environmental justice movement has highlighted the disproportionate number of ecological health hazards confronting communities of color. Not only are the health resources of the inner city demonstrably more constrained than those that are available to other areas, inner-city neighborhoods are also more likely to be themselves unhealthy because of the illnesses associated with poverty and population density and because these neighborhoods are more likely to be the locations for waste disposal facilities and other toxic sites. What the environmental justice movement has largely failed to recognize is that the other effects of the spatialization of race examined thus far—in terms of poorer educational support, employment opportunities, and health facilities for ghetto residents—are also forms of environmental racism that need to be addressed even more urgently than the Not-In-My-Backyard (NIMBY) issues that tend to dominate urban environmental activism.

These various forms of space-based racism are bound together by the very formation of ghetto environments in the first place through the ongoing housing discrimination and increasing segregation experienced by inner-city blacks. In their important study of *American Apartheid,* Massey and Denton maintain that "residential segregation is the principal structural feature of American society responsible for the perpetuation of urban poverty and represents a primary cause of racial inequality in the United States" (viii). The authors point out that the supposed response to segregation during the Civil Rights era—the Fair Housing Act of 1968—was stripped of its enforcement mechanisms, thus making it virtually useless. Since that time, the isolation of African Americans in urban Bantustans was actually aided by government housing policy. This reality makes the notion of "American apartheid" much more than a metaphor. Goldberg maintains that the segregation of African Americans from the rest of the population could not have been more efficient if the United States had actually passed a version of South Africa's Group Area Act, which assigned blacks to particular neighborhoods and homelands during the height of apartheid. In the American context, Goldberg argues, "the construct of separate (racial) group areas, in design or effect, has served to constrain, restrict, monitor and regulate urban space and its experience" (52). Analysts of the environmental justice movement (e.g., Bullard, Godsil) note that segregated housing patterns also facilitate the placing of environmental hazards in poor black communities, which have less political power to resist these hazards.

Federal efforts to address this racial divide by integrating housing collapsed in the 1980s as spending on public housing declined to almost nothing. Between 1981 and 1988, federal spending on low-income housing was cut from thirty-seven billion to seven billion dollars, "the greatest cut endured by any major federal program" during the Reagan years (Boger 33). What little money was made available for public housing only added to the inequity: "Government housing programs perpetuated racial divisions by placing public housing in already poor urban areas and bankrolling white suburbanization through discriminatory housing subsidies" (Sugrue 9–10). Massey and Denton detail the ways in which, far from combatting the forces of segregation, federal policies actually aided them:

> Discrimination in home lending originated in the Federal Housing Administration and its predecessor agencies. White suburbanization was subsidized by mortgage interest deductions and encouraged by FHA policies that denied credit to inner cities. White flight was enabled by massive federal investment in freeways, often constructed strategically to form barriers between black and white areas. Federal urban renewal programs and public housing projects were used by local governments, with federal acquiescence, to contain and isolate urban blacks. (186–87)

The sharp decrease in low-income housing was paradoxically matched by a sharp increase in low-income families, which led to a desperate housing shortfall. Boger traces this housing crisis to four causes: the almost total lack of new public housing construction; the destruction of 3.3 million older, low-income rental units; gentrification; and the withdrawal of existing housing from the low-income market.

The problem with gentrification (the process of reinvestment of capital in urban areas) is that it actually begins with the process of disinvestment that clears the land and makes it available to up-scale developers. In this way, the so-called unfettered private market actually destroys low-rent property by providing "tax breaks for people whose housing can be undervalued or written off in various ways in the tax system" and by encouraging "windfall profits from the process of what is called 'milking' of properties—doing no repair and no maintenance and turning the property over every few years" (Smith 111). Thus, the supposedly neutral process of gentrification takes on a clear cultural meaning through its contribution to the racialization of space: "efforts by city planners to gentrify and redevelop downtown [are] a deliberate attempt to regulate and control racial difference in terms of the city's visual space" (Haymes 102). As gentrification accelerates, many cities will experience the shifting of poor populations of color from urban areas to the nearest and financially ravaged suburbs, where the process of disinvestment and reinvestment will start all over again (barring some sort of public intervention). In the history of urban space, the 1960s and 1970s were the era of white flight to the suburbs and the 1980s and 1990s have been the era of urban renewal and gentrification. However, underlying all of this has been a shifting form of residential apartheid. Without much exaggeration, one could argue that the effect of denying low-income African Americans access to private home ownership or even rental opportunities outside of inner-city areas, combined with the funneling of this same population into substandard housing projects, has been to keep the majority of black families penned into ghetto areas where they have largely been dispensed with as a public-policy concern.

If these increasingly isolated neighborhoods are adversely impacted by the lack of financial resources, they are also starved of social capital, which Coleman defines as "any aspect of informal social organization that constitutes a productive resource for one or more actors" (170). The cumulative effect of the discrimination against inner-city residents in terms of education, employment, health and safety, and housing is magnified by this lack of informal networks of social organization. Despite the difficulty in quantifying the production of "social capital," Galster cites studies that indicate that "minorities bear a disproportionate share of socially isolated neighborhoods" ("Polarization" 202), largely because of the spatial concentration of poverty in these neighborhoods. The deteriorating physical infrastructure contributes to a deteriorating social infrastructure, which is then read by policymakers as a cause rather than an effect of the disproportionate hazards of urban living. In the absence of a federal urban policy to address the increasing decline of inner-city neighborhoods, we are left with privatized solutions: gentrification, urban renewal (which has aptly been nicknamed "Negro removal" by urban activists), and business improvement districts.

Beyond nimby

All of these privatized "solutions" to the increasing ghettoization of African Americans do not eliminate the problem; they simply displace it, feeding the distinction between cities and inner cities while promoting an anti-urbanism that is specifically focused on nonwhite neighborhoods. What is considered the "true city" is marked by a fluid boundary that moves to make room for islands of white wealth amid seas of poor people of color. Many critics have pointed to the ideological underpinning of gentrification as a remodulated form of the myth of the frontier. In this new form, the city becomes the landscape on which "urban pioneers" wrest valuable but wasted territory away from the "savage natives." Neil Smith reminds us of the seriousness of this metaphor: "Native Americans were seen as virtually part of the existing landscape, and they could be displaced or wiped out, and it is exactly that mentality that is being incorporated in describing the contemporary urban setting" (Smith 110). Gentrification's ongoing transformation of former ghettos into trendy neighborhoods indicates the constantly shifting turf of racial spatialization. Because of this fluidity, a nimby approach to environmental justice will prove futile unless there is a full-scale assault on the coded racism of public policy.

Despite the many merits of the environmental justice movement, one of its chief limitations is that it tends to be site specific, rather than focusing attention on larger issues of public policy that impact environments across the United States. In this sense, the collapse of an urban policy has become one of the most significant challenges for the environmental justice movement, and anti-urbanism is revealed as one of the most virulent forms of environmental racism.

Retooling the environmental justice movement to become a staging ground for such a dual program of integration and spatial equity may provide part of the answer. The grassroots nature of the environmental justice movement is suited for forms of community empowerment at the same time as the movement has been a locus for personal empowerment. In examining organizational efforts of a group of working-class minority women in Los Angeles to prevent the placement of a waste incinerator in their neighborhood, Cynthia Hamilton discovered that not only did these women come together as an effective political group, but "individual transformations accompanied the group process"; "new levels of consciousness" were achieved by these women at the same time as their collective effort "transformed the political climate of a major metropolitan area" (654–55). In fact, the environmental justice movement could be the legitimate heir to 1960s organizations like the National Welfare Rights Organization (NWRO), which Thomas F. Jackson has called that decade's "most successful attempt to join local client-based movements in an organization that could lobby and protest at the national level" (434). Like the NWRO, environmental justice movements work to create the necessary bridge between direct empowerment of those affected by racist public policy, community response, and pressuring the government to act.

Whatever form urban environmental activism takes to deal with the problems outlined here, it needs to move beyond NIMBY politics to confront the spatialization of race and to build coalitions capable of placing real urban revitalization back on the public agenda. These sociopolitical developments will not be possible unless concerned environmentalists—from environmental justice activists to members of the Sierra Club to ecocritics—contest the very visible anti-urban ideology that permeates our culture (including much of mainstream environmentalism and ecocriticism) and reveal the often invisible social effects of this ideology as it is used to construct and enforce the increasingly fortified boundaries of America's ghettos.

NOTES

1. The term "environmental racism" apparently was first used to describe the disproportionate targeting of minority communities for environmental hazards in the 1987 United Church of Christ Commission for Racial Justice report *Toxic Wastes and Race in the United States,* written under the supervision of Benjamin Chavis. This report superseded a 1983 General Accounting Office report that discovered that three out of four hazardous waste landfills in the southeastern United States were located in predominantly black communities. The United Church of Christ report revealed that this pattern was consistent across the nation and that race was more significant than socioeconomic status in determining the placement of such facilities. In 1990, the Environmental Protection Agency also released a study indicating that racial minorities are disproportionately exposed to environmental toxins. Academics, notably Robert Bullard, have provided independent corroboration of the existence of environmental racism. Bullard has revealed the discriminatory placement of landfills and garbage incinerators in Houston *(Invisible),* analyzed toxic dumping in African American communities throughout the South *(Dumping),* and edited the excellent collection *Confronting Environmental Racism.* These sources provide further information on the environmental justice movement, as well as the comprehensive collection *We Speak for Ourselves: Social Justice, Race, and Environment,* edited by Dana Alston.

2. The Great Migration from the rural South to the urban North during the early twentieth century has continued during the last half-century, such that eighty-two percent of blacks now live in urban areas (Rosler). These black urbanites are increasingly concentrated in areas where at least eighty percent of their neighbors are also African American, with the majority living in all-black locales (Massey and Denton). At the same time, eighty-six percent of white suburbanites live in communities where less than one percent of the population is black (West).

3. This critique of the ideology of the urban "wilderness" is a strategy mentioned in my interview with Andrew Ross (chapter 2) and developed by Andrew Light (chapter 8).

WORKS CITED

Alston, Dana, ed. *We Speak for Ourselves: Social Justice, Race and Environment.* Washington, D.C.: Panos Institute, 1990.

Aronowitz, Stanley, and William DiFazio. *The Jobless Future: SciTech and the Dogma of Work.* Minneapolis: U of Minnesota P, 1994.

Bluestone, Barry, and Bennett Harrison. *The Deindustrialization of America.* New York: Basic Books, 1982.

Boger, John Charles. "Race and the American City: The Kerner Commission Report in Retrospect." Boger and Wegner. 3–76.

Boger, John Charles, and Judith Welch Wegner, eds. *Race, Poverty, and American Cities.* Chapel Hill: U of North Carolina P, 1996.

Bullard, Robert D. *Confronting Environmental Racism: Voices from the Grassroots.* Boston: South End Press, 1993.

——. "Dumping in Black and White." Alston. 4–7.

——. *Dumping in Dixie: Race, Class, and Environmental Quality.* Boulder, Colo.: Westview Press, 1990.

——. *Invisible Houston: The Black Experience in Boom and Bust.* College Station: Texas A&M UP, 1987.

Carmichael, Stokeley, and C. V. Hamilton. *Black Power.* New York: Vintage, 1967.

Cater, John, and Trevor Jones. *Social Geography: An Introduction to Contemporary Issues.* London: Edward Arnold, 1989.

Coleman, James S. "A Rational Choice Perspective on Economic Sociology." *The Handbook of Economic Sociology.* Eds. N. J. Smelser and R. Swedberg. Princeton, N.J.: Princeton UP, 1994. 166–80.

Cross, Malcolm, and Michael Keith. "Racism and the Postmodern City." Cross and Keith. 1–30.

——, eds. *Racism, the City, and the State.* New York: Routledge, 1993.

Davis, Mike. *City of Quartz: Excavating the Future of Los Angeles.* New York: Verso, 1990.

Dreier, Peter. 1992. "Bush to Cities: Drop Dead." *The Progressive* 56 (July): 20–23.

Eitzen, D. S., and Maxine Baca Zinn. *Social Problems.* 6th ed. Boston: Allyn and Bacon, 1994.

Galster, George C. "More Than Skin Deep: The Effect of Housing Discrimination on the Extent and Pattern of Racial Residential Segregation in the United States." *Housing Desegregation and Federal Policy.* Ed. J. M. Goering. Chapel Hill: U of North Carolina P, 1986. 119–38.

——. "Polarization, Place, and Race." Boger and Wegner. 186–227.

Godsil, Rachel D. "Remedying Environmental Racism." *Michigan Law Review* 90 (November 1991): 394–427.

Goldberg, David Theo. " 'Polluting the Body Politic': Racist Discourse and Urban Location." Cross and Keith. 45–60.

Gregory, Steven. *Black Corona: Race and the Politics of Place in an Urban Community.* Princeton, N.J.: Princeton UP, 1998.

Hamilton, Cynthia. "Women, Home, and Community: The Struggle in an Urban Environment." *Rereading America: Cultural Contexts for Critical Thinking and*

Writing. 3rd ed. Eds. Gary Colombo et. al. Boston: St. Martin's Press, 1995. 650–57.

Haymes, Stephen Nathan. *Race, Culture, and the City: A Pedagogy for Black Urban Struggle*. Albany: State U New York P, 1995.

Institute of Medicine. *Homelessness, Health, Human Needs*. Washington, D.C.: National Academy Press, 1988.

Ivie, Sylvia Drew. "Ending Discrimination in Health Care: A Dream Deferred." *Civil Rights Issues in Health Care Delivery*. Ed. U. S. Commission on Civil Rights. Washington, D.C.: U.S. Commission on Civil Rights, 1980. 282–317.

Jackson, Thomas F. "The State, the Movement, and the Urban Poor: The War on Poverty and Political Mobilization in the 1960s." *The "Underclass" Debate: Views from History*. Ed. Michael B. Katz. Princeton, N.J.: Princeton UP, 1993. 403–39.

Jargowsky, Paul A. "Ghetto Poverty among Blacks in the 1980s." *Journal of Policy Analysis and Management* 13 (1994): 288–310.

Kantor, Harvey, and Barbara Brenzel. "Urban Education and the 'Truly Disadvantaged': The Historical Roots of the Contemporary Crisis, 1945–1990." *The "Underclass" Debate: Views from History*. Ed. Michael B. Katz. Princeton, N.J.: Princeton UP, 1993. 366–402.

Kasarda, John D. "Cities as Places Where People Live and Work: Urban Change and Neighborhood Distress." *Interwoven Destinies: Cities and the Nation*. Ed. Henry G. Cisernos. New York: Norton, 1993. 81–124.

Katz, Michael B. *Improving Poor People: The Welfare State, the "Underclass," and Urban Schools as History*. Princeton, N.J.: Princeton UP, 1995.

Katznelson, Ira, and Margaret Weir. *Schooling for All: Race, Class, and the Democratic Ideal*. New York: Basic Books, 1985.

Kirshenman, Joleen, and Kathryn M. Neckerman. " 'We'd Love to Hire Them, But . . .': The Meaning of Race for Employers." *The Urban Underclass*. Eds. Christopher Jencks and Paul E. Peterson. Washington, D.C.: Brookings Institution, 1991. 203–32.

Kozol, Jonathan. *Savage Inequalities: Children in America's Schools*. New York: Harper, 1991.

Marable, Manning. "Black (Community) Power!" *The Nation* 22 December 1997: 21–24.

Massey, Douglas S., and Nancy A. Denton. *American Apartheid: Segregation and the Making of the Underclass*. Cambridge, Mass.: Harvard UP, 1993.

Rosenbaum, James E., and Susan J. Popkin. "Employment and Earnings of Low-Income Blacks Who Move to Middle-Class Suburbs." *The Urban Underclass*. Eds. Christopher Jencks and Paul E. Peterson. Washington, D.C.: Brookings Institution, 1991. 342–56.

Rosler, Martha. "Fragments of a Metropolitan Viewpoint." *Wallis*. 15–44.

Ross, Andrew. *The Chicago Gangster Theory of Life: Nature's Debt to Society.* New York: Verso, 1994.

Sage, Alan. "The Closure of Hospitals That Serve the Poor: Implications for Health Planning." *Extension of Health Planning Program: Hearings on Extension of HHS Aid before the Subcommittee on Health and the Environment of the House Committee on Energy and Commerce.* Ed. U.S. House Committee on Energy and Commerce. 97th Cong. 2nd sess., 1982, H. Doc. 126. 530–44.

Schiller, B. R. *The Economics of Poverty and Discrimination.* Englewood Cliffs, N.J.: Prentice Hall, 1989.

Smith, Neil. "Housing: Gentrification, Dislocation and Fighting Back." Wallis. 93–123.

Sugrue, Thomas J. *The Origins of the Urban Crisis: Race and Inequality in Postwar Detroit.* Princeton, N.J.: Princeton UP, 1996.

United Church of Christ Commission for Racial Justice. *Toxic Wastes and Race in the United States: A National Report on the Racial and Socio-Economic Characteristics of Communities with Hazardous Waste Sites.* New York: United Church of Christ, 1987.

Wallis, Brian, ed. *If You Lived Here: The City in Art, Theory, and Social Activism.* Seattle: Bay Press, 1991.

Walljasper, Jay. "Portland's Green Peace: At Play in the Fields of Urban Planning." *The Nation* 13 October 1997: 11–15.

West, Cornel. *Race Matters.* Boston: Beacon Press, 1993.

Wilson, William Julius. "Public Policy Research and *The Truly Disadvantaged.*" *The Urban Underclass.* Eds. Christopher Jencks and Paul E. Peterson. Washington, D.C.: Brookings Institution, 1991. 460–81.

——. *When Work Disappears: The World of the New Urban Poor.* New York: Alfred A. Knopf, 1996.

5

ECOFEMINISM AND THE CITY

11

AN ECOFEMINIST PERSPECTIVE ON THE URBAN ENVIRONMENT

Catherine Villanueva Gardner

Although the contribution of women in grassroots urban environmental protests in the United States has been both significant and acknowledged, a survey of ecofeminist literature reveals that the urban environment itself has not been a locus of attention.[1] In "Ecofeminism and Grassroots Environmentalism in the United States," Barbara Epstein has even suggested that ecofeminism—despite its link between the environment and women—has little at present to offer women involved in grassroots urban politics. Epstein claims that ecofeminism offers a theoretical approach when the need is for a point of leverage, "a way of focusing the widespread discontent over the degradation of the environment and the hazards posed by toxics especially in communities of working-class people and people of color" (150).

Although I do not intend to reply directly to Epstein's comments, they are a useful way to begin a discussion of what an ecofeminist perspective on the United States urban environment, and the problems peculiar to this environment, would look like and what it can offer. An ecofeminist perspective on grassroots protest can allow us to see the complex interconnections of race, class, gender, and the environment. The "inclusivity" of ecofeminism has both a theoretical and a practical strength; it can both inform the analysis of grassroots protest and provide a theoretical structure that can include these voices of protest. Moreover, an ecofeminist perspective on the practical problems of the urban environment is not merely an appropriate one, but these problems actually call for just such a perspective.

Yet, it may seem that Epstein's concern over the theoretical nature of ecofeminism still stands and that it may cut even deeper than Epstein realizes. While ecofeminism helps the academic engaged in a theoretical analysis of grassroots protest in the urban environment, it may do so by privileging persons "outside" the environment studied. In fact, it may appear that those living in inner-city environments are excluded from gaining an ecofeminist perspective because it is fundamentally connected to a position of white, middle-class privilege and because it may involve a problematic essentializing of nature and even of race. Although I argue for the importance of an ecofeminist perspective on the urban environment, I also recognize that this argument is conditional on carefully analyzing and reconceiving the ecofeminist perspective itself.

Ecofeminism: A Brief Account

The majority of work to date in ecofeminism has been in the field of "environmental ethics," specifically work on the development of an appropriate feminist value system, although it would be a mistake to begin by trying to state *the* ecofeminist ethical perspective. Because ecofeminism entails both a feminist and an environmentalist ethic and because it engages in theoretical philosophy analyzing issues that are of central practical importance, ecofeminism contains a wide range of diverse thought. Moreover, a search for *the* perspective implies that there is a single ecofeminist theory or at least that one may be sought. Marti Kheel suggests that we instead understand ecofeminist theory as "a number of theories or stories that, when woven together into a fabric or tapestry, help to provide a picture or 'portrait' of the world in which we currently live" (244). Within this tapestry, however, there are several patterns that continuously reappear. It is these that I shall discuss to provide an account of the typical features of an ecofeminist ethic.

All ecofeminist theories agree that there are important connections between the oppression of women and the oppression of nature and that, to bring out an ecofeminist ethical perspective, we must first understand these connections. To accomplish this task, our initial focus must be not on offering a (simplistic) *causal* account of the connections between ecological destruction and the oppression of women, but on exposing and revising the oppressive conceptual framework that sanctions the joint subordination of women and nature.[2] A key feature of this conceptual framework is the dualistic classification of reality, with the disjuncts not only being seen as oppositional and exclusive (mind/body, man/woman, human/nature), but as organized on what Elizabeth Dodson Gray calls a spatial metaphor (up/down), with a lesser value attributed to the lower (20). Thus, body, woman, and nature are put "down" or given a lesser value. Furthermore, the assumption is that the perceived moral superiority of one group over the other *justifies* the oppression of the "inferior" group.[3]

In understanding the way that this conceptual framework functions to oppress women and nature, ecofeminism can begin to draw conceptual connections between sexism and racism, classism, heterosexism, etcetera. Because of its commitment to end sexism and naturism, ecofeminism is also committed at a conceptual level to ending these other forms of oppression. As Karen Warren states, "it is by clarifying this conceptual connection between systems of oppression that a movement to end sexist oppression— traditionally the special turf of feminist theory and practice—leads to a reconceiving of feminism as *a movement to end all forms of oppression*" (132; original emphasis).

The mind/body and human/nature dualisms are present in traditional moral theory as its pivotal dualism: the valuing of "the rational" over "the emotional." According to this view, the moral life is one of rationality, a life that is potentially impeded by the needs of the body and the pull of the emotions. The emotions will affect/distort our rational decisionmaking; if our emotions are allowed to affect moral choice, the high degree of separateness and independence necessary for the moral agent is threatened. Thus, the truly rational moral agent is one who is unrestricted by the demands of the attachments and relationships that are part of the emotional or affective "side" of our nature. This superiority accorded to rationality underpins a view of morality in which the moral agent is an individual free to choose from a range of alternative relations, attachments, and goals. However, this freedom of choice may be restricted by the choices and ends of other moral agents, thus, the moral agent is an individual potentially in competition with other individuals over the ends for which they choose to aim. One central aim of any moral theory that accords superiority to the rational is to allow this collection of individuals to form a productive community; such individualistic moral concepts as rights and justice are pivotal to such a theory. Clearly, the type of community that will be built on this model is one that only demands a minimum moral commitment: a willingness to consider the needs of others in conjunction with one's own.

The rejection of the framework that justifies the up/down hierarchy of the emotional/rational dualism removes the underpinning of many of these aspects of traditional moral theory. If we reject the fundamental notion based on this dualism that moral activity is comprised of decisionmaking procedures between potentially competitive abstract individuals, we shall be able to recognize previously ignored pivotal features about human moral life. We shall be able to see that human ethical life and action occurs within a *web* of relationships. Moreover, the recognition of the existence of this web allows the re-estimation of values appropriate for its maintenance: cooperation, friendship, love—values that fall within the scope of the previously undervalued "emotional."[4] This framework allows us to recognize that ethical action (and interaction) occurs between diverse humans living in varied historical/social contexts. Ethical activity is no longer restricted to the making of rational choices. Although ecofeminism *can* still allow a place for the traditional/patriarchal individualistic moral concepts of rights and justice, its focus on understanding relations and making connections involve a shift toward an ethics of community, an ethics that emphasizes our relations to each other and the context in which we live and that involves perception as a moral activity as much as it does choice or action. Thus, ecofeminism expands the moral community. Rejecting the moral superiority of the mental over the physical means that the exclusion of the nonhuman world from our moral consideration will have lost its original justification.

Thus we can see that a rejection of the conceptual framework that has served to justify the oppression of women and nature facilitates sweeping changes in moral theorizing. Our concept of the moral self and its relations to other moral selves and entities, our notion of the moral community and who will be included in that community, and our understanding of what constitutes moral activity all undergo a dramatic shift in perspective. If the moral agent is no longer a fixed abstract entity, but is instead contextualized, then ecofeminism prescribes an ethic that includes diverse experiences rather than being based on a unified experience.

Although it is possible to outline basic values that are common to ecofeminist ethical views, the rejection of traditional moral theory does not entail the need to replace it with a formal or essential ecofeminist moral theory.[5] There is no one way that ecofeminists arrive at a rejection of the conceptual framework that oppresses women and nature, nor (once this framework is rejected) is there only one way that ecofeminists can develop new ways of moral perception. Typically, ecofeminists refer to their sense of relationship with the natural environment as conducive to producing an ecofeminist ethical consciousness. As I will discuss later, this may raise potential difficulties for the development of an ecofeminist perspective for the urban dweller.

An Ecofeminist Analysis of Grassroots Protests

Now that I have outlined the scope of ecofeminist thought, I can begin to examine what it can offer women involved in grassroots protests. Much of the grassroots activism that has emerged recently in both urban environments and in rural areas has been led by women. One survey indicated that seventy to eighty percent of local leaders involved in protests related to toxic-waste issues were women (Zeff et al. 25). What is particularly significant about women's involvement at this level of environmental protest is that while they may become involved with a single-issue protest, such as the location of a toxic-waste dump, there appears to be a transformation of the political consciousness of these women:

> Women in Texas, for example, organized against the pollution they believed was causing brain cancer in their children. A mother of a child born severely retarded became a leader in a movement against a battery recycler in Throop, Pennsylvania, that contaminated her neighborhood with lead. . . . Although these leaders became involved because of a single issue or problem, they quickly recognized the interconnections with other injustices they face daily . . . deteriorating neighborhood conditions, poverty, and race. (Gibbs ix–x)

As a perspective on environmental protest in the urban environment, ecofeminism is able to make visible parts of this process of politicization and change of consciousness that may be missed by a nonenvironmental feminist perspective. This becomes clear if we compare a feminist analysis with an ecofeminist analysis of a similar grassroots protest.

In "Blue-Collar Women and Toxic Waste Protests," Celene Krauss offers an analysis of this process of politicization through the lenses of feminist theory and new social historiography. Krauss shows that the original impetus for the protest often comes from the fact that these women see themselves as performing the traditional roles of protecting and caring for their family and home: They are prepared to protest because they see toxic-waste dumps as a threat to the health of their family. Krauss argues that as these women bring their personal and particular concerns into the world of policymaking, they come into conflict with policymakers, who are traditionally white, male, and middle class. These women come to see the gulf between the actions of the policymakers and the lip service these policymakers pay to the importance of family and home. They also come to recognize the gender and class inequalities of traditional political power. Krauss claims further that these women begin to see these relations reflected in the traditional gender roles of the patriarchal family and to question the underlying power relationships of the family.

In "Women of Color on the Front Line," Krauss extends her analysis to an exploration of working-class, African American women. Krauss claims that although the impetus for the protest—protection of the family—remains the same, African American women typically begin from a greater political awareness, which is grounded in race, and they have a more community-based approach because their protest comes out of a history of civil rights activism. Krauss maintains that the process of consciousness and empowerment for African American women activists mirrors that of the white activists, but that for women of color "it is the link between race and environment, rather than between class and environment, that characterizes definitions of environmental justice" (270). Clearly, a feminist analysis of this kind can allow us to see the politicization of the private and the way it can be used to affect public policymaking. Yet, I would argue that it cannot make visible all the facets of a woman-based environmental protest. If we compare the aspects of women's grassroots protests that are brought out through a feminist perspective with those that are made visible through an ecofeminist perspective, we find that the latter allows a recognition of the interconnections of sexism, classism, racism, and naturism.

In "Women, Home, and Community," Cynthia Hamilton gives the case history of a group of low-income, black women in Los Angeles who were able to prevent the installation of a solid-waste incinerator in their community. Like Krauss, Hamilton notes that what began as a pragmatic concern for a localized threat to homes and families—traditionally the domain of women—became a locus for the development of the political consciousness of the women protesters.[6] Furthermore, these women encountered the same lack of support (or even hostility) as their individual relations with husbands and family were affected by this change in consciousness.

However, Hamilton brings out some aspects of the Los Angeles protest that remain invisible in Krauss's analysis of grassroots protests, an invisibility that would appear to be a function not just of the individual protests examined, but of the lens through which they are examined. Hamilton allows us to recognize that the process of politicization of the protesters involves more than an understanding of race, gender, and class inequities; it contains an understanding of our relationship to the environment: "The principles of feminism and ecology . . . found expression and developed in the consciousness of these women: the concern for Earth as a home, the recognition that all parts of a system have an equal value" (221).

It is this concern for the Earth that the protesters saw as allowing their protest to cut across racial, class, and neighborhood lines as the original protesters were joined by women from all over the city. It is here that we can start to see the differences between Hamilton's ecofeminist analysis and Krauss's feminist analysis. For Krauss, political consciousness develops as particular environmental concerns of the individual or group become linked to class or race issues, whereas, for Hamilton, particular environmental concerns leads to an awareness both of Earth as a home and of the problem of its degradation. This sense of a shared Earth or home that is under threat leads to a unity of purpose that joins together women across class, race, and location. Moreover, this concern for the Earth allowed the protesters to see the issues involved in a woman-based process of the location of a toxic-waste dump in a working-class, minority neighborhood as comprising resistance to interconnected forms of oppression. Hamilton quotes one of the protesters as saying, "This fight has really turned me around, things are intertwined in ways that I hadn't realized. . . . All these social issues as well as political and economic issues are really intertwined" (221).

It would then appear that Hamilton's analysis moves, in a way that Krauss's does not, beyond particular environmental problems toward a more general (and potentially fruitful) discussion of our relationship with the Earth. Furthermore, Hamilton's analysis, unlike that of Krauss, allows a potentially productive understanding of the development of political consciousness that need not be restricted to the awareness of a particular form or forms of oppression, but instead develops (at least in part) from the awareness of their interconnections. Thus, Hamilton's analysis allows us to see that an ecofeminist perspective may have potential to help women actually involved at the grassroots level to focus their protests.

It still could be maintained, however, that an ecofeminist perspective may ultimately have little to offer the women protesters. The sense of interconnectedness that is so central to an ecofeminist perspective may not be readily available to those living in urban environments. Although the protesters that Hamilton interviewed may seem to have developed an ecofeminist ethical consciousness, it can still be asked whether an ecofeminist perspective is fundamentally privileged. The importance of contact with the Earth and the possibility of being in a relationship with the natural environment are central ethical experiences for an ecofeminist. Such experiences and connections are clearly unavailable to many living in urban areas.

Charlene Spretnak discusses how important for the development of an ecofeminist understanding "is a willingness to deepen our experience of communion with nature. This can be done in the mountains, at the ocean, in a city park, or a backyard garden. . . . Nature has given me gifts, teachings, and revelations, but none more intense than those times in the wilderness I approached in silence, simply observing and being aware of the sensations I was experiencing, until eventually I was enfolded by the deep, deep silence and the oneness that is almost palpable" (7–8). Although inner-city gardens and summer wilderness camps for children are praiseworthy experiences, such things cannot easily replicate the type of experience of the nonhuman world described by Spretnak—an experience that she argues can transform ethical understanding. Moreover, the chance to reflect on and to experience a oneness with one's surroundings, which is so important to Spretnak's ethical perception, does not seem to be available to the inner-city inhabitant who is in the process of protesting the very inequities and inadequacies of her environment.

Underlying Spretnak's description of her experiences in the wilderness is a fundamental ecofeminist claim about the importance of a human relationship with nature. This relationship, which leads to ethical transformation, is not one where nature is "instrumental" (where nature is the *means* to a *human end*), rather change comes about through a shift in perception of nature: We move from seeing the nonhuman world as something to "master" to loving and respecting that world. This shift in perception of the world is important for our shift in perception of the moral community: We move from upholding hierarchy to respect for difference, from maintaining separation to recognition of ties and connections.

However, if an ecofeminist perspective of the moral community is contingent on this kind of experience of "nature," the urban dweller is potentially excluded from the purview of ecofeminism, which creates a tension for the inclusivist nature of ecofeminism.[7] If an ecofeminist perspective on the urban environment excludes—directly or indirectly—the "voices" of those living in an urban environment, then it cannot be, by its own definition, a true ecofeminist perspective. Yet, if we do not allow for the inclusion of these voices or if we assume that the urban dweller's voice is no different than that of a woman alone in the wilderness, then we have presumed to speak for others, a typical assumption of the kind of universalizing world view that ecofeminism aims to confront. A closer examination of this tension is productive because it brings out important aspects not only of an ecofeminist perspective on the urban environment, but of the ecofeminist perspective itself.

THE URBAN ENVIRONMENT AND AN ECOFEMINIST PERSPECTIVE

Initially, it would seem that there cannot be a human relationship with the urban environment in the way that the nature enthusiast has a loving relationship with the wilderness. In fact, the urban environment seems hostile to such a relationship. The nature enthusiast's sense of oneness with, and the sense of caring for, her environment may seem to be at odds with the discord of many urban areas. Insofar as we cannot have a sense of connection with our environment, we may be kept from the possibility of the development of a moral community. Thus, an ecofeminist perspective could allow a critique of the urban environment: that the conditions under which some people live in urban environments are not merely unjust, but that the "soulless" context of some urban environments threatens moral life itself. It could be argued that the potential exclusion of the urban dweller from the development of an ecofeminist consciousness is due to some fundamental inadequacy of the urban environment itself—its inability to sustain human life and community. This approach could be fruitful, but at the expense of theoretical inclusiveness: Ecofeminism can then only be a theory *about* or *for,* but not *of,* urban dwellers.

However, it could also be argued that those who adopt this perspective misunderstand the potential of the urban environment to touch the "soul." Although the urban environment may potentially threaten moral connections, it does not *necessarily* preclude the sense of oneness that is a catalyst for a shift in moral perception. In "Goddess in the Metropolis," Irene Javors argues that we can find spirituality even in urban decay. Javors describes how the hungry and the homeless are reminders of what we fear in life: disease, poverty, and our own mortality. Yet, she claims, we must not run from these "gifts" of the goddess Hecate/Kali, nor must we disassociate ourselves through dualisms: good/bad, beautiful/ugly.[8] Instead, we must transcend this fearful way of thinking. Indeed, we must see the most beleaguered of urban dwellers as part of a whole of which we too are part: "Hecate/Kali destroys the ego. In so doing, she opens us up to our true being—our spiritual essence. She wants us to become one with her, with nature. She teaches us that we heal ourselves when we accept and reunite with the cycles of the natural world. The city is nature. The people are holy. The land is sacred. In so loving the world, the Goddess in the metropolis dances amidst the concrete and the garbage, embracing us all" (214). Thus Javors suggests that the sense of oneness that leads to a shift in perception of the moral community may be available even to one who lives in the most ravaged of urban environments. If Javors is offering us a cogent possibility, then we must return to our original understanding of a sense of oneness with nature as the precondition for a shift in perspective and explore what is shared by both Javors and Spretnak.

What appears to be central to both experiences is that the self is seen as continuous, rather than discontinuous, with its environment. As Val Plumwood shows, seeing the self as discontinuous reinforces the rationality/emotion dualism. As discussed above, it is this dualism that underpins conceptions of the moral community and moral relationships that are rejected by ecofeminism. Here we should understand "environment" to cover not just the wilderness or national parks, but our homes, our communities, and their interactions. Thus, the sense of oneness that can lead to a ecofeminist ethical consciousness can be understood in terms of discontinuity/continuity; it need not be framed in terms of nonnatural/natural. When understood in this way, an ecofeminist ethical consciousness is clearly available to urban dwellers.

Thus, although experience of wild nature may be more conducive than the urban environment for the development of an ecofeminist ethical consciousness, the former type of experience is not necessary for a shift in moral perception. This is an important point because, as Victoria Davion argues, there is a tendency in some ecofeminist thought to make a claim about the existence of an essential "feminine" connection with nature. The assumption that underpins this claim is clear: There is some kind of unified woman's experience of, or connection with, nature. To hold that such a unified experience exists is to ignore differences between women, and, in this case, specifically to ignore the differences between those who live in urban and nonurban areas. A claim that emphasizes uncritically the connections between woman and nature (even if this claim purports to celebrate such connections) may serve to reinforce the dualisms that ecofeminism needs to uproot.

Unfortunately, however, one could argue that this solution to the problems of privilege and inclusivity in an ecofeminist perspective on the urban environment still relies on dualisms of the type that ecofeminist theorizing is committed to removing. In her book *Ecofeminist Natures,* Noel Sturgeon claims that work such as Javors's can underpin the dualism between the "civilization" of the United States and the real or mythologized "indigenous" cultures of Asian Indians, Native Americans, or European pagan cultures. Ecofeminist approaches similar to Javors's work may avoid gender essentialism while unwittingly substituting the category of race in its place. Such approaches see members of certain groups of women—such as pagan women, tribal women, or "Third World" women—as having a close, essential connection with nature. Women who are not members of those groups—specifically white, "civilized" women—are then to learn from these typically nonwhite, "more ecofeminist" modes of acting and being within the world and nature. Sturgeon argues that this is potentially exploitative because women of color and nonmodern women become "natural resources for the betterment of white people" (130). In the particular case of Javors's work, Sturgeon claims that "the idea that poverty, homelessness, and social isolation are part of 'cycles of nature' is a particularly egregious example of the way essentialist feminist spirituality can be used to mask white middle-class privilege" (222, fn. 61).

Cecile Jackson also demonstrates how ecofeminism may contain such racial essentialisms. She argues that the romantic essentializing of "Third World" women ignores the many differences and divisions between these women created by class, age, geographical region, and other factors. This perspective also obscures the fact that the environmentally friendly practices of women may be dictated as much by their particular needs at that time as by some close connection to nature. Jackson notes, for example, that women may be willing to collect dead wood for firewood and replant trees near their homes for convenience's sake, but, given a shortage of firewood, they will just as "naturally" chop down living trees. Jackson claims that "women have no inherent or definitive closeness to nature, but socially constructed relations to natural resources which vary for different groups of women, and for individual women during the course of a lifetime" (405).

A further problem with such racial essentialisms of "indigenous" women as being more "natural" (and thus more ecofeminist) is the accompanying implicit essentialism of nature and the natural. The meaning of "nature" and "the environment," as Jackson claims, are no more biological facts than "woman." We must recognize that the nature/culture dichotomy is a construct of a culture that has a particular social, economic, and intellectual history: Our concept of "nature" is neither universal nor timeless. As Elly Haney argues, we must recognize the way our heritage defines and shapes the ways in which we conceptualize nature, conceptualizations that will then dictate how we "do" environmental ethics. Haney shows that two centuries ago nature was a threat to American (white, middle-class) "civilization" and—like its Native population—was in need of taming, whereas today nature offers the privileged (white, middle-class) members of our society a spiritual escape from the rigors of civilized life. Despite their differences, Haney sees these two conceptions of nature as "rooted in the same racist legacy" (86). In short, both conceptions posit nature as the object of control or use by a particular group.

This nature essentialism is deeply problematic not just for the particular case of Javors or my attempt to reconcile the tensions created by an ecofeminist perspective on the urban environment, but, as Sturgeon argues, for ecofeminist theorizing itself. Sturgeon claims that if ecofeminists did not make the ideological separation between culture and nature, they would not need to rely on these indigenous groups or aim to become like them, "rather they would be challenged to creatively deal with the politics of their daily technologies. . . . White ecofeminists would have to start imagining nature as including the urban and constructed landscapes in which many people live (including Native American and Third World women)" (132). It may initially appear that this approach to the urban landscape is precisely what Javors is offering, because her way of seeing the self as continuous with the environment does not make a separation between the inner city and the wilderness. Yet the way in which the inner city is understood as an environment that produces an ecofeminist perspective is problematic. One type of experience—of the "natural" environment—is still valorized over the other kind—of the "urban" environment. The latter is only valued or accepted insofar as it approximates the former; moreover, the "urban" environment remains dependent for this value on the value of the "natural" environment.

This theoretical problem has clear repercussions for our analysis of the urban environment. Given a choice, most people would not choose to live in decaying inner cities or near target zones for toxic-waste sites, yet they often do not have the social or economic power to "vote with their feet" and leave. If we are too quick to identify a "natural" affinity between women and environmental protection, we may come to believe that it is their role to remain and preserve those areas, a preservation that ultimately benefits those who have the social and economic power to not have to live in areas of environmental degradation.

Environmental Justice, Ecofeminism, and the Urban Environment

These difficulties for developing an ecofeminist perspective on the urban environment—in tandem with the problems of privileging a middle-class perspective and forms of nature and racial essentialism—may then lead us to believe that we should instead examine an approach that confronts these problems head on: the movement for environmental justice. The particular strength of the environmental justice movement is that it unites both environmentalism and social justice into one framework. It is clear that environmental problems do not affect us equally and that specific environmental concerns are not universal. Unfortunately, as Nathan Hare argues, the ecology movement has often failed to recognize not only the dynamics of class, but also the differences between black and white environments. For Hare, white ecology has as its central focus aesthetic conditions: clean rivers and beaches. Whereas for black ecology, pollutants and overcrowding are not simply experienced in a greater degree, but are tied into racial oppression and economic exploitation, which make a call for a cleaner environment a call for social justice and specifically racial justice.

To give an example of the differences between black and white environments, I need look no further than my current hometown of Flint, Michigan. During the 1990s, one predominantly black neighborhood—which already houses harmful factories and dumps—was threatened by illegally dumped pesticides that contaminated a creek in the area and was chosen to be the site for a refuse-disposal factory that burned lead-contaminated wood from demolished buildings. Only two or three miles away, there are predominantly white neighborhoods in the outskirts of Flint where the houses cost ten times as much and where the threat of pollution in one's home is equated with the installation of a carbon-monoxide detector.[9]

A recognition of the differences between the environments where the majority of residents are people of color and areas that are predominantly white demonstrates the way in which the environmental justice movement has rejected not only the equivalency of "environment" with "nature," but the notion that "the environment" is a static, unitary concept. For example, in October 1991, the First National People-of-Color Environmental Leadership Summit offered this explicit redefinition of the environment: "the totality of life conditions in our communities—air and water, safe jobs for all at decent wages, housing, education, health care, human prisons, equity, justice" (Szasz 151–52). This redefinition of the environment, Hare's characterizations of black and white environments, and others like them make it clear how and why the environmental justice movement is committed to combating environmental racism. Once we recognize that the environment is not to be equated with "nature" and that not all environments are created equal, then we become committed to combating the factors that produce racial inequalities and to identifying and resolving problems specific to particular minority-dominated environments.

The struggle for environmental justice is a social movement that cuts across racial boundaries in two distinct ways. First, the movement is not set up on the basis of a simplistic opposition between black and white communities. It is not arguing that these forms of injustice should instead be visited on white communities, but rather that *no* community should be a target for environmental degradation (Chavis 5). Second, the movement's emphasis on the connections between racism and environmental issues (and how those connections work) and its conception of the environment itself can allow the inclusion of the diversity of racial environmental problems: from the lead poisoning of inner-city African American children to attempts by multinational corporations to mine Native American land. Moreover, as Dorceta Taylor shows, the movement itself is racially diverse: "Environmental justice groups range from those that are all, or primarily, African-American, Native-American, Puerto Rican, Latino, and Asian to multiracial coalitions, some including European Americans as members. For instance the Labor/Community Strategy Center in Los Angeles is a multiracial coalition, while Mothers of East Los Angeles is all Latina, and Concerned Citizens of East Los Angeles is made up primarily of African Americans" (57).

The clear connections between racism and environmental problems mean that a struggle against the latter must also become a struggle against the former. However, the connections between sexism and the environment (and between sexism and racism) are not an explicit part of this struggle. This oversight becomes even more evident in light of the fact that women are typically the leaders of grassroots movements for environmental justice and that much of the membership tends to be women (Zeff et al. 25).[10] Andrew Szasz claims that the additional challenge of sexism—whether on the part of government officials, mainstream environmentalists, or other members of their own movement—has been recognized and work is being done to integrate a call for women's liberation into the environmental justice movement (152).

Yet I would argue that although this "reaching out" or "integration" is a worthy attempt to address these issues, the movement for environmental justice does not appear—unlike ecofeminism—to be able to provide the framework that will allow us to examine the connections between the oppression of women and the oppression of the environment or the connections between sexism and racism. We are left with an "additive" analysis that claims that these women are under environmental attack because they are minorities *and* that their protest is then hindered by their gender. We cannot see the interlocking connections between gender, race, and socio-economic status. Nor can we see the particular vulnerability of areas with a predominance of female-headed minority families or understand that these women's experience of environmental threat is not "as minorities" or "as women," but as minority women.

The common ground that the environmental justice movement tries to establish between all those fighting for social justice does create an important solidarity for political activism and allows us to explore fully the connections between racism and environmental degradation. However, it does not offer us an opportunity to explore the connections between oppressions. I want to argue that ecofeminism can offer just such an opportunity. However, as is now clear, this opportunity will be conditional on ecofeminism's ability to eschew essentialism, whether in terms of nature, race, or gender.

What an Ecofeminist Perspective on the Urban Environment Offers

The ability of ecofeminism to provide a strong theoretical framework within which the connections between oppressions can be explored and analyzed is due to its respect for difference and recognition of the diversity of voices. As Lee Quinby argues, it would be "masculinist" to form a total politics. Quinby points to Wilmette Brown's "Roots: Black Ghetto Ecology" as a distillation of the ecofeminist web (125). Brown analyzes her experiences as a cancer survivor by presenting different political perspectives: from her personal experience as a black, working-class, lesbian, feminist living on welfare in a polluted inner city, as well as through the lenses of her involvement in the black Civil Rights movement, the ecological movement, the peace movement, and the holistic health movement. Instead of attempting to combine these perspectives into one viewpoint—at the potential cost of devaluing one or more of them—Brown allows these different and often conflicting perspectives to work both with and against each other. In so doing, she is able to show the links between the health of an environment, gender, race, and class; she concludes that "getting well means organizing to defeat the power relations of sex, race and class that make cancer, illness and disease possible" (76).

Here the strength and value of ecofeminism is that it has developed from an alliance of shared resistances, not from the imposed coherence of a centralized theory. This strength comes both from the shared insights of this alliance and from the tensions between the different political insights contained within the alliance. Quinby argues that ecofeminism is at its strongest when it is challenging its own assumptions and that this type of challenge is important if we are to avoid essentialist tendencies (126–27).

It is in this way that we must understand the concept of "inclusivity" for ecofeminism. Inclusivity does not mean that oppressions other than the oppression of women are recognized and integrated into the ecofeminist framework. Because then, as we have seen with the environmental justice movement's integration of sexism as a concern, we will not be able to see the connections between oppressions or the potential tensions between these oppressions within women's experiences in the grassroots environmental movement. If we merely mean by "inclusivity" that ecofeminism is theoretically flexible enough to include other voices while maintaining difference, then we may return to the problems encountered earlier. To achieve this desired inclusivity, there is either a privileged "we" who may allow other voices to become one of "us" if they share a common ground (decided by the privileged group) or "we" create foundations for a common ground with others by appropriating the real or mythologized experiences of other groups.

It may still seem that no matter how inclusive ecofeminism is, an approach that takes women's perspectives as pivotal may—by definition—be limiting and restricted to specifically "women-centered" issues such as the inadequate resources available for the disproportionately high numbers of low-income, single, young mothers of color living in urban areas. When we examine some of the many factors that have produced this situation in urban areas, we start to see connections between race, gender, high rates of unemployment and crime, and deteriorating infrastructure. Nor should it be forgotten that these women may require medical and financial support for children whose poor health can be directly or indirectly traced to the environment in which they live or that pollution, such as lead poisoning, affects the children of the inner city disproportionately—particularly black children living below the poverty level.[11] Thus, the issues confronting these young female heads of households and the support systems needed to subsist in these conditions become issues of the complex interaction between the oppressions of race, class, gender, and the environment. Given ecofeminism's understanding of feminism as a movement to end *all* forms of oppression, it allows a perspective on the problems of the urban environment that can incorporate all these issues.

However, it is not merely that ecofeminism can provide a productive perspective on many of the problems of the urban environment, it can allow us to see that many of these problems are ones that are specifically problems for women. Environmental health hazards—from pollution to lack of adequate medical care—can take a greater toll on women because of their heavier work loads (the "double shift," full-time work and full-time household duties) and because of the extra physical and emotional demands created by pregnancy (Steady 14, 104). The combined effects of poverty and pollution will also affect women indirectly. Whether it is the women, men, or children who are sick, it is the women who are typically the primary caretakers; family health care is still very much "women's work." While the urban environment creates these greater demands on women as mothers and caregivers, it also serves to frustrate them in fulfilling these roles. Penelope Leach argues that the buildings and streets of the city are, in a sense, the work environment for an urban mother, but the streets are designed for cars not for pedestrians, and parks and other open public areas are often home to trash and broken bottles.

Not only *can* the problems of the urban environment be analyzed through an ecofeminist perspective, but the urban environment *calls for* such an analysis. Ecofeminism can highlight the complex interactions between oppression due to gender, class, race, and environment while demonstrating how women as a group are often the most affected—directly or indirectly—by the problems of living in cities. If, as it would appear, many of the problems of the urban environment are problems for women, then we must search for "feminist" solutions and avoid simplistic "masculinist" solutions to the problems of the urban environment. Although the "clean-up" of the inner cities is of tantamount importance, we must not forget human needs for home and community or the forces that produced segregation into polluted areas. Finally, ecofeminism as an ethical approach is able to demonstrate that although calls for social and racial justice (such as those of Hare and Chavis) are appropriate, it is not simply urban dwellers' rights that are under threat. The moral community and the fundamental human relationships of that community (such as the mother-child relationship) are also under threat. Without this community, talk of rights and justice will become empty goals.

Insofar as an ecofeminist perspective is available to urban dwellers, ecofeminist theory can offer a productive perspective on both the political protests of those who live in the urban environment and the problems they may face in that environment. Although ecofeminism may remain fundamentally a theoretical perspective, it is clear that it is committed in practice as well as theory to the removal of sexism, classism, racism, and naturism. Yet, as we have also seen, the ability of ecofeminism to offer a cogent analysis is conditional on a reconceiving of some of its central aspects: the link between women and nature and the ideological separation of nature and culture. Given this caveat, ecofeminism has the potential to play an important role in demands for change in the urban environment, for if we cannot truly understand the nature of the problem, we shall be unable to provide a solution.

NOTES

1. For example, see Zeff et al., Hamilton, Riley (198–201), Pardo, Shiva, and Mies and Shiva (85, 87–97).

2. Karen Warren defines conceptual frameworks as socially constructed sets of "beliefs, values, attitudes, and assumptions which shape and reflect how one views oneself and one's world" (127). A conceptual framework is an oppressive framework when it "explains, justifies, and maintains relationships of domination and subordination" (127).

3. For example, see Warren, Griffin, Plumwood, and Birkeland.

4. The specifics of the revaluing of the emotional are a question for concern. Some ecofeminists focus on Gilligan's ethic of care. Others are concerned about using a moral paradigm that has grown out of human experience in an oppressive society. Underlying this concern is the question of the identification of women with the emotions.

5. The attempt to outline the basic values of ecofeminist ethics has been carried on in greater detail by Warren and Birkeland. Warren sets out eight "boundary conditions" that offer minimal conditions for an ecofeminist ethic. Birkeland sets out nine "basic precepts" present in most ecofeminist ethics.

6. To claim here that the protest began from an acceptance of traditional female roles need not be seen as implying that such roles should not be challenged.

7. Although this particular claim is not part of Warren's or Spretnak's work, some such understanding acts as an underlying premise for much work in ecofeminism.

8. For Javors, nature is symbolized by the triple goddess of life, death, and rebirth. In the West, this goddess is known as Artemis (creatrix), Selene (preserver), and Hecate (the crone or destroyer). In the East, specifically India, this goddess is Shakti, Karuna, and Kali, respectively.

9. For example, houses in predominantly black neighborhoods can cost as little as thirteen thousand to twenty thousand dollars, whereas housing costs in predominantly white neighborhoods tend to begin around seventy-five thousand dollars.

10. See Bullard (30).

11. For instance, one recent study suggests that pregnant women living closer to waste sites have a higher risk of birth defects, although the study did not attempt to show a direct chemical causal relation (Geschwind et al.). A 1990 report by the Environmental Defense Fund claims that ninety-six percent of black children and eighty percent of white children in poor families in the inner city have levels of lead in their blood sufficient to reduce IQ, stunt growth, and affect ability to concentrate. In families with annual incomes above fifteen thousand dollars, eighty-five percent of black children and forty-seven percent of white children have unsafe lead levels (Florini 11).

WORKS CITED

Birkeland, Janis. "Ecofeminism: Linking Theory and Practice." *Ecofeminism: Women, Animals, Nature.* Ed. Greta Gaard. Philadelphia: Temple UP, 1993. 13–59.

Brown, Wilmette. "Roots: Black Ghetto Ecology." *Reclaim the Earth: Women Speak out for Life on Earth*. Eds. Leonie Caldecott and Stephanie Leland. London: Women's Press, 1983. 73–85.

Bullard, Robert D. "Anatomy of Environmental Racism and the Environmental Justice Movement." *Confronting Environmental Racism: Voices from the Grassroots*. Ed. Robert D. Bullard. Boston: South End Press, 1993. 15–39.

Chavis, Benjamin F., Jr. Foreword. *Confronting Environmental Racism: Voices from the Grassroots*. Ed. Robert D. Bullard. Boston: South End Press, 1993. 3–5.

Davion, Victoria. "Is Ecofeminism Feminist?" *Ecological Feminism*. Ed. Karen Warren. New York: Routledge, 1994. 8–28.

Epstein, Barbara. "Ecofeminism and Grassroots Environmentalism in the United States." *Toxic Struggles: The Theory and Practice of Environmental Justice*. Eds. Richard Hofrichter and Lois Gibbs. Philadelphia: New Society Publishers, 1993. 144–52.

Florini, Karen, et al. *Legacy of Lead: America's Continuing Epidemic of Childhood Lead Poisoning*. Washington, D.C.: Environmental Defense Fund, 1990.

Geschwind, Sandra A., et al. "Risk of Congenital Malformations Associated with Proximity to Hazardous Waste Sites." *American Journal of Epidemiology* 135 (1992): 1197–1207.

Gibbs, Lois. Foreword. *Toxic Struggles: The Theory and Practice of Environmental Justice*. Eds. Richard Hofrichter and Lois Gibbs. Philadelphia: New Society Publishers, 1993. i–xii.

Gilligan, Carol. *In a Different Voice: Psychological Theory and Women's Development*. Cambridge, Mass.: Harvard UP, 1982.

Gray, Elizabeth Dodson. *Green Paradise Lost*. Wellesley, Mass.: Roundtable Press, 1979.

Griffin, Susan. *Women and Nature: The Roaring Inside Her*. San Francisco: Harper and Row, 1978.

Hamilton, Cynthia. "Women, Home, and Community: The Struggle in an Urban Environment." *Reweaving the World*. Eds. Irene Diamond and Gloria Orenstein. San Francisco: Sierra Club Books, 1990. 215–22.

Haney, Elly. "Towards a White Feminist Ecological Ethic." *Journal of Feminist Studies in Religion* 9 (1–2): 75–93.

Hare, Nathan. "Black Ecology." *Environmental Ethics*. Ed. K. S. Shrader-Frechette. Pacific Grove, Calif.: Boxwood Press, 1981. 229–36.

Jackson, Cecile. "Women/Nature or Gender/History?" *Journal of Peasant Studies* 20.3 (April 1993): 389–418.

Javors, Irene. "Goddess in the Metropolis: Reflections on the Sacred in an Urban Setting." *Reweaving the World*. Eds. Irene Diamond and Gloria Orenstein. San Francisco: Sierra Club Books, 1990. 211–14.

Kheel, Marti. "From Heroic to Holistic Ethics: The Ecofeminist Challenge." *Ecofeminism: Women, Animals, Nature*. Ed. Greta Gaard. Philadelphia: Temple UP, 1993. 243–71.

Krauss, Celene. "Blue-Collar Women and Toxic Waste Protests." *Toxic Struggles: The Theory and Practice of Environmental Justice*. Eds. Richard Hofrichter and Lois Gibbs. Philadelphia: New Society Publishers, 1993. 107–17.

——. "Women of Color on the Front Line." *Unequal Protection: Environmental Justice and Communities of Color*. Ed. Robert D. Bullard. San Francisco: Sierra Club Books, 1994. 256–72.

Leach, Penelope. "Greening the Cities: Creating a Hospitable Environment for Women and Children." *Reclaim the Earth: Women Speak out for Life on Earth*. Eds. Leonie Caldecott and Stephanie Leland. London: Women's Press, 1983. 115–24.

Mies, Mari, and Vandana Shiva. *Ecofeminism*. London: Zed Books, 1993.

Pardo, Mary. "Mexican American Women Grassroots Community Activists: 'Mothers of East Los Angeles.'" *Frontiers: A Journal of Women's Studies* 11 (1990): 1–7.

Plumwood, Val. "Nature, Self, and Gender: Feminism, Environmental Philosophy, and the Critique of Rationalism." *Hypatia* 6.1 (Spring 1991): 3–27.

Quinby, Lee. "Ecofeminism and the Politics of Resistance." *Reweaving the World*. Eds. Irene Diamond and Gloria Orenstein. San Francisco: Sierra Club Books, 1990. 122–27.

Riley, Shamura. "Ecology is a Sistah's Issue Too: The Politics of Emergent Afrocentric Ecowomanism." *Ecofeminism and the Sacred*. Ed. Carol Adams. New York: Continuum, 1993. 191–206.

Shiva, Vandana. *Staying Alive: Women, Ecology and Development*. London: Zed Books, 1988.

Spretnak, Charlene. "Ecofeminism: Our Roots and Flowering." *Reweaving the World*. Eds. Irene Diamond and Gloria Orenstein. San Francisco: Sierra Club Books, 1990. 3–14.

Steady, Filomena. "In Sickness and Health." UNICEF *News*. No. 2. New York: UNICEF Information Division, 1980. 11, 14–15.

Sturgeon, Noel. *Ecofeminist Natures*. New York: Routledge, 1997.

Szasz, Andrew. *Ecopopulism: Toxic Waste and the Movement for Environmental Justice*. Minneapolis: U of Minnesota P, 1994.

Taylor, Dorceta E. "Environmentalism and the Politics of Inclusion." *Confronting Environmental Racism: Voices from the Grassroots*. Ed. Robert D. Bullard. Boston: South End Press, 1993. 53–61.

Warren, Karen. "The Power and the Promise of Ecological Feminism." *Environmental Ethics* 12 (Summer 1990): 125–46.

Zeff, Robbin Lee, Marsha Love, and Karen Stubbs, eds. *Empowering Ourselves: Women and Toxics Organizing*. Arlington, Va.: Citizens Clearing House for Hazardous Wastes, 1989.

12

"YOU MAKE ME FEEL LIKE A NATURAL WOMAN"

The Political Economy of Contemporary Cosmetics Discourse

Laura L. Sullivan

"Beauty Is an Act of Nature"

The above Aveda slogan reflects the increasing appeal to nature and the "natural" in contemporary beauty discourse. For example, an advertisement for Freeman Botanical Hair Humectant Conditioner announces, "Nature . . . it works!" (*Cosmopolitan* November 1995). Similarly, Biolage equates "The Goodness of Nature" with "The Beauty of Youth" (1995). The new cosmetics line Naturistics promises us "Natural Beauty," "Natural Ingredients," and a "Natural Glow" (*Glamour* January 1995). This trend is reminiscent of the beauty industry's appropriation of the "natural look," which evolved as an offshoot of the late 1960s/early 1970s women's movement and was based on the desire of many Western women to be/look more earthy and less artificial, to reject standards (including beauty standards) defined by patriarchy, and to set our own standards—to be who we "really" are. Ever looking to ensure the creation of new markets and the continuation of sales and profits, cosmetics companies tapped into this concept and turned it into a practice that still requires the mediation of cosmetics products. From the 1970s onward, the discourse of beauty has appealed not to an actual natural look, but to an *ideal* one, equating "natural" with "flawless" and "perfect." In this way, an appeal to nature was applied to standards for the female consumer of beauty products. Today, there is a further appeal to the "natural" as a crucial characteristic of the ingredients and products themselves.

The emphasis on nature and "natural" products is characterized by environmentalist rhetoric. Such an environmentalist emphasis is only possible within the context of a renewed imperialism. Granted, the imperialism of much contemporary beauty discourse harks back to the "nativism" of Western beauty culture of the 1920s and 1930s. However, this nativism is lent a new twist by its combination with the "progressive" discourse of environmentalism in the contemporary discourse of beauty. Thus, nativism and a philosophy of organicism that privileges nature, which were both present in previous eras of beauty culture in the West, are currently combined in new ways, most particularly meshing with what has become one of the primary ideological trajectories within contemporary beauty discourse: environmentalism. The beauty industry has attached itself to a host of industries that are representationally (and financially) capitalizing on the current rise of "green" thinking and knowledge. As Andrew Ross notes, "eco-marketing" has become increasingly ubiquitous as "socially responsible" businesses seek to find ways to produce values campaigns that resonate with consumers (1–2).

Within beauty discourse, this environmentalist rhetoric has two trajectories. On the one hand, companies such as The Body Shop and Aveda explicitly objectify and commodify indigenous peoples, and, on the other hand, some texts feature the erasure of the indigenous peoples and highlight a commodified nature. Yet, even in beauty texts that foreground a natural world to be used respectfully and responsibly by Western urban consumers, as I will attempt to show, the figure of the non-Western indigenous native (particularly the native woman) never quite leaves the rhetorical scene.

As Frederic Jameson explains, in our increasingly image-driven society, "we consume less the thing itself, than its abstract idea, open to all the libidinal investments ingeniously arrayed for us by advertising" ("Reification" 12). While drawing on the work of Norman Holland, Jameson proposes that mass-cultural texts contain mechanisms of both "repression" and "wish-fulfillment"; he recommends that we "grasp mass culture not as empty distraction or 'mere' false consciousness, but rather as a transformational work on social and political anxieties and fantasies which must then have some effective presence in the mass cultural text in order subsequently to be 'managed' or repressed" ("Reification" 25). Thus, there is a "utopian" appeal in the texts of mass culture, including (perhaps especially) advertisements, one that is ultimately recuperated by other elements of the text itself. Jameson explains that such textual recuperation requires "strategies of containment" (*Political* 53). Elements of contemporary beauty discourse, namely an appeal to the "natural" and an imperialist objectification of non-Western native peoples, both project and contain the utopian horizons of politically progressive ideas and goals, such as liberal feminism and environmentalism. Such projection and containment is predicated on an entrenched semiotic opposition between urban, Western women consumers and non-Western, "native" women, an opposition with implications and effects beyond the discursive or consumptive realms.

"Trading with Communities in Need"

Texts produced by cosmetics companies that promote themselves as champions for improving the lives of indigenous peoples and for helping the environment use a rhetorical strategy that positions potential consumers as advocates for these "causes."[1] Caren Kaplan relates the textual and economic strategies of The Body Shop, the British international company run by cofounder and spokeswoman Anita Roddick, to those of other companies, such as The Banana Republic, that rely on "safari" discourse and appeal to imperialist logic. Yet, Kaplan asks neither "Why do First World women buy these products?" nor "Why are subaltern women important signs in the discourse of beauty?" Thus, she is unable to offer a critique that connects these two groups of women. It is my goal here to make connections between the exploitation and personal experiences of women in the West and women in the developing world and to examine the way that both groups of women experience effects produced and perpetuated by beauty discourse.

Body Shop literature makes its neocolonialist and pseudofeminist logic manifest and clearly constructs its intended "progressive" consumer: "Increasingly, we are attempting to buy our ingredients from communities in need, mostly in the majority or developing world, who can use our business to help build a future for themselves. Handouts don't always work—it's much better to provide people with the tools and resources they need to help themselves. . . . A company that makes shampoos and skin creams [can] really help the world . . . by breeding a sense of responsibility and communal obligation in their customers" (*The Body Shop Book* 13). This policy (called "trade not aid" in other Body Shop literature) serves the purpose of tapping into some of the various utopian desires of potential customers. Roddick and The Body Shop recognize that contemporary cosmetics consumers *do* have the desire to make the world a better place; this desire gets tapped in different ways in the discourse of cosmetics. As if to indicate his approval of Roddick's philosophy, a Brazilian Indian is rather obnoxiously pictured on the same page giving the thumbs-up sign (13).

"A Mexican Tip"

The Body Shop Book provides us with this "Mexican tip": "wet the hair with aloe vera, allow to dry, rinse out at night. Adds lustre and manageability to the hair and acts as a partial sunscreen" (89). Beauty discourse is filled with the trendy notion that products made with "secrets" of indigenous peoples (particularly those of native women) are superior to Western industrial products—that indigenous practices are more "authentic." A large blurb in the "Body" chapter says, "Chinese women use a scrub of rice husks as a fragrant exfoliator. The Body Shop Rice Bran Scrub has ground rice to exfoliate, and rice bran oil to moisturise" (21). "What Chinese women?" we ask. Presumably, poor rural women use rice husks in this way, while the text implies that Western urban women will buy the product from The Body Shop and continue the practice in a more sophisticated form. In other words, all of these "secrets" are not just beauty "tips." Rather, they are marketing tools and product signifiers whose role is to encourage consumption and to set up a hierarchy between Third World women providers of beauty "secrets" and First World women consumers of high-tech versions of such "secrets."

Texts in this trajectory primarily rely on indigeneity as a sign and often use indigenous peoples to invoke exoticism. Non-Western and Western beauty practices are presented as part of an ethnographic array of a variety of beauty standards cutting through geographical and historical boundaries. Under the heading "Decorating the Body" comes this description:

In tribal culture, the body can be a blank canvas for intricate patterning caused by nicking the skin with thorns and other sharp implements to cause welts. The process is called scarification. In Southern Sudan, these scars on a Dinka woman's back are a sign of great beauty. . . . Scarification is strong visual evidence of the key moments in an individual's experience, a map of a life which is patterned with skin souvenirs of significant stages. The scars also relate to one's identity within a group. Other groups can read where someone comes from by the marks on his or her skin. In Scotland, where the climate is less friendly, the same function was filled by the intricate, elaborate knitting patterns of Arran sweaters, which originated so that drowned sailors could be identified by their families. (20)

Such a description demonstrates the romanticism-gone-awry of much of this discourse. In making a parallel between African scarification and Scottish sweater-knitting practices, the fact of African women's bodily pain goes unremarked upon because African (women's) bodies are *already* viewed as objects in this discourse.

Many of these texts also employ an environmentalism that paints the Third World as mere locale. Nature itself is commodified, and the non-Western world is then depicted as pure nature. As consumers are urged to "do right" by the planet, native peoples disappear. This environmentalist beauty discourse often appeals to a globalist philosophy that promotes the picture of the planet as one harmonious unit. For instance, an Earthsource Perfume advertisement features the phrase "Global Releaf" atop its globe logo. Many advertisements, such as one for Aveda Uruku lipstick (March 1995), emphasize that their products are made with ingredients gathered from "all over the world." The Body Shop, as Kaplan explains, represents a trend in contemporary media representations to promote a transnational geopolitics, one in which "the 'national' is increasingly destabilized" and "the representation of the 'world' in these forms of advertising signals a desire for a dissolution of boundaries to facilitate personal freedom and ease of trade even as it articulates national and cultural characteristics as distinct, innate markets of difference" (49). However, unlike the globalism of contemporary advertisements for Internet providers and telephone companies, in which technology is promoted as creating a world in which all people are connected and equalized, beauty discourse and the industry behind it depict and unequally distribute power in ways that reflect colonialism. Contemporary beauty discourse contains not only a transnational dimension, but also an invocation of the "national" that divides the world into the powerful First World nations and the powerless, exploitable Third World.

In beauty discourse, the globalist aspect is merely an overlay for a pervasive neocolonialist thrust in which scenes of colonial exploration are evoked. For instance, Africa is depicted in mainstream beauty discourse as a continent to be explored by the First World. The Clinique Aromatics Elixir advertisement uses a "tribal" theme, with the product pictured among an ebony carving of a head, bones, and other African "trinkets," spoils from a safari adventure—a theme that is also exemplified by Ralph Lauren Safari perfume advertisements (as Kaplan notes) and by the discourse of The Banana Republic stores and catalogues analyzed by Paul Smith. In the same vein, *British Harper's & Queen* encourages readers to "dress for an Encounter with Africa," which was the theme of a safari party at the National Portrait Gallery (Barwell 36).

Beauty discourse also invokes the role of the male colonial explorer, as vividly exemplified in the advertising for two new men's colognes, Avatar and Navigator. Navigator's advertisement (*Glamour* October 1996) features the slogan "Chart Your Own Course" surrounding an image of a young, white, Michael Stipe look-alike. Lest the viewer miss the neocolonialist connotations, there is a map of the world, with latitude and longitude lines included, drawn on the man's shaved head. Similarly, advertisements for Avatar describe the cologne as "The Fragrance of Possibilities" and assert for the male consumer "Today the Beginning. Tomorrow the World."

This neocolonialism extends to a world beyond the discursive. Contemporary critics often forget both the materiality of language and the force of discursive fields in the material world. For example, Jonathan Rutherford claims that in the marketplace of cultural difference, "The power relation is closer to tourism than imperialism, an expropriation of meaning rather than materials" (Kaplan 50). However, in the case of the beauty industry and its discourse, the raw materials are being expropriated as well. Thus, in a rhetorical and economic climate that resembles the heyday of imperialism, First World companies such as Aveda roam the Third World for rare, exotic, and "natural" raw materials—plants and flowers in particular—that are then brought back to the First World for consumption. There is, in other words, a *real* extraction of resources. The practice of "sourcing"—traveling to Third World countries to find and obtain "exotic" ingredients for "natural" beauty products—is the literal manifestation of this rhetorical neocolonialism.[2]

There are the literal explorers as well. The founder and president of Aveda, Horst Rechelbacher, is a good example. A European scientist and entrepreneur who set up the Aveda company in Minneapolis, Rechelbacher travels the world, much like The Body Shop's Roddick, as the company's head trader with native populations. This relationship is spelled out on Aveda's on-line "Sourcing" page, where Aveda's "unique business partnership" with the Brazilian Yawanawa Indians is described: "Located in a remote region of the Amazon rain forest, the Yawanawa are working toward their economic sustainability, including the planting of organically grown Bixa—a bush-like tree with pods that contain red powder. The ingredient was the inspiration for and is a perfect natural coloring agent in Aveda's Uruku Lip Colours. . . . After personal meetings with Rechelbacher and Aveda representatives, the tribe was assured of Aveda's sincerity and true desire for a new eco-nomics [sic]." Indigenous peoples, in the words of Kathryn Vanspanckeren, "are imaged as freely having chosen tradition or modernity as if their lives were commodities" (171). Moreover, a simple neoliberal version of success is depicted here, one that paints the Yawanawas as self-motivated business mavericks who just need markets for their products to be a "sustainable" community.

In actuality, the logic of "preservation" and "protection" upon which these discourses draw serves precisely a politics opposite to their communicated intentions. Both the narrative of imperialism and its literal practices are being drawn upon here. As the knowledge of non-Western, native peoples is expropriated, its use value transformed into exchange value, the profits resulting from such commodification are never equitably shared with the people whose knowledge is viewed as common property.[3] In the words of Vandana Shiva, "the labour of Third World farmers has no value, while the labour of Western scientists adds value" ("Biotechnological" 210). For instance, the "Sourcing" page of Aveda's web site begins with this epigraph from founder Rechelbacher: "Our most valuable resource is indigenous peoples, for they are the living libraries of ancient wisdom and ways." This extraction of indigenous knowledge is explicitly related both to the gendered dimensions of such imperialist conditions and to international trends in intellectual property rights.

THE FRENCH CONNECTION

In the neocolonialist ideology of beauty discourse, Western, especially European, nations are constructed as justified and helpful explorer-diplomats—the experts on an evolved beauty as artifact and the bearers of civilized, sophisticated taste—whereas Third World cultures are the sources of "natural" beauty. Throughout the discourse of beauty, certain European countries (particularly France and Switzerland) are invoked as the places where knowledge, technical and scientific ability, and expertise are used to create the "breakthrough" products. Nationalism is still a major force within the "globalization" of the current stage of capital. The two states—globalization and nationalism—are not mutually exclusive, but rely on and play off of each other in complex ways.[4]

This logic of Europeanicity romanticizes European spas and invokes wealthy, aristocratic European women, such as Princess Marcella Borghese or Lancome spokesmodel Isabella Rossellini, as the bearers of the highest standards of beauty. European male scientists and doctors are proposed everywhere as the authority figures on Western woman's beauty. Natural "extracts" are taken from the Third World to the First, where European scientists improve upon them to make them usable or better. Ultimately, the elitism of the beauty industry's "Europeanicity" reinforces a north-south domination model.

Nationalism and the corresponding belief in the urban superiority of the West accompanied the global explorations of colonial times and are found in the neocolonialist aspect of the discourse and industry of beauty as well. Thus, the metropolis in beauty discourse is not the generic city; instead, certain cities—particularly Paris, but also London, Geneva, and Milan—are presented as the premier centers of fashion and cosmetics development and production. Raw materials extracted in foreign, exotic lands are brought "home" to be refined and manufactured in industrialized cities such as Montreaux, Switzerland, home to Clinic La Prarie where "targeted cellular skincare treatments are formulated" (*Vogue* January 1990). One modern-day American example of these urban beauty centers is Minneapolis, the site of Aveda's headquarters, which includes its production facilities and training centers.

In these textual constructions that perpetuate a myth of the superiority of the "civilized" north (First World) and the "primitive" south (Third World), the First World woman is a sophisticated urban consumer, as opposed to the Third World, mythic, "natural" woman who gives away her secrets. A *Glamour* magazine fashion spread (October 1996) entitled "Urban Studies" depicts a European woman to demonstrate how "Classic camel gets a contemporary edge in work clothes with a citified sensibility—sleek, chic and utterly sophisticated" (232). Reflecting this assumed dichotomy, one contemporary cosmetics line is called "Urban Essentials" and the title of one of the most popular Western women's magazines is *Cosmopolitan*. Nowhere in this discourse does the urban appear in the Third World. The Western world is a place in which nature has been transformed into total urbanity, a world where there is no "untamed nature" left to be enjoyed or ravaged. In this discursive terrain, the line between the urban and the rural is firmly demarcated. In actuality, however, the very definitions of "urban" and "rural" are fluid and open to contestation.[5]

In the contemporary discourse of beauty, the city (particularly the Western European city, such as Paris) is not only constructed as the mecca of scientific, high-tech expertise, it is also depicted as a hostile place for women, who are advised to use products to "defend" ourselves against pollution. The "environment" itself in the West is depicted as similarly unsafe, as another element from which women need protection. For example, we are warned in an advertisement for Oil of Olay's Daily uv Protectant (*Vogue* June 1991) about the danger of harsh ultraviolet rays that has resulted from depletion of the ozone layer. We are told to "detoxify" with skin care products in the advertisement for Intelligent Skincare Cosmetics (*Vogue* May 1991). Thus, according to beauty discourse, the only safe environment from which First World women can draw sustenance is the "nature" of the Third World.

"BECAUSE LOOKING GOOD IS EVERY WOMAN'S RIGHT"

Even progressive elements present in the discourse of beauty still enact this imperialist desire. One of the primary utopian, progressive appeals of contemporary beauty discourse involves the appropriation of women's liberation rhetoric. As Kaplan notes, "Current advertising is replete with references to bourgeois feminist concerns" (51). For example, the slogan for Pond's skin-care line is "Because Looking Good Is Every Woman's Right." One strain of appropriated women's liberation rhetoric is the rhetoric of ecofeminism, in which the body of "woman" is equated with the body of the Earth and environmentalism and feminism come together. Carol Stabile explains that ecofeminism employs a "universalizing perspective": "By insisting that women—across race, class, and national lines, across history—have a more intimate and stable relationship with nature and the natural, ecofeminism flattens out and ultimately ignores race and class distinctions, not to mention history" (52). Ecofeminism in beauty discourse relies heavily on essentialist, nostalgic tendencies and promotes a notion of preindustrial, "authentic" woman. In this prelapsarian world, renewal and rejuvenation are emphasized, a trend reflected in product names such as Philip B.'s botanically based Rejuvenating Oil ("Beauty" column, *Elle* December 1995). We are encouraged to go back to an earlier time and way of life. An EarthSource fragrances advertisement (*Bazaar* April 1993) tells us, "Today we know natural smells are mood changers, reminding us of another time, a better place." Nostalgically connecting women to nature in a typically Edenic fantasy, hair-care maker Biolage features advertisements with a white, blond, blue-eyed mother and daughter in various nature scenes; a Biolage television commercial tells women, "There is a need in all of us . . . to get back to our beginnings . . . a way to renew, a way to look back without going backwards."

This viewpoint exclusively equates the environment with nonurban areas. As Stabile notes, "In ecofeminist thought as well as mainstream environmentalism, what counts as an environment generally does not extend to urban areas" or to "toxic work places" (58). She explains that representations such as advertisements for beauty products work to keep in place this dangerous misconception of what constitutes the "environment" as a place of protection and care: "The general association of environmental concerns with leisure-time activities is thus legitimated through a representational framework that rigidly distinguishes between a pre-industrial, romanticized environment and industrialized non-environments inhabited on a daily basis" (58). Just as the equation of "environment" with "nature" is misleading, the equation of "environment" with Third World, "native" peoples is also inaccurate. According to the logic of ecofeminism, native people are more knowledgeable and respectful of the environment. Not only does this view elide the industrialization and urbanization of Third World areas, it also obscures the fact that native people have a much more complex relationship with their environments than this picture suggests.

In this way, these neocolonialist beauty texts set up a rigid contrast between the First World, urban woman and the Third World, "natural" woman. The former comes to occupy the vacuum provided by the commodification of the latter, which has rendered her invisible. The Western white woman frequently appropriates the "exotic" beauty of the Third World woman, as when "supermodel" Cindy Crawford appears in the Revlon Exotika! advertisement wearing dark lipstick and large beads. Similarly, in a fashion spread entitled "Island Girl" (*Marie Claire* May 1996), a blond-haired, white woman, "supermodel" Amber Valleta, is pictured lounging among tropical greenery wearing floral prints.

If the Third World woman is present, she is only a sign, not the interpellated consumer of the product or an agent in her own right. For example, the Benetton Tribu perfume advertisement (*Vogue* November 1993) draws upon tribalism. Opposite an image of the product is a picture of two "tribal" women carrying large loads above their heads, bathed in the orange glow of sunset. First World, urban women are encouraged to desire the romanticized connotations of the images through the use of the perfume, and the very real labor of Third World women, much of which involves manual labor such as the pictured hauling of large bundles for long distances, is rendered unreal, another "sign" to be taken up for Western commodification and consumption. The ideology of beauty discourse as reflected in a text such as this Tribu advertisement mirrors the way that "from the dominant standpoint, 'nature' is everything that should be available free or as cheaply as possible. This includes the products of social labour. The labour of women and Third World farmers is said to be non-labour, mere biology, a natural resource; their products are thus akin to natural deposits" (Shiva "The Seed" 140).

While contemporary beauty discourse does commodify the non-Western woman and her labor, as in the Tribu advertisement, this discourse simultaneously works to efface the non-Anglo woman. A complex, yet telling, example is the advertisement for Revlon's Ajee perfume (*Glamour*

March 1994). The left page features a picture of the product and its box against the backdrop of an African landscape. The text first announces, "From The Heart Of Africa Comes A Fragrance To Capture The Heart Of Every Woman." Next, we are instructed—in large, bold, purple letters—to "Experience The Essence of Africa. Feel The Power Of Woman." The second page provides the context for interpreting these words. If, as Barthes asserts in *Image-Music-Text,* words "anchor" images in a text and inflect them with a particular range of meanings (39), so, too, do images anchor words. In this case, the arrangement of the second-page picture speaks to the earlier text. A picture of a black woman and a white woman, both naked and bare-shouldered, is placed on top of the photograph of the African landscape. The black woman has hair cropped very short and close to the head; the white woman has long, flowing blond hair. The layout of the advertisement suggests that the black woman is to be read as "the essence of Africa" (which parallels the trend in beauty discourse directed specifically at African Americans), whereas the white woman represents "the power of woman." This text mirrors the way "black female figures often appear in Orientalist paintings" where "usually the pairing of a light- and dark-skinned woman prioritizes a reading in which the white woman is the object of desire" (Lewis 172). Clearly, the white woman does not possess the "essence of Africa," although the advertisement implies that using the product will give her access to the power provided by such an essence.

This advertisement indicates that racism underlies much of the discourse of substitution, and such racism has become increasingly overt in the last few years. An advertisement for Jovan White Musk fragrance (*Self* September 1996) shows a large white flower and reads, "White . . . Unpredictable in Spirit / Pure in its Essence / Exquisite in its Delicacy / Discover its Unexpected Nature." There are also advertisements, such as those for the African Pride hair relaxer line, which—despite being directed specifically to African American female consumers—also rely on a nostalgic, ahistorical view of Africa and its peoples.[6]

"Isn't Technology Beautiful?"

Thus, the Third World woman imparts natural wisdom, the product of her labor, and even parts of herself to the First World, middle-class woman struggling to negotiate this age of post-1970s feminism. Joining the boys in the capitalist rat race leads some women to feel completely stressed out and overwhelmed. If you are one of these stressed-out women, you can buy Biolage with its "purifying botanicals and herbal extracts" to help you "rejuvenate your hair as soothing aromas clear your mind." Nature invites us, via the tour of the Third World woman hostess, to relax, nurture ourselves, and feel good about who we are and what we are doing. The non-Western, native woman's closer connection to nature is offered to the Western woman, as the "you" in the Aretha Franklin song, "You Make Me Feel Like a Natural Woman," used in a Clairol hair color television commercial. "You" is a reference not only to the product, but also to the non-Western woman herself, who *enables* the Western woman ("me") to feel better, that is, more "natural."

Non-Western, native women make us offerings: wisdom, nurturing, exotic sex appeal. We borrow the information, techniques, and energy they offer and use them as tools with which to negotiate our chaotic First World lives. We remember them when we use the products inspired by their knowledge. I wash my face with The Body Shop's Pineapple Facial Scrub and think of the Sri Lankan woman whose knowledge formed the basis of the product—good for exfoliation, the woman knows.[7] I thank her as I swirl the cool, yellow-white cream around in circles on my face. The return to the "female" realm of nature does not occur in an unmediated way. Rather, it is achieved both semiotically and materially through the figure of the non-Western, "natural" women, as her spirit and labor/knowledge provide the (typically white) Western urban woman's comfort and relief, as when Aveda gives us its Purescriptions "for Stress Relief" (*Vogue* November 1995).

The advertisement for Nivea Visage moisturizer (*Bazaar* April 1993) asks, "Isn't Technology Beautiful?" The contemporary discourse of beauty answers in contradictory ways. On the one hand, technoscience plays a powerful role in the discourse of beauty, because the First World, urban woman is depicted as upwardly mobile and technologically hip. She is the first to buy new products, especially those related to skin care—the most rapidly changing area of cosmetics—to signify her ability to avoid obsolescence.[8] On the other hand, the discourse of beauty recognizes that the world of "male" culture and technoscientific "progress" is not purely beneficial to Western women, with its harmful effects such as pollution and stressful working conditions, which are often compounded by commitments to work as homemakers, wives, and mothers. Drawing upon an ecofeminist paradigm that upholds "the binarism between technology, as the monstrous, phallic present, and the environment, as matriarchal past" (Stabile 51), beauty discourse implies that to fight the conditions found within male technoculture politically is a bankrupt strategy. Instead it provokes Western women to turn back to the primeval woman's energy offered by the (figure of the) native woman, who possessed a knowledge prior to and superior to that of Western technoscience in its gentle, holistic effectiveness. Such energy and knowledge have the added bonuses of being bathed in exoticism and possessing the "politically correct" environmental effects.

Western women are not being asked to occupy the Third World woman's *current* subject position—we do not have to give up the social and economic gains that we have worked so hard to obtain (or at least we can hold on to our *claim* to these gains for which we still continue to struggle). As Biolage tells us, we can have "a way to look back without going backwards." Thus, in this case, we are not going "back to nature." Rather, we are borrowing what it offers us in negotiating our position as alienated workers in a late capitalist system. This women's liberation–saturated discourse encourages us to "just do it" and to claim our power in our lives. In this vein, the advertisement for Sarah Michaels Moisturizing Bodywash asks, "What do women want? We want everything" (*Glamour* September 1996). However, tapping into contemporary, Western, middle-class women's recognition that getting power in our lives is not happening in the way feminism predicted, the advertisements set us up to obtain this power only through the consumption of particular products.

Contrary to the picture presented in contemporary beauty discourse, Western technoscience is not the exclusive province of the West. Not only have "nature" and the "native" never existed in an unmediated way, as environmentalist beauty discourse would have us believe, the natural world and native populations in the non-Western world have been devastated by Western technoscience and its role in carrying out the imperatives of transnational capital. Additionally, the construction of non-Western, native women as more connected to the Earth and thus more "natural" than Western, urban women belies the real position of many non-Western women as laborers producing goods marketed to Western consumers of beauty products. For example, Aveda emphasizes its use of pure, natural ingredients—most "sourced" from the Third World—and its use of "the most advanced flower and plant technology" to make its products. Aveda's Plant & Flower Pure-fumes are made with "no artificial fragrances or petrochemicals." The production of flowers, however, is not a pretty picture. As Sarah Stewart documents in "The Price of a Perfect Flower," seventy-two thousand mostly female workers work in a flower industry in which "over 450 companies nationwide export . . . over 3.5 billion flowers a year." These workers are exposed to often toxic levels of pesticides—many of them banned in the United States or Europe—which lead to major health problems such as "fainting, dizziness, skin irritations, respiratory ailments, neurological problems, premature births," and contaminated breast milk (132–33, 135).

CONCLUSION

The dualistic nature of beauty discourse—which, although fluid, still maintains traditional Western binaries—leads to a sense of the impossibility of resistance to capitalism and its raced and gendered manifestations. The discourse provides a further denial of the possibility of building alliances among women who occupy different positions in terms of geography and the global political economy. The contemporary discourse of beauty contributes to a *fantasy* of consent, and thus denies the agency of non-Western women engaged in struggles of resistance to global capital, including those organized around environmental issues. Non-Western women are at the forefront of resistance efforts the world over. For example, Gail Omvedt provides a picture of non-Western women that contrasts greatly with their image as passive embodiments of an ecofeminist link to nature in the discourse of beauty. She specifies that in their resistance efforts as leaders of both the environmental and farmers' movements in India, women's "agitations tend to be directed against the state, or sometimes large corporations, the forces behind displacement, land take-overs, etc." (103). A rally organized by women-led Indian organizations to fight for alternatives to Green Revolution agriculture was attended by 300,000–400,000 people (109).

The imperialist inflection of beauty discourse mystifies the targeted consumers of such discourse, who are encouraged to rechannel our liberation-directed energies into more individualistic, consumptive concerns as we search for products to help fill the gaps in our postliberation lives. This supplementation, which is never completed, leads to perpetual disappointment. In turn, this disappointment leads to perpetual acquisition of products designed and marketed as potential fix-its. These products assuage the sense of frustration that such perpetual disappointment brings by providing a muted sense of satisfaction at the level of self-nurturing, helping the planet, and sometimes "helping" indigenous women/people. However, such a sense of satisfaction is neither stable nor permanent; it must still be continually renewed because "assaults" by the "world" (from environmental forces, but more often from social forces such as industrial pollution or powerlessness in the male world of capital) are continuous. Thus, we have an incessant need to consume these "natural" and "soothing" products. The Calgon moment must be expanded to all areas of life for the ever-more-worn-out, Western, middle-class, urban woman, who needs such a moment more often and in an increased variety of forms. White, middle-class consumers of beauty products feel bad about ourselves, having experienced and internalized the effects of the "backlash" Susan Faludi so thoroughly documents. Otherwise, we would not participate in the objectification of the Other for our own sense of self-satisfaction. We are seduced by the belief that perhaps we will finally one day come upon the one "secret" of the non-Western, "natural," native woman, which will turn out to be the key to a way out of our painful, stressful situation: a *real* way *back* to a perceived better time before the conditions of "progress" ran rampant. This hope drives both us and the discourse that produces and capitalizes upon it. This illusory state of total nurturance through a reconnection with nonurban nature is necessary for the ideological priorities of beauty discourse and the exigencies of advertising and capital involved in the beauty industry itself.

NOTES

1. "Trading with Communities in Need" is the title of one of The Body Shop's many brochures based on philanthropic environmentalism.

2. Both The Body Shop and Aveda use the term "sourcing" to refer to their companies' practice of finding and using materials (usually plants) from all over the world in making their products.

3. Most sources on this topic claim that indigenous peoples do not directly benefit much, if at all, from such relationships with cosmetics companies. See, for example, Jon Entine's web site.

4. For example, see Paul Smith's *Millennial Dreams* for an analysis of the operation of nationalism within the current stage of contemporary capitalism.

5. For example, as non-Western cities expand, governments routinely redesignate agricultural land as urban space or ecological "preserves." See Nick Caistor.

6. Furthermore, the complexity of race-related beauty products is belied by such "black-and-white" advertisements. As Lisa Jones (1994) documents, there is presently a thriving "hair trade" in which rural women, mostly from Third World countries such as China and India, sell their hair to be processed in factories and made into hair extensions and the like.

7. I originally remembered her as an African woman, which demonstrates the way that confusion and inaccurate information reign in the reception of this discourse. The Southern Hemisphere became a lump of a place; I knew she was from somewhere "down there."

8. See Evan Watkins for an analysis of consumption as a strategy for avoiding obsolescence.

WORKS CITED

Aveda web site. http://www.aveda.com.

Barthes, Roland. *Image-Music-Text*. Trans. Stephen Heath. New York: Noonday, 1977.

Barwell, Carolyn. "Painting an Exciting Portrait of Africa." *British Harper's & Queen* April 1996: 36.

The Body Shop Book: Skin, Hair and Body Care. Introduction by Anita Roddick. Boston: Little, Brown, 1994.

Caistor, Nick. "San Salvador: The City Versus the Forest." Collinson. 210–14.

Collinson, Helen, ed. *Green Guerillas: Environmental Conflicts and Initiatives in Latin America and the Caribbean*. London: Latin American Bureau, 1996.

Entine, Jon. "The Messy Reality of Socially Responsible Businesses." http://www.betterworld.com/BWZ/9512/cover2.htm#1.

Faludi, Susan. *Backlash: The Undeclared War Against American Women*. New York: Crown, 1991.

Jameson, Fredric. *The Political Unconscious: Narrative as a Socially Symbolic Act*. Ithaca, N.Y.: Cornell UP, 1981.

——. "Reification and Utopia in Mass Culture." *Signatures of the Visible*. Ed. Jameson. London: Verso, 1991. 9–34.

Jones, Lisa. *Bulletproof Diva: Tales of Race, Sex, and Hair*. New York: Anchor Books, 1994.

Kaplan, Caren. "A World without Boundaries: The Body Shop's Trans/national Geographies." *Social Text* (43): 45–66.

Lewis, Reina. *Gendering Orientalism: Race, Femininity and Representation*. London: Routledge, 1996.

Omvedt, Gail. " 'Green Earth, Women's Power, Human Liberation': Women in Peasant Movements in India." Shiva *Close*. 99–112.

Ross, Andrew. *The Chicago Gangster Theory of Life: Nature's Debt to Society*. London: Verso, 1994.

Shiva, Vandana. "Biotechnological Development and the Conservation of Biodiversity." Shiva and Moser. 193–213.

——, ed. *Close to Home: Women Reconnect Ecology, Health and Development Worldwide*. Philadelphia: New Society Publishers, 1994.

——. "The Seed and the Earth: Biotechnology and the Colonization of Regeneration." Shiva *Close*. 128–43.

Shiva, Vandana, and Ingunn Moser, eds. *Biopolitics: A Feminist and Ecological Reader on Biotechnology*. London: Zed Books, 1995.

Smith, Paul. *Millennial Dreams: Contemporary Culture and Capital in the North*. London: Verso, 1997.

——. "Visiting the Banana Republic." *Universal Abandon?: The Politics of Postmodernism*. Ed. Andrew Ross. Minneapolis: U of Minnesota P, 1988.

Stabile, Carol. *Feminism and the Technological Fix*. Manchester, U.K.: Manchester UP, 1994.

Stewart, Sarah. "The Price of a Perfect Flower: Environmental Destruction and Health Hazards in the Colombian Flower Industry." Collinson. 132–39.

Vanspanckeren, Kathryn. "The West and the Rest in TechniColor." *American Quarterly* 48.1 (March 1996): 167–77.

Watkins, Evan. *Throwaways: Work Culture and Consumer Education*. Stanford, Calif.: Stanford UP, 1993.

6

THEORIZING URBAN SPACE

13

DARWIN'S CITY, OR LIFE UNDERGROUND

Evolution, Progress, and the Shapes of Things to Come

Joanne Gottlieb

R ecently, utopia has undergone a revival. Coinciding with the explosive growth of the World Wide Web and the expansion of multimedia and interactive technology, the discourse of utopia has been resurrected in the rhetoric of liberatory cybernetic technology and has found expression in such enterprises as Utopia Technologies, developers of interactive and real-time 3D games; Internet Utopia, a web and graphic design firm; Utopia Inc., "cyberspace architects"; and the Utopia CyberMall. The 1996 "Anthem" television spot for MCI Network contemplates an idealized democracy devoid of all social distinctions (except that of the electronically well-endowed and everyone else), a place where "there are only minds. Is this place Utopia? No. The Internet." In a cryptic 1996 advertising campaign on Manhattan phone banks and bus shelters aimed at Chelsea-area high-tech graphic design and publishing firms, Appleton Papers proclaimed "Utopia is Right Around the Corner."[1] While offering a utopian prospect both urban and pedestrian, the statement holds peculiar frustrations: easily accessible yet slightly displaced, utopia is never quite there. But then has utopia ever really been there?

From the late nineteenth century, the invented nature of the technological utopia persistently has been associated with evolutionary themes. By combining the idea of a transformed nature with the modern fantasy of limitless progress through rational processes, evolutionary narratives have a powerful resonance for technological utopia and for the narrative of urban development generally: "The idea of *the city* has been so central to the linear narrative of 'civilization' that urban growth, or urbanization (customarily used to described a less agreeable process), is often conceived in evolutionary terms, either analogous to biological processes or as organic development of an advanced social and political community" (Ross 114).[2] By offering a natural justification for continuous progress while threatening to cause transiency and obsolescence, evolution evokes temporal considerations that inform and trouble the spatial imagination of the technological utopia. These contradictions in the basic concept of the technological utopia are played out in the symbolic space of the urban underground.

THE RAILWAY AS TIME MACHINE

The city of the future has its roots in the nineteenth-century underground. The significance of the underground for the urban imagination accompanies the nineteenth-century shift in the imagination of the underground as a space of exploration to a place of habitation (Williams 10). This shift occurred within a context of developments in mining and tunneling; the rise of the new scientific disciplines of geology, archeology, and paleontology; and the excavation of the urban underground per se for the emerging technologies of sewage and water systems, railways and underground railways, gas, telegraphy, telephony, pneumatic tubes, steam, and electricity. The urban underground acquired a particular resonance with the rapid growth of underground rail systems in the late nineteenth century. The railway introduced its connotations of progress in time into the new spatialization of the modern city.

Even before the full development of technologies like the railroad and the underground railway, which both defined modernity and later promised the improvement of urban life, there was a connection between underground and urban qualities, a connection that expressed anxieties around modernization. The increasingly elaborate underground space of the coal mine was analogized to the great town, whereas the developing urban space of industrialization came to be viewed as an expansion of the hellish qualities of underground space (Bobrick 80–85).[3]

Ultimately, the railway was the "agent of [this] transformation" of surface into underground space (Bobrick 85). The railroads that eventually found their way into the London underground had their origins in the mine (the first railroads served to haul coal from Newcastle's coal mines). As the railways grew, Lewis Mumford argues, "the environment of the mine, once restricted to the original site, was universalized by the railroad" (*Culture* 150). More than any other invention of the period, the railroad embodied and epitomized industrial technology, not only in material technology per se, but also in implementing an organizational form and a structure of efficiency that came to characterize the industrial factory.[4] The genealogy of the railway out of mining suggests an organic connection between railways, the urban undergrounds where they eventually lodged, and coal-driven industrialization itself. Because they were derived from the railroads that developed in the coal mines and fueled industrialization, the underground railways installed this industrial ur-technology in the urban infrastructure— and symbolically foregrounded the thorough imbrication of industrial technology in the foundations of the city.

The railway both defined the modern city and was instrumental in the nineteenth-century transformations of space and time. David Harvey traces the rationalization of space and time from its origins in the Renaissance to its culmination in the Enlightenment project as a means to achieve human emancipation and enable utopian thinking (242). The conquest and control of space require the production of networks of transport and communications, among which were the railway networks that gave rise to the global standardization of time. These rationalizations paradoxically generate a spatiotemporality that is disrupted, compressed, or annihilated. The railroad eroded distance and disrupted earlier perceptions of space and time (Schivelbusch 41). The railroad may have been the first modernizing technology to effect what Harvey calls the annihilation of space through time (232, 264).[5]

According to Susan Buck-Morss, the railroad became a metaphor for the false equivalency of technological and social progress: "Railroads were the referent, and progress the sign, as spatial movement became so wedded to the concept of historical movement that these could no longer be distinguished" (90).[6] Mumford similarly observes, "Progress was the equivalent in history of mechanical motion through space: it was after beholding a thundering railroad train that Tennyson exclaimed, with exquisite aptness, 'Let the great world spin forever down the ringing grooves of change'" (*Technics* 184). The spatialization of progress—in mechanical motion through space, in the city shaped by the railroad—presents a paradox, a fundamental tension between the understanding of social possibilities in time and in space. Time in this formulation can be identified with a large trend in modernity toward historical and projective thinking, the modern mode of thought that privileges time over space and that fundamentally informs the very periodizing notion of modernity itself. In a period in which time connotes progress and movement and technological changes seem to accelerate the course of history itself, the problem becomes how to understand the effects of these changes in the spatial and social spheres, especially given that "progress entails the conquest of space, the tearing down of all spatial barriers, and the ultimate 'annihilation of space through time.' The reduction of space to a contingent category is implied in the notion of progress itself" (Harvey 205). The notion of progress contains a central ambiguity: progress as a deterministic unfolding through time, the inevitable attainment of ever-more-complete levels of technological development and scientific knowledge versus progress as the material improvement of human lives. Lewis Mumford implies the fundamental contradiction at the heart of progress when he characterizes it as "motion toward infinity, motion without completion or end, motion for motion's sake" (*Technics* 184).

As a figure for the relationship between modern technology and the possibility of social progress, the urban underground poses a conceptual problem for the technological utopia. The penetration of the spaces underneath the nineteenth-century city represented a triumph for technological rationality, the rationalization of urban space, at the same time that the underground was the locus of certain nightmares about progress, nature, and the city—the place where repressed or unforeseen consequences of technological development were revealed. In Richard Jeffries's future history *After London* (1885), the waste matter of "ancient" industrial London contributes over time to a vast stoppage of the river Thames, which therefore wells up through the elaborate underground spaces of the city. The upturned sewage fills a giant swamp, which reeks of disease and death, in the place of the old city. Jeffries's image evokes the origins of modern urban technology in sewage and fears of contagious disease: London's massive sewage systems, the city's first large-scale exploitation of underground space, underwent construction in the 1840s and again after 1855 in the wake of two calamitous cholera epidemics. In Paris, according to Christopher Prendergast, the sewers and catacombs served to rationalize urban space: through the "fantasy" of odorless sanitation, concerns about disease and contagion are elided with an ideal of social order and discipline (79).[7] In these structures, Prendergast traces the imaginative exchange between fears of contagion and transgression associated with the lower depths of the city and the technologies implemented to contain these forces. The structures of rationalized circulation that these technologies brought to the city, and that culminated in the Metro, both addressed and generated the risks of bourgeois contact with poverty, criminality, disease, and insurrection (Prendergast 99–100). Michel de Certeau writes that restrooms on trains provide "a little space of irrationality, like love affairs and sewers in the *Utopias* of earlier times" (111). The comparison is particularly apt: The occupation of the urban underground culminates with the appearance of railways in the space of sewers.

Underground spaces figure prominently in numerous science fiction texts from the late nineteenth century, including stories by Edward Bulwer-Lytton, Jules Verne, Villiers de l'Isle Adam, H. G. Wells, the French sociologist Gabriel Tarde, and E. M. Forster, all of whom marveled at the power and sophistication of a realm permeated with technology. A culminating statement of the underground as technological sublime can be seen in the 1936 film *Things to Come* (based on Wells's 1933 novel). Evolutionary themes also feature in the nascent utopian-futuristic imagination of this time, with 1871 a watershed year that saw the emergence of both Edward Bulwer-Lytton's *The Coming Race* and Samuel Butler's *Erewhon*. Edward Bellamy's paradigmatic urban utopia *Looking Backward* (1888) hinges on eugenic processes. H. G. Wells is undoubtedly the central figure in this tradition, with his utopias and scientific romances showing the life-long influence of his biology professor, the Darwinian apologist T. H. Huxley. Near the turn of the century, H. G. Wells produced two texts within as many years that figured the relation between evolutionary processes and city space in ways that have vastly different consequences for the status of the city. The remarkable point about London in *The Time Machine* (1895) is its thorough obsolescence, whereas *War of the Worlds* (1897) features the city's swift devastation and then redemption.

The Time Machine provides a paradigmatic statement of the space/time paradoxes of the railroad that culminate in the urban underground: the underground imaginatively links modern urban space with progress in time, the ambivalence of which is expressed in its uncomfortable evolutionary associations. Although evolution rationalizes time, thus making possible a linear narrative of progress toward a goal, it makes equally possible the inversion of this narrative, decline instead of progress.[8] If the railroad represents the possibilities of limitless progress in time at odds with the spatial nature of the city, that is, a form of progress that ultimately achieves nothing, evolution comes to represent a similar historical impasse, constant change without necessary improvement. Both signify the conflict between a continuous historical process—the temporal register itself—and the space of the city. The future is at odds with the city.

The Call of Nature

The evolutionary underground marks the unexpected appearance of nature in a realm tenuously appropriated by technology. Underground space already lends itself symbolically to the conflation of natural and technological registers, with its telluric associations combining both organic and inorganic nature, gestation and growth as well as death and decomposition. Didier Gille associates "underground powers" with "natural forces that work on substances in a mysterious and uncontrollable way and that make time appear as a productive force" (243). Gille explicitly contrasts these transformative processes with the circulation that characterizes the modern city, which is premised on the purely abstract movement in space, "in which no metamorphosis can take place" (246). The controlled and orderly technologies of pipe and conduit replace the qualitative transformations of the soil (Gille 247). The deformed nature that emerges after the penetration of technology into nonhuman space expresses a fundamental uneasiness about the growth of technology, an anxiety about human intervention in received nature.

In an episode of *The X-Files* entitled "The Host" (first aired 23 September 1994), a half-human and half-flatworm (or "fluke") monster, which is the product of a bizarre evolutionary process, attacks workers in the Newark County sewer system. The creature makes its debut appearance in the septic system of a Russian cargo freighter sailing two miles off the New Jersey coast; the freighter evacuates the contents of its septic tanks into the ocean. As the episode unfolds, we learn that the course of evolution had been locally accelerated by exposure to radioactive sewage from the freighter, which had been used for the disposal of material from the meltdown at Chernobyl. FBI Special Agent Dana Scully tells her partner, Fox Mulder, "Nature didn't make this thing; we did."

In an episode pervaded by effluvia and excrement, the search for the creature leads the agents to plumb the Newark County sewage system. A trail of waste links urban, rural, and oceanic environments, all filtered through the giant Newark County sewage-processing plant that forms the symbolic center of the episode. A sequence in which Mulder first visits the plant thematizes the hundred-year interval from the origin of the system at the turn of the century: The sewage administrator speculates, "No telling what's been breeding down there in the last hundred years." No longer associated with the inevitable progressive development of the modern city, the evolutionary paradigm now marks the changing conceptualization of urban space in that hundred-year span. Mulder tells the sewage administrator of his visit to an older section of sewer, built around the turn of the century, which he associates with the capacious Parisian catacombs. The newer, concrete pipes are "not more than 24 inches across" and indicate a change in scale from human to inhuman or marginally human.

The episode refigures the technological utopia as a sewage-processing plant and offers as a primary urban paradigm an elaborate technological system based in excrement, an irony that is also historically appropriate to the sewer-based origins of the urban underground. The sewage administrator quips, "560,000 people a day call my office on the porcelain telephone." The sewage system supervenes the modern networks of communication that both define and threaten to dissolve the city and inform an obsessive leitmotif of the show, the trill of Mulder's and Scully's incorporeal communications via cellular phone that continually traverse the episodes. The shift between these two modalities of urban circulation has significant repercussions for the concept of the city. The technologies of the sewer and the sewage-processing plant epitomize the narratives and technologies of circulation, speed, and technological progress premised on the rationalization and repression of sewage, the dark underbelly of the urban environment. However, the creature represents the return of just such primal fears, which are associated with such urban mythologies as wildlife in the sewers and monsters that lurk in toilets.

Moreover, the reinstatement of sewage system as urban paradigm resituates the city in the unmistakable physicality of the body and the environment, as well as in an increasingly imperiled public municipalism. The flow of sewage provides a material counterpoint to what Manuel Castells terms the "space of flows."[9] The sewage-treatment plant forms the nucleus of the city, as well as of a much larger region. Whatever the city is, the production and distribution of waste (rather than of capital or of information) is the primary process that binds it to the region and the world, a quasi-symbiotic matrix ambivalently symbolized by the parasitic nature of the creature itself, whose life cycle establishes a manifest continuity between the bodily process and the urban process. The attacking creature implants a larva in its victim's bile duct; we watch as an attacked worker later vomits up the matured form of this developmental stage, which slithers down the drain. After being absorbed into the Newark County sewer system from the Atlantic Ocean, the creature is spotted near the sewage plant's overflow system that dumps into the harbor during heavy rainfall. It will head back out to sea.

The episode concludes its investigation of the status of the city and its technologies with a video montage of a murky Newark: an illuminated cityscape at night, a solitary car on a wet nighttime street, and several shots within the sewers, including a final shot of the human flatworm as it opens its eyes. The status of the creature from the underground forms the focus and culmination of the episode: Mulder tells his superior at the FBI, "This is not a man. It's a monster. You can't put it in an institution." Skinner replies, "Well what do you do with it, Agent Mulder? Put it in a zoo?" The creature troubles the categories of both human and nature; it is the product of the urban processes of the last century—the period of time representing the future of the modern city, the history of the promise and effects of modern urban technologies, as well as the movement from the modern industrial city to the so-called posturban. If the modern industrial city in its heyday generated a crisis around subjectivity in the form of urban anomie—the facelessness of the denizen of the modern city—the contemporary city creates ambiguities of identity having to do with the creature's status in the natural world, the incomprehensibility of its human potential or of its place in the urban environment.

EVOLUTION IN OUR TIME

Evolution once offered a paradigm of a natural, and therefore inevitable, historical development and progress into the future. However, the evolutionary process thematized here thwarts any possibility of a "natural" narrative of evolution and troubles the boundaries between natural and built environment, the human and the nonhuman, natural processes and the products of human intervention. This episode of *The X-Files*, Michael Crichton's novel *Jurassic Park* (1990), and Terry Gilliam's film *12 Monkeys* (1995) are significant for their revival of the particular conjunction of evolutionary processes and underground spaces. The reappearance of these spaces in contemporary texts suggest a renewed inquiry into the utopian imaginary and its implications for the city.

Jurassic Park offers a meta-utopia in the form of a theme park modeled on the natural-history museum that would be the ultimate testament to the parallel between evolutionary and technological progress: a living recreation of the prehistoric past premised on the cloning of dinosaurs. The status of utopia is a central problem of the story. Because it is situated on Isla Nublar off the coast of Costa Rica, a New World locale of the kind regularly "discovered" by European explorers, the sophisticated theme park reverses the fundamental nineteenth-century reorientation of utopia from a remote place to a future time. In pointed ways, *Jurassic Park* recapitulates an ur-text of the genre, Wells's *The Island of Dr. Moreau* (1896), which is an anti-utopia set on a classically exotic and isolated no-place. Wells's story hinges on the tension between the suggestion of human devolution and the forcible evolution of animals at the hands of the island's vivisectionist doctor.

As a theme park, Jurassic Park issues from a tradition of visionary urbanism ranging from world's fairs to Disney's Epcot Center. According to Michael Sorkin, this tradition developed into two strains in the modern period, the Corbusian celebration of rationality and engineering and the Garden City of Ebenezer Howard.[10] *Jurassic Park* draws on both strains to present a spectacle of technological achievement in the form of genetic engineering, an achievement symbolized by its ability to evoke the pre-historic past: "My colleagues and I determined, several years ago, that it was possible to clone the DNA of an extinct animal, and to grow it. That seemed to us a wonderful idea, it was a kind of time travel—the only time travel in the world. Bring them back alive, so to speak. And since it was so exciting, and since it was possible to do it, we decided to go forward" (Crichton 305). Jurassic Park creates an environment so deeply technological that it can pre-sent a perfect simulacrum of a pristine natural world. The ultimate theme park no longer depends on the explicit thematization of the ideal city; the rationalist urban paradigm is so implicit that it can locate in a remote region and forge its transport technologies out of actual life forms. The domestica-tion of nature for the urban environment is a key part of this visionary tradition: "At its core, the greenhouse [i.e., urban winter gardens like the Crystal Palace]—or Disneyland—offers a view of alien nature, edited, a better version, a kind of sublime. Indeed, the abiding theme of every park is nature's transformation from civilization's antithesis to its playground" (Sorkin 210).

In its aspirations toward rational control, Jurassic Park represents a con-tinuation of modernist urbanism in a postmodern guise. It raises the ques-tion of whether the greater hazard resides in the success of this model or in its breakdown. The rational utopia of Jurassic Park is fundamentally un-stable; it eventually succumbs to nonlinear, chaotic, irrational processes, the tightly controlled technological reconstruction of the evolutionary past transformed into tense struggles for the survival of the fittest. The novel offers a moral tale about the violent recuperation of technological hubris by nature as flawed technological control gives way to productive biological chaos. The novel's critique is articulated by bad-boy mathematician Ian Malcolm: "The history of evolution is that life escapes all barriers. Life breaks free" (159). This creates a narrative peculiarity in that the source of threat for the suspense novel is the same as the element of redemption. The outcome offers reassurance that there is an irreducible life force with an innate rebelliousness that ensures its ultimate autonomy from technological control and financial exploitation.

The park's aspiration to total technological control rests on the recon-stitution of the evolutionary past, that is, a gesture that undermines the linear evolutionary process at the same time that it tries to mobilize it as a sign of technological mastery. Even while it plays on the impulse behind the natural-history museum that documents the evolutionary ascent of man, Jurassic Park indicates the exhaustion of the progressive paradigm in multiple ways. The park harks back to utopias of spatial exploration and focuses on the recreation of the past rather than the creation of the future. The technological recreation of the evolutionary past signifies both a fascination with this linear narrative and its destruction. The evolutionary process is reestablished only in the failure of the park as rational utopia.

Terry Gilliam's *12 Monkeys* (1995), which is based on Chris Marker's time-travel movie *La Jetée* (1962), is an extended meditation on the possibility of the future. Both films follow a hero from a postapocalyptic future who is sent back to the time and city of his childhood as part of a technocratic project to prevent or ameliorate the story's originary apocalyptic event. If earlier time-travel narratives were employed to explore a future transformed beyond recognition by historical forces, these films are emblematic of a later tendency to stage struggles in the present over the shape of the future, a future typically threatened by the misuse of technology. Both types of time-travel narrative manifest a central concern with the status of the future. On one level, they assert the significance of the future and its linear relation to the present, they trouble the future's very conception by undermining the unidirectional unfolding of time and the basic dynamics of cause and effect. *La Jetée, 12 Monkeys,* and the related *Terminator* movies are additionally distinguished by the apocalyptic quality of their futures: Their returns to the present are engineered to deter these bad outcomes and thus recuperate the future. However, the fact remains that the only futures they are capable of imagining are deeply compromised.[11] The backward direction of their time travel signals the diminished possibilities in the future, a rejection of forward motion or progress.

The crux of both Marker's and Gilliam's films resides in an ambiguity about which dimension constitutes the site of emotional investment. The heroes of both ultimately choose to inhabit the past rather than the future, with the result that memory and personal narrative replace the sweeping futuristic concerns that characterize science fiction as a genre. There is no question of asserting dystopian horrors against utopian progress; the future no longer represents an ideal to be striven toward or a concept to be imagined (Pfeil 84). For all its bleakness, the 1962 version is able to anticipate a redeemed future (in the form of a city whose vastly intricate structure is represented by the natural cross-hatching of a piece of wood), even if it ultimately rejects it. The reorientation of utopian concerns from the future to the present/past signals both the loss of the utopian project as well as a form of its recuperation.

The 1995 film *12 Monkeys* is set in 1990, late 1996, and 2026, with most of the action unfolding in December 1996, a future so near that it serves merely as an extension of the present. This fact illustrates both the already thoroughgoing permeation of the present with bewildering new technology as well as this technology's lack of redemptive potential. In *12 Monkeys,* this reduction or loss of the future accompanies the unraveling of the linear narrative and breaching of any definitive ending in favor of an unstable circularity.[12] That is, the principal ending of the narrative—the annihilation of all but one percent of the world's population by a genetically engineered ebola-like virus that forces the survivors underground—is a *fait* almost casually *accompli.* The futility of the film's "outcome" evokes Fredric Jameson's assertion that the imaginative work of science fiction, optimistic or pessimistic, is not about the future at all, but rather offers a strategy by which to compensate for our diminished ability to perceive the present ("Progress" 147–58).[13] Jameson's insight provides a persuasive theoretical framework for reading *12 Monkeys,* wherein the struggle between the events leading up to the genetically engineered pandemic and the equally dystopian attempts at recuperation are elements in a narrative that continually gravitates toward a fragile central moment in the quasi-present where perfect happiness is always already lost. The phenomenon that Jameson observes may in fact mark a distinct and relatively recent change, a historically specific loss of the ability to imagine a progressive future achieved through technology.

The project of the narrative in *12 Monkeys* is to recover information that would lead to a cure for the virus and the eventual retaking of the surface, which is now arrogated to the animals—a reascent of man. The narrative is propelled by the desire to change the past, although this aim directly contradicts the future scientists' asserted goal of simply tracking the virus, rather than intervening in its release, and the film's repeated assertions that the past cannot be changed. The film makes the frequent, unnerving suggestion that the hero's interventions in the past introduce the very elements that precipitate the apocalyptic events. However, whether this demonstrates free will or determinism is unclear. Despite the continual tension between the film's determinism and its shifting and unstable temporal matrix, the emotional force of the narrative leans heavily toward the impossibility of change: The narrative both revolves around and culminates in a tragic moment that remains the same, the shooting death of James Cole (Bruce Willis) and the dissemination of the deadly virus. The extent to which we accept a stable time line is also the extent to which we are enslaved to bureaucratic forces of control.

The film stages not only the loss of a progressive future, but the future altogether. Not only are humanity and its achievements obliterated, temporal sequence itself is hopelessly indeterminate. The inability to untangle these threads is paralleled by evolutionary confusions from which it is impossible to recover origins or make claims for progress. The film's opening statement, "Once again the animals will rule the world," describes a straightforward reversal of the evolutionary process—the undoing of human ascendancy by a "natural" catastrophe (or boon, depending on one's perspective)—while the genetically engineered virus confounds the very notion of such an evolutionary process. The evolutionary interventions of genetic engineering are balanced in the narrative by a reversionary ecologism. A narrative chiasmus emerges between the animal-rights activism of the demented Jeffrey Goines (Brad Pitt) and the genetic experiments of his father (Christopher Plummer), a Nobel prize–winning virologist. This chiastic structure establishes parallel, alternate explanations of the film's apocalyptic events: deep ecological zeal that aims to eliminate the human population versus the unleashed virus as a logical extension of the rationalism of high-tech laboratory experiments.

In the loss of these certainties, or even possibilities, of progress or regress, the film's focus becomes the utopian imagination itself, both the unrealizability of utopias and their desirability. The film is a meditation on utopian and dystopian modes of thought and is littered throughout with utopian and apocalyptic references drawn from artworks, popular songs, and cartoons. The film's opening sequence presents something like the imaginative remains of the futuristic city, which are comprised primarily of an elaborate technological underground, the deepest level of which is a warren of human cages that evoke a combination of prison, hospital, and animal research laboratory. Unwillingly "volunteered" to aid with the scientific investigation of the virus, Cole ascends through intricate layers of the underground until he reaches the city's deteriorated, subterranean infrastructure (where he orients himself with the aid of a city map). Finally, he attains the surface via a manhole. While sealed off from the dangers of nature, biology, infection, and disease by full latex body armor, Cole is assigned to gather specimens of surviving animals, mostly rats and insects. Emblematizing urban investigation at the start of the film, the scene focuses ironically on the natural life of the dead city.

The wintry abandoned Philadelphia of 2026 is significantly not a futuristic city, but the city of 1996, both frozen and decayed. What is the status of the city given the loss of the future? The film has a particular focus on urban space and on how to make sense of the urban given the loss of utopian/dystopian narratives. Spatial considerations emerge from the breakdown of time as the present replaces the future as the site of Cole's utopian (or apocalyptic) fantasy and projective possibility.[14] Utopian and dystopian possibilities are anticipated by extremes of opulence and degradation in the Baltimore and Philadelphia of 1990 and 1996: The same neoclassical building (the real Philadelphia Museum of Art) represents a posh university lecture hall in Baltimore and a homeless encampment in Philadelphia. The film balances the opening sequence with a second emblematic urban vision, something like a fantasy of utopian possibilities in the present, with the release of the animals from the Philadelphia Zoo. This release of the animals engineered by the "Army of the 12 Monkeys" (in lieu of releasing the virus— a narrative twist that offers a temporary reprieve from inevitable apocalypse) is one of two fragile utopian moments in the film. The other is the moment of Cole's death, the revisited trauma that allows for the momentary reintegration of past and present, dream and reality. The image of the animals in the city is as fleeting and dreamlike as the doomed embrace that closes the circular narrative: Giraffes bound across an I-95 overpass, emus block traffic, flamingos take flight from a skyscraper. This utopian image of the city frustrates a narrative of redemption. It is significantly not futuristic, although it draws on the visual lexicon of the monumental futuristic cityscape. The anomalous introduction of these animals into urban space marks the reintroduction into urban space of a nature that is anything but native or originary, a reintegration of nature and city that, albeit glorious, is either tragically misguided or simply fantastical. The rebellious gesture of the animal-rights activists points to a larger dilemma about nature after modernity—the attempt to recuperate an originary nature is impossible, we are left instead with anomalous conjunctions—whereas the introduction of an exotic and anomalous nature is an act of detournement—defamiliarizing, halting, foregrounding, and questioning the nature of the city.[15]

The scene poses a question about the status of the present and its relation to utopian possibilities. The film constantly raises the possibility that the whole elaborate plot is a form of madness or paranoia, a dangerous escape from reality that risks creating its own, self-fulfilling prophesies. Living in the present represents a psychological challenge to decipher the tangled layers of real and unreal, reason versus fantasy. Although the familiarity of the present offers a saner counterpoint to the film's apocalyptic or utopian obsessions, these projective possibilities provide the very elements that structure and give meaning to the present. The film's investigation of the failed remnants of an obsolete and largely pernicious utopianism offers one redemptive possibility (among multiple contradictory ones) in the reinvestment of the present with emotional and utopian possibilities: Our vision of the urban environments of Baltimore and Philadelphia through Cole's eyes is suffused with wonder, terror, and joy.

CITIES IN SPACE

Transformations in the contemporary city are marked by the loss of the ability to conceptualize urban space, to attach meaning to the urban. Much of postmodern urbanism thematizes the loss of a recognizable notion of the city to forces like privatization or globalization, the curtailment of municipal services, the loss of public space, the rise of edge and virtual cities and of gated communities, and the increasing polarities of rich and poor—in other words, the erosion of the kinds of progressive municipalism that accompanied the rise of the utopian urban imagination in the 1890s. What is the connection between the state of the contemporary city and urban representation? In Jameson's famous account, postmodern space is characterized by the loss of the means to conceptualize or abstract from it—the inability to map it. As products and microcosms of multinational capitalism, postmodern cities defy the kind of representation that allows the orientation of the urban subject with regard to the whole and yields instead a kind of interpretive vertigo (*Postmodernism* 44). If, according to Paul Patton, cities "are complex objects which include both realities and their description" (112), then one can argue that projective ideas about the city are crucial to its conceptualization: The status of the city is inextricable from the urban imaginary. To what extent is it possible to imagine the city without a utopian model? How are these spaces meaningful in its absence?

In "Mythicizing the City," Leslie Fiedler describes a different kind of urban destruction that is emblematic of a previous generation of urban concerns. As the embodiment of artifice, the city in this account severs human life from nature and becomes a kind of overgrown, yet decaying, monstrosity:

> It is a sense of the contradiction implicit in this insight between what our conscious needs demand, i.e., civilization, the city-as-world, and what our instinctive, impulsive undermind yearns for, i.e., nature, the persistence of the pre-human, a world we never made, which nurtures our underground resentment of the City and our image of it as a Hell to which we are self-condemned. . . . Do those who imagine the end of the City, whether in fire or ice, wish it or dread it—or, like me, dread they wish it, wish they dreaded it? Certainly, I . . . am caught in an unresolvable ambivalence. And I suspect that those others, too, endure fantasies bred by their love/hate for the City the world threatens/promises to become. (118–20)

This discussion sounds a note of both inevitability and centrality—above all, the city is important. Modernity moves toward increasing urbanization, even as the urban infrastructure crumbles and burns. For good or for ill, the apocalyptic metropolis represents the coalescing of technological and social forces.

The supersession of these narratives suggests the loss of this kind of social imagination. What is left is the city as the site of social residuum—the remains and human consequences of new forms of wealth and exchange, new spatial organization or despatialization—as in the remove from space to cyberspace. Michael Sorkin writes that "the new city . . . eradicates genuine particularity in favor of a continuous urban field, a conceptual grid of boundless reach" (xii). For Scott Bukatman, this grid becomes literalized, or rather, fully metaphorized, in the matrix of cyberspace: "The result [of the rise of a global communications network involving an avalanche of data] is an intensification of the dissolution of the boundaries between public and private realms, physical and electronic spaces. . . . 'This is an Information Era,' proclaims a world leader in an SF [science fiction] novel, 'and our lack of territory—mere topsoil—no longer restrains us' " (105). Cyberspace is both the logical extension of the disappearance (implosion, diffusion, emptying) of the traditional city amid the rise of communications and information technologies and a compensatory function for the intolerable illegibility of contemporary urban space. At a moment when urban space is being transformed beyond the bounds of comprehensibility, the urban is reduced to a metaphor. The disappearance of the real city and the obsolescence of utopia are entirely commensurate in this account as the monumental urban forms that marked the utopianism of the old modern era become empty and inert (Bukatman 123–26). Ironically, in describing the loss of a real, referential city amid the multiplication of representations, Michael Sorkin identifies an obverse process, in which the utopian imagination overtakes real urban space.

If linear evolutionary narratives express the troubling tension between progress into the future and urban space, nonlinear evolutionary narratives reorient the focus on the city to the present. In its recent, nonlinear manifestations, evolution marks a basic confusion about linear time and it signals the ascendancy of space, of postmodern spatialization. Ironically, this increased and increasing spatialization is concomitant with the loss of the ability to conceive of the city as material, social, and referential. If the future is at odds with the city, it seems that the loss of the conceptual possibility of the future is equally stymieing. Two outcomes suggest themselves.

First, the waning of the utopian imagination may bring diminished urban aspirations, specifically a retreat from the urban technological sublime of either sophistication or degradation. Postmodern urbanism of the Scott Bukatman/Paul Virilio variety risks the dangerous presupposition of the loss of a material urbanism outside of cybernetic "spaces." These cybernetic constructs lend themselves to forms of utopian thematization that, like earlier technological utopias, slight the material realities of the existing city. In response to this conceptualization, numerous critics have suggested alternatives to a utopian notion rooted in an Enlightenment universalism—viewing the city instead as participatory, contestatory, diverse, and civic.

The second outcome is that some type of utopianism may be necessary for a coherent understanding of the city as a humanistic political project, that is, the city comprising the possibility of the improvement of social life: "Spatialization, then, whatever it may take away from the capacity to think and History, also opens a door onto a new domain for libidinal investment of the Utopian and even the protopolitical type" (Jameson *Postmodernism* 160). This is not to propose the recuperation of the absolutism of technological utopia from earlier in this century, but rather that the possibility of reading urban spaces seems to rest implicitly on utopian impulses inherited from a previous era.

NOTES

1. Appropriately, Appleton's Utopia line of papers is marketed to producers of advertising and glossy publications. The Appleton Papers web site explains: "For centuries, people have tried to describe UTOPIA. Appleton Papers has managed to get it down on paper."

2. In particular, the notion of the "evolution of cities" designates a historicist, anthropological strain of urban analysis, which originates from the work of archaeologist V. Gordon Childe, who traced the rise of modern cities in the history of human development from the paleolithic era to industrialism in *Man Makes Himself* (1936), or equally (if less inclined to a progressive narrative of development) from that of Patrick Geddes, who published *Cities in Evolution* in 1915.

3. Bobrick cites Louis Laurent Simonin, who in his 1869 *Underground Life* makes an extended analogy between the network of tunnels in a French mine and the streets of a great city (81).

4. "The railroad was the first industry to benefit by the use of electricity; for the telegraph made possible a long distance signalling system and remote control; and it was in the railroad that the routing through of production and the timing and interrelationship of the various parts of production took place more than a generation before similar tables and schedules and forecasts made their way into industry as a whole. The invention of the necessary devices to ensure regularity and safety, from the air-brake and the vestibule car to the automatic switch and automatic signal system, and the perfection of the system for routing goods and traffic at varying rates of speed and under varying weather conditions from point to point, was one of the superb technical and administrative achievements of the nineteenth century. . . . [W]ithin the social limitations of the period, the railroad was both the most characteristic and the most efficient form of technics" (Mumford *Technics* 199).

5. Stephan Graham offers a variation on this account by arguing that the intensive communications infrastructure in and around the industrial city served to "overcome time constraints by minimizing space constraints," whereas contemporary telecommunications technologies "overcome *space* constraints by minimizing *time* constraints," which is to say, " 'annihilate space with time.' " In other words, Graham associates the apparently paradoxical effects of this general class of technologies with a shift between two periods and two stages of technological development (32, 48).

6. This statement rests on a confusing use of the terms referent and sign; it might be better to say that railroads were the signifier and progress was the signified.

7. For a similar process in England, see also Stallybrass and White 130–31, 140–43.

8. By cataloguing proliferating narratives of decline that coincided with optimistic or active visions of the future, Stephen Kern identifies unresolved contradictions between progressive and regressive worldviews at this time (104).

9. Castells writes of "the historical emergence of the space of flows, superseding the meaning of the space of places. By this we understand the deployment of the functional logic of power-holding organizations in asymmetrical networks of exchanges which do not depend on the characteristics of any specific locale for the fulfillment of their fundamental goals" (348–49). Castells argues that new information technologies are instrumental to the rise of the space of flows. These networks of information flows are used to evade the control of local governments and other place-based forms of control.

10. "Reaching the scale and density of small cities, the fairs also became models, adopted visionary urbanism as an aspect of their agendas, both offering themselves as models of urban organization and providing, within their pavilions, panoramic visions of even more advanced cities to come" (Sorkin 210, 212).

11. In this, *12 Monkeys* differs from *La Jetée,* which attributes to the future its own redemptive futurity—the purpose of the time-travel experiments in this case is ultimately to plumb a future for the means to effect the salvation of the film's postnuclear (and underground) present. However, both films turn on their protagonist's rejection of the postapocalyptic "present" reality in favor of the nostalgically charged "past" (i.e., the filmmakers' present). Constance Penley suggests the relation between *La Jetée* and *The Terminator* (79).

12. The film's narrative circularity is troped in its opening credits, which portray a mechanism that combines the antiquated technologies of magic lantern and analog timepiece. The nature of the temporal issues in the story, especially the documentation of the past through video images, has strong implications for the film medium itself. See Penley (66, 77).

13. Drawing on a Marcusian understanding of the utopian imagination as "the imagination of otherness and radical difference" ("Progress" 153), Jameson equates the imagination of the future with the utopian imagination. The answer to his

question "Can we imagine the future?" is no. It is unclear in this essay whether Jameson reads the failure of the utopian imagination as such to be a historically specific loss or a structural impossibility. Structurally, he argues that utopias from Sir Thomas More to the present are characterized by a central repression of negativity that serves to undermine their basic premises. Instead, utopian texts (like modern texts) are fundamentally about interrogating their own conditions of possibility. A utopian possibility paradoxically emerges from this very process, by which we can "contemplat[e] . . . our own absolute limits" ("Progress" 153). The strength of this insight rests in the examples Jameson draws from the twentieth-century capitalist milieu: Science fiction, like Raymond Chandler's detective stories, enable us to see a present obscured by "the systemic, cultural, and ideological closure of which we are all in one way or another prisoners" because "humankind . . . is able to bear very little of the unmediated, unfiltered experience of the daily life of capitalism" ("Progress" 152–53).

14. Fredric Jameson suggests that "the distinctiveness of SF as a genre has less to do with time (history, past, future) than with space" ("Science" 58). The suggestion again seems motivated both by longstanding formal qualities and by recent changes in the genre.

15. The translator's notes to the *Situationist International Anthology* defines the French word *détournement* as "diversion, deflection, turning aside from the normal course or purpose (often with an illicit connotation)." The entry continues by noting that "It has sometimes been translated as 'diversion,' but this word is confusing because of its more common meaning of idle entertainment. I have chosen simply to anglicize the French word, which already has a certain currency in America and England" (Knabb 371).

WORKS CITED

Bellamy, Edward. *Looking Backward 2000–1887*. 1888. New York: New American Library, 1960.

Bobrick, Benson. *Labyrinths of Iron: Subways in History, Myth, Art, Technology, and War*. New York: Henry Holt, 1986.

Buck-Morss, Susan. *The Dialectics of Seeing: Walter Benjamin and the Arcades Project*. Cambridge, Mass.: MIT Press, 1989.

Bukatman, Scott. *Terminal Identity: The Virtual Subject in Postmodern Science Fiction*. Durham, N.C.: Duke UP, 1993.

Bulwer-Lytton, Edward. *The Coming Race*. 1871. London: Routledge, 1886.

Butler, Samuel. *Erewhon: or, Over the Range*. London: Trubner, 1872.

Castells, Manuel. *The Informational City.* Oxford: Basil Blackwell, 1989.

Childe, V. Gordon. *Man Makes Himself.* London: Watts, 1936.

Crichton, Michael. *Jurassic Park.* New York: Ballatine Books, 1990.

de Certeau, Michel. *The Practice of Everyday Life.* Trans. Steven Rendall. Berkeley: U of California P, 1984.

Fiedler, Leslie. "Mythicizing the City." *Literature and the Urban Experience.* Eds. Michael C. Jaye and Ann Chalmers Watts. New Brunswick, N.J.: Rutgers UP, 1981. 113–21.

Geddes, Patrick. *Cities in Evolution.* London: Williams, 1915.

Gille, Didier. "Maceration and Purification." Trans. Bruce Benderson. *Zone* 1/2 (1986): 226–81.

Graham, Stephen. "Imagining the Real Time City." *Imagining Cities.* Eds. Sallie Westwood and John Williams. London: Routledge, 1997. 31–49.

Harvey, David. *The Condition of Postmodernity.* Oxford: Basil Blackwell, 1990.

Jameson, Fredric. *Postmodernism, or, the Cultural Logic of Late Capitalism.* Durham, N.C.: Duke UP, 1991.

——. "Progress Versus Utopia; or, Can We Imagine the Future?" *Science Fiction Studies* 9.2 (1982): 147–58.

——. "Science Fiction as Spatial Genre: Generic Discontinuities and the Problem of Figuration in Vonda McIntyre's *The Exile Waiting.*" *Science Fiction Studies* 14.1 (1987): 44–59.

Jeffries, Richard. *After London.* 1885. Oxford: Oxford UP, 1980.

Kern, Stephen. *The Culture of Time and Space 1880–1918.* Cambridge, Mass.: Harvard UP, 1983.

Knabb, Ken. Translator's Notes. *Situationist International Anthology.* Ed. and trans. Knabb. Berkeley, Calif.: Bureau of Public Secrets, 1981. 371–77.

Mumford, Lewis. *The Culture of Cities.* San Diego: Harcourt Brace Jovanovich, 1938.

——. *Technics and Civilization.* San Diego: Harcourt Brace, 1934.

Patton, Paul. "Imaginary Cities: Images of Postmodernity." *Postmodern Cities and Spaces.* Eds. Sophie Watson and Katherine Gibson. Oxford: Basil Blackwell, 1995. 112–21.

Penley, Constance. "Time Travel, Primal Scene, Critical Dystopia." *Close Encounters: Film, Feminism, and Science Fiction.* Eds. Constance Penley et al. Minneapolis: U of Minnesota P, 1991. 63–79.

Pfeil, Fred. *Another Tale to Tell.* London: Verso, 1990.

Prendergast, Christopher. *Paris and the Nineteenth Century.* Oxford: Basil Blackwell, 1992.

Ross, Andrew. *The Chicago Gangster Theory of Life: Nature's Debt to Society.* London: Verso, 1994.

Schivelbusch, Wolfgang. *The Railway Journey: The Industrialization of Time and Space in the 19th Century.* Berkeley: U of California P, 1986.

Sorkin, Michael. "See You in Disneyland." *Variations on a Theme Park: The New American City and the End of Public Space.* Ed. Michael Sorkin. New York: Noonday, 1992. 205–32.

Stallybrass, Peter, and Allon White. "The City: The Sewer, the Gaze and the Contaminating Touch." *The Politics and Poetics of Transgression.* Ithaca, N.Y.: Cornell UP, 1986. 125–48.

Virilio, Paul. *The Lost Dimension.* Trans. Daniel Moshenberg. New York: Semiotext(e), 1991.

Wells, H. G. *The Island of Dr. Moreau.* 1896. New York: New American Library, 1988.

——. *The Time Machine.* 1895. New York: Airmont Books, 1964.

——. *War of the Worlds.* 1898. New York: Harper, 1926.

Williams, Rosalind. *Notes on the Underground: An Essay on Technology, Society, and the Imagination.* Cambridge, Mass.: MIT Press, 1992.

14

NATURE IN THE APARTMENT
Humans, Pets, and the Value
of Incommensurability
David R. Shumway

The American environmental movement traces its intellectual lineage back to Henry David Thoreau and John Muir.[1] They are remembered not as ecologists, but as romantic philosophers whose beliefs are closer to pantheism than to biology. They were famous not mainly for what they told us about the natural world, but for their having lived apart from human society in what they called the wilderness. "In Wildness," says Thoreau, "is the preservation of the World" (609). As a result of this heritage, environmentalism in this country has assumed a version of the nature/culture binary that is a specification of the more generally held opposition. According to Kate Soper, "In its commonest and most fundamental sense, the term 'nature' refers to everything which is not human and distinguished from the work of humanity" (15). When defined in opposition, "culture" refers to everything that is the work of humanity. In the American environmentalist version, nature is located in particular spaces defined by their relative lack of human habitation or intervention. Soper acknowledges this conception of nature when she says "for the most part, when 'nature' is used of the nonhuman, it is in a rather more concrete sense to refer to that part of the environment which we have had no hand in creating" (16). Culture, or the human, is then identified with everywhere else, especially urban areas. We now speak of going off to enjoy, experience, see, or even to visit nature.

A little reflection reveals this to be a very odd way of speaking, because it renders unnatural human beings and the spaces we occupy and create. If "nature" only meant that which is not human, this would simply be a tautology. However, "nature" carries another set of meanings that identify it with what is good, normal, and real.[2] Environmentalists do not value nature merely (if at all) *because* it is the other of humanity. "Nature" for them names the order of life—healthy, proper, and scientifically verified. To call something "natural," in this sense, is to say that it is the way it ought to be. Conversely, to call human spaces unnatural is to offer the opposite moral and political judgment. Moreover, the opposition of nature to culture works at cross-purposes to another premise of environmentalism, that human beings are a part of nature and ultimately bound by its limits. The traditional nature/culture opposition has removed human beings from nature by placing them in a separate metaphysical category by virtue of their having souls and/or rationality. Environmentalism need not deny that humans and other animals differ in significant ways, but it cannot support an absolute distinction. As Soper puts it, "ecology would have us revise our attitudes to 'nature' and the place of humanity within it, along the lines that would reintroduce some of the conception of the Chain [of being]; rather than view 'nature' as an external and inorganic context, we should regard the ecosystem as a plurality of beings each possessed of its particular function and purpose in maintaining the whole" (25).

It follows from these assumptions that a genuinely ecological perspective must begin with the assumption that human activities are no less natural than are those of other species. One could start to develop this approach by deconstructing the nature/culture binary. Because *Homo sapiens* is an animal species, and thus just as natural as wolves or spotted owls, human culture is nature. We now have good reason to believe that culture, defined as a web of socially transmitted behaviors, is not restricted to human beings and thus must be deemed natural. If this is the case, humans' cultural activity distinguishes them less than previously thought. However, it also provides a different perspective on cities and other "unnatural" spaces that humans have constructed. Like ant hills and beehives, such spaces should be understood as environments humans naturally construct. Conversely, the spaces we deem nature (wilderness preserves, national parks, etc.) are defined precisely by their cultural value, as are museums, monuments, and other specially preserved spaces, which thus renders the spaces most identified with nature as culture. Indeed, we might call such places "nature museums" to emphasize that preservation itself is a distinctly cultural act. Thoreau to the contrary, we have not preserved wilderness to save the planet, but in response to ethical or aesthetic beliefs and values that have only recently become influential.[3] Moreover, even if we grant a certain distinct otherness to some few wilderness areas, we must recognize "how difficult it is to refer to the landscape one is seeking to conserve simply as 'nature.' For if nature is conceptualized and valued, as it sometimes is in environmental philosophy, as that which is independent of human culture, then rather little of the environment corresponds to the concept: hardly anything we refer to as natural landscape *is* natural in this sense, and its supposed value might therefore be put in question" (Soper 152). In fact, this argument is often used in the United States by those arguing against preservation of a particular piece of land because statutes sometimes make preservation dependent on the land existing in a pristine state.

One sort of space that often is taken to be natural, but that is not at all independent of human culture, is the bucolic or pastoral landscape. For a long time the designation of these landscapes as natural was unproblematic, and there has been a long history of the celebration of such spaces by city-dwelling poets and intellectuals to whom they were indeed other. Farms have been taken to be more natural than cities, yet they are every bit as much a cultural achievement. Although explicit pastoralism is no longer in intellectual fashion, farms are still often taken to be natural, a fact that may stem from the misperception that farms do not much alter the environment. However, agriculture is perhaps the single most important way in which humans have affected their environment, and the changes it entailed made possible towns, cities, superhighways, and nuclear power. Ecologists have recognized the massive and potentially disastrous effects that contemporary factory farming has had on the land, and environmentalists have not located nature on the farm. However, it is likely that the agricultural landscape continues to be perceived by many people to be more natural because it is defined by the presence of many other living things, that is, nonhumans. Cities, by contrast, are imagined as lacking such nonhuman life.

If you have been following my argument so far, you understand that I am not denigrating agriculture or wilderness preserves by emphasizing their cultural status, just as I do not mean to endorse, say, building houses on the steep slopes of Los Angeles's canyons when I describe cities as natural. Nor is my object in deconstructing the nature/culture binary to do away with those terms, as if one could ever achieve that. Rather, by showing the dependence of the terms upon one another, I want to suggest that a successful ecology must take account of their inseparability.

It is not just environmentalists who have persistently misunderstood the complexities of the interdependence of nature and culture. As I have suggested above, one of the most salient facts about the human niche as it has evolved since the era when hunting and gathering were dominant is the importance of domesticated plants and animals. Until the advent of factory farming, environmentalists tended to see this activity as unproblematic. However, as Vicki Hearne points out, "People who claim to speak for animal rights and/or animal liberation are increasingly devoted to the idea that the very keeping of a dog or a horse or a gerbil or a lion is in and of itself an offense" (213). While such people tend to be more exercised about the keeping of wild animals, they often depict domestic animals as oppressed, especially if, like dolphins, they have only recently come to be domesticated.[4] There are many recent instances of "animal liberation" that demonstrate that such reasoning very often causes great harm to animals because most captive animals cannot survive in the wild.[5] However, in my view, such reasoning also reflects a misunderstanding of the place of *Homo sapiens* in the Earth's ecosystem because it assumes that it is possible for humans and animals to live independently from each other. This assumption seems to be yet another version of the thinking that has insisted on asserting an absolute difference between humans and other animals, in that it also claims a moral superiority for animal-independent humans. It is my argument that the interdependence of humans and other species defines human ecology. Thus, relations of humans and animals should be understood as a central instance of the inseparability of nature and culture.

While those outside of the respective movements may tend to lump together those who want to preserve the wilderness and those who want to free Willy, insiders have recognized considerable tension between the positions the two represent.[6] In fact, there are three positions in the debate because animal-welfare advocates are divided into liberationist and rights camps. Although the two animal-welfare positions have significant theoretical differences, they share many practical goals. The liberationist position is radically anti-interventionist and is rooted in the utilitarian doctrine of reducing suffering as much as possible for the greatest number of beings. Liberationists need not assert that animals have rights. Their view differs from that of rights advocates in that the latter hold that rights pertain to individuals. The environmentalist critique of both positions has focused on their failure to attend to ecosystems. J. Baird Callicott suggests that both positions imply "the ecological nightmare of a policy of predator extermination" and he notes that liberationists have actually gone so far as to question whether carnivorous animals should be eliminated to alleviate the suffering of herbivores ("Back Together" 260–61, fn. 15). For their part, animal-rights advocates have accused environmentalists of neglecting individuals; leading spokesperson Tom Regan has described Aldo Leopold's land ethic as "environmental fascism" (361–62).

This is not the place to offer a full-scale critique of animal rights/liberation theory. My concerns are rather to suggest why the liberationist position, which would ultimately mean "freeing" domestic animals and pets, actually works against the interests and welfare of those animals and to suggest that sympathy for animals can in fact serve as the basis for environmental awareness—that interaction with pets and other animals should be properly understood as an aspect of urban ecology.

Each of the three positions I have mentioned fails in some way to capture the complexities of human-animal relations. Being the least adequate, liberationism fails to recognize the interdependence of humans and other animals. Environmentalism, which takes "natural" or nonhuman biota as its norm, also has trouble depicting this relationship robustly, although it is represented in a highly mediated form. Animal-rights advocates do assume the interdependence of humans and other animals and offer a program to regulate that interdependence. However, the animal-rights position typically ignores ecological concerns entirely and it can only deal with the relations of predator and prey judgmentally. Thus the "natural" or nonhuman gets left out of animal-rights theory, which projects the human world on to animals.

What we need is a theory that recognizes both the value and reality of the otherness of the nonhuman, while at the same time acknowledging that that otherness is not absolute and that any value we find in otherness will nevertheless be value *to humans*. A good place to start thinking about how to construct such a theory is the work of Mary Midgley. Her discussion of "speciesism" effectively demonstrates the mistake of extending the notion of racism to cover species: "Race in humans is not a significant grouping at all, but species in animals certainly is. It is never true that, in order to know how to treat a human being, you must first find out what race he belongs to. (Cases where this might seem to matter always really turn on culture.) But with an animal, to know the species is absolutely essential" (98).

However, in rejecting the notion of speciesism, Midgley does not mean to return to a position in which the differences between humans and other animals are the basis for an "absolute dismissal" of our interest in the welfare, happiness, and moral standing of other species. Rather, her position leads to the recognition of the reality and value of species loyalty, but also to the recognition of interspecific bonds. One could illustrate Midgley's account of an individual human's relation to other beings in a Venn diagram. One circle, which defines the human species, would represent the species loyalty that makes other humans more important than animals in general. As Midgley suggests, such a preference is not an irrational "prejudice," but a natural preference. Other circles, however, would represent the fact that we do not show the same level of concern about all humans. The individual is understood as rightly more concerned with his or her own family and community—but also with his or her pets and other domestic animals—than with those beings that are less directly related to the individual. In other words, here some animals are likely to be of greater concern to an individual than most people.

However, Midgley recognizes that our relations with the animals we own are not simply a matter of property interests. We do not merely own these animals, we bond with them just as we form bonds with family members and other humans. Animals matter because they are part of what Midgley calls "the mixed community": "All human communities have involved animals. Those present in them always include, for a start, some dogs, with whom our association seems to be an incredibly ancient one, amounting to symbiosis. But besides them an enormous variety of other creatures, ranging from reindeer to weasels and from elephants to shags, has for ages also been domesticated" (112). Midgley notes that most of these animals were exploited for meat, milk, wool, hides, or their ability to control vermin, but she also notes the paradox that "exploitation requires sympathy" (113). She observes that a farmer would not beat an ox unless he assumed it could feel and that we routinely address horses and dogs by name and expect them to understand what we say to them. She concludes that such examples show "a direct capacity in man for attending to, and to some extent understanding, the moods and reactions of other species" (114). Midgley concludes that sympathy for animals is a normal consequence of the mixed community in which humans are raised.

Midgley's explanation suggests that such sympathy will most often be felt for animals that are part of the community. Thus, it is not readily apparent that such sympathy extends to wild animals. I want to argue that sympathy for one's pet is likely to extend to wild beasts as well and from them to the environment that supports them. Lawrence Buell argues that "Human denizens of the modernized world are most likely to move toward ecocentric ways of thinking when the sympathetic bond is activated" (386). John Fisher observes that "Sympathy for animals clearly plays an important role in generating concern for the environment" (236). This is an important insight, but one that cuts against the conception of nature as other. Although hard-core environmentalists may feel a deep concern for wilderness itself, even Thoreau found it alienating when he actually encountered it in Maine. The "poster children" for the environment are most often birds and large mammals. It is easier to mobilize folks to save spotted owls and wolves than to save less appealing species or merely a tract of "empty" land. Leopold's land ethic expresses concern for ecosystems, not individuals or even particular species: "A thing is right when it tends to preserve the integrity, stability, and beauty of the biotic community. It is wrong when it tends otherwise" (225). However, in "Thinking Like a Mountain," Leopold describes the dawning of his ecological consciousness as an experience of sympathy not with the mountain, but with an animal:

> In those days we had never heard of passing up a chance to kill a wolf. In a second we were pumping lead into the pack. . . . When our rifles were empty the old wolf was down, and a pup was dragging a leg into impassable slide rocks.
>
> We reached the old wolf in time to watch a fierce green fire dying in her eyes. I realized then, and have known ever since, that there was something new to me in those eyes—something known only to her and to the mountain. I was young then, and full of trigger-itch. I thought

that because fewer wolves meant more deer, that no wolves would mean a hunter's paradise. But after seeing the green fire die, I sensed that neither the wolf nor the mountain agreed with such a view. (130)

Leopold uses the trope of personification here to render a biota, itself represented by the metonymy of the mountain, more sympathetic to the reader than it otherwise would be. Later he continues the trope: "I now suspect that just as a deer herd lives in mortal fear of its wolves, so does a mountain live in mortal fear of its deer" (132). Mountains, we presume, do not really think or feel, but, aside from behaviorists, most of us normally grant wolves and deer these abilities. It is that common assumption that explains the rhetorical power of "Thinking Like a Mountain." Notice that it is not all wolves that Leopold depicts sympathetically. The passage turns on the creation of an individual "old wolf" with whom the narrator bonds and whose death affects him and us because she has become a subject. Although the founders of the American environmentalist tradition rarely make sympathy for animals a significant element of their rhetoric, we do find it in some other texts that Buell rightly regards as a part of the environmental literary tradition. Faulkner's "The Bear," for example, depicts the loss of the Mississippi wilderness most centrally in the form of the bear, Old Ben, and Lion, the dog that finally enabled the hunters to kill the bear. Environmentalist writers who do not rely on our bonds with animals render the environment sympathetic by inviting our identification with a narrator whose feelings and thoughts we are asked to share. We may rationally agree about the value of a landscape or biota, but these remain abstractions unless they can be shown to affect a thinking, feeling subject.

Just as the old wolf mediated Leopold's identification with the mountain, companion animals, especially cats and dogs, represent a means by which urban dwellers can come to have sympathy with the larger nonhuman environment with which they otherwise have quite limited direct contact. It is beyond the scope of this essay to try to determine how often pets do in fact function in this way, but it is obvious that they do not always do so. Dogs kept for hunting and cats to control vermin have not traditionally produced sympathy for other species, much less the landscape itself. While not wishing to deny that significant bonds did often develop between a hunter and his dog, I want to suggest that animals kept purely for companionship are a more likely starting point for the production of a more general sympathy with the nonhuman. As long as the animal is kept for utilitarian motives, the animal is liable to be taken primarily as an object, just as human employees are often treated as objects. Exploitation may require sympathy, but it also limits it.

Pets are of ecological interest for more than their potential for moral education. A very large percentage of American households include pets, yet they remain oddly invisible to accounts of both society and ecology. In fact, pets seem to be something of a cultural embarrassment, like masturbation, perhaps—a habit that is common, but best not acknowledged, much less investigated:

> [The] view of pet-keeping as a 'gratuitous perversion' of natural behavior has been reiterated time and again throughout history and, nowadays, is most often expressed either by means of caricatures of postmenopausal women and poodles or by a general tendency to regard people's relationships with their animal companions absurd, sentimental and somewhat pathetic. As psychiatrist Aaron Katcher points out 'we are taught to despise the sentimental, to think of it as banal or as a cover for darker hidden emotions.' (Serpell 20)

Hearne notes that various psychologists deny that the death of a pet is a big deal. Indeed, the same Katcher quoted above believes that when an animal dies there are no regrets, no rehearsal of the wail "If only I had . . . ," because when we mourn animals "we are only mourning a personal loss and not 'the loss of life and potential' " (Hearne 95). One could easily argue almost the opposite claim, that we mourn the loss of a pet more unambiguously than we do the loss of a human companion because we always experience ambivalence about other humans. Because we grant animals innocence in their motives if not in their behavior, we rarely carry grudges against them. We imagine their affection for us to be unambivalent and lacking in ulterior motives in a way that we do not with regard to people. The loss that many feel when a pet dies is all the more painful because of the general refusal of society to accept the legitimacy of such mourning. The frequency of such feelings is a testament to the depth of the bond that many owners feel for their pets.

Of course not all pet owners feel so deeply for their animals. Yi-Fu Tuan claims that "approximately 15 percent of the total estimated dog population is destroyed yearly in dog compounds and animal shelters" and that "a majority of Americans keep their dogs only two years or less" (88). If we as a culture do not usually feel ambivalent about individual pets, we are of two minds about them as a class. A sizable minority of Americans probably continue to believe, as their farming ancestors typically did, that animals do not belong in the house. Even those who have given up this view or have not held it may feel its pull in the face of the damage, dirt, or inconvenience that pets often cause. If it is a choice between nice furniture or the cat, the furniture may win. The real difficulties of pet-keeping are not understood by many who undertake the enterprise, so it is not surprising that such relationships often do not work out. Although the idea that pets are child substitutes has become a familiar joke of late, the parallel should be taken more seriously. A puppy may not need as much attention as a human child, but if it is abused or neglected it will become an equally unsuccessful member of its family and mixed community.

This leads to the issue of the necessary inequality in human-animal relationships. Liberationists, who take human slavery as their paradigm, regard this inequality as a similar evil that must be ended. Cavalieri and Singer, for example, have urged that we must treat the great apes as if they were human. As Soper argues, however, plans to "extend the 'community of equals' to include the great apes are certainly well intentioned, but the bonds they seek to cement are arguably too little respectful of the quality of ape life and the ways in which it must be allowed to differ from our own" (172). Liberationists and animal-rights activists have attacked animal training on similar grounds. Trainers are assumed to abuse the animals they train, probably because what the animals do is perceived to be so unnatural. However, when Bobby Berosini, a Las Vegas animal trainer and showman, was forced to defend his treatment of his orangutans in court, he was exonerated; one of the jurors said that she felt that it would be "abuse" to take the animals away from him (Hearne 190). Berosini's act itself calls into question the idea that training is an expression of pure domination. Its theme is "how I train them," and the running joke is that the orangutans actually train the trainer. According to Berosini, the joke works because the animals are comedians; that is, they understand that they are playing and playing to an audience. Some of their responses, such as a "wonderfully timed grin," could not be coerced, and, in fact, could not be taught unless the grin already had an interspecific meaning or unless the orangutans were capable of manipulating that meaning (Hearne 186–87).

Most pets are not trained animals in the sense in which Berosini's orangutans are. With certain exceptions, such as guide dogs, we do not normally ask a companion animal to work, but merely to keep us company. Yet the relationship between pet owner and animal involves the same processes of communication. The behaviorist position would limit these processes to one direction, from human to animal, the latter being capable only of responding to the owner's stimulus. However, if this were the case, why would people not be happy with machines as "pets"? We talk to our pets because they "talk" back, although not in a human language and often not vocally. What they say is often not what we expect. It is the unreliability of the stimulus-response system that makes pets interesting. Their needs and desires, their stimulation of us, make them companions and not mere wards.

Behaviorism is a dogma of epistemological convenience. Its postulates are those needed to allow us to have certainty about animal psychology and other minds in general. Because we do not have direct access to those minds, we cannot know them as we can the physical world. Behaviorism solves this problem essentially by denying that other minds exist. It is a counter-intuitive denial and one for which there is no convincing evidence. On the contrary, most of what we know about mammals suggests that their minds should be more like ours than not. Why not start with that assumption, rather than the assumption of absolute or fundamental difference? The only explanation for the tenacity of the latter assumption is a dogma much older than behaviorism, that humans are essentially and radically distinct, by virtue of either religion or reason, from other living beings.

The most-cited current dividing line between "brute" animals and "rational" humans is, of course, language. We do know that animals do not use language in the same way as we do. This fact is sometimes the grounds for denying animals consciousness—or thought—or of rendering their minds entirely incommensurable to ours. The first point that needs to be made here is that human consciousness consists of much that is not language; presumably, mammals with similar brains might share these aspects of consciousness even if they do not speak. The notion of animals' incommensurability with humans is perhaps most famously stated by Wittgenstein, who said in *Philosophical Investigations* that if a lion could talk, we would not be able to understand him. Like most philosophers, Wittgenstein really was not interested in lions or other animals. His lion is a metonymy for all of those beings whose world is incommensurable with our human one.

Donald Davidson has contributed what has become the current defining text on the issue of incommensurability, "On the Very Idea of a Conceptual Scheme." Davidson argues against the existence of incommensurable schemes or untranslatable languages—they amount to the same thing, he tells us—on the grounds that if such things existed they would be unrecognizable: "Nothing, it may be said, could count as evidence that some form of activity could not be interpreted in our language that was not at the same time evidence that that form of activity was not speech behavior" (185). Languages are translatable, Davidson believes, because the world that humans share is largely the same and because humans have substantially the same beliefs about it:

> [I]f all we know is what sentences a speaker holds to be true, and we cannot assume that his language is our own, then we cannot take even a first step toward interpretation without knowing or assuming a great deal about the speaker's beliefs. . . . The method is not designed to eliminate disagreement, nor can it; its purpose is to make meaningful disagreement possible, and this depends entirely on a foundation— some foundation—in agreement. . . . Charity is forced on us; whether we like it or not, if we want to understand others, we must count them right in most matters. (196–97)

Davidson would have to argue that if a lion could talk, we would understand him, because to recognize his talk as such would make it translatable. But, like most philosophers, Davidson thinks that because lions, dogs, and other animals are not capable of "speech behavior," they are therefore incapable of "thought," that is, things like beliefs, intentions, desires, and attitudes ("Thought and Talk," "Rational Animals").[7] On these grounds, Davidson objects to characterizing a dog who, after chasing a cat into the woods, barks up a particular tree as "believing the cat is in that tree." The scenario of a dog chasing a cat into some woods is likely for a pet owner to yield any number of what seem like perfectly sensible attributions of beliefs, desires, and attitudes: The dog intends to kill the cat; the dog just wants to play with the cat; the dog desires to eat the cat; and so on. Once having established that dog's interest in the cat, it is reasonable to assume that its barking is predicated on the assumption that the cat is in the tree. Davidson's problem with all of these attributions is not primarily that the dog has not explicitly stated his "thoughts." Presumably, Davidson would allow us to attribute to a human who had been chasing a cat and now standing and calling at the bottom of a tree the belief that the cat was in the tree even if the person had not told us so. That is because the human could utter the sentence "the cat is in tree" and thus could have that belief. Davidson makes all kinds of mental states dependent on the power of language to represent the world in propositional form.

However, what if animal consciousness represented the world in other ways? The fact is that no one knows how or if animals other than humans represent things. Until someone invents a way to make *Star Trek*'s Vulcan mind meld a reality, we will never know. Prior to such time, any hypothesis will be a mere guess. Philosophers like Davidson base their guess on the single, but very striking, fact that animals do not speak. However, there is other evidence that animal minds make representations. Anyone who has been around sleeping dogs or cats know that they often behave as if they were dreaming. A dream is clearly a mental representation. Animals have been shown by numerous sorts of experiments to have memory, and memories are also forms of mental representation. Yet these representations, unlike language, are not shared or public. In recent years, however, some researchers have begun to suggest that animals have culture. Elizabeth Marshall Thomas argues that the lions she studied in southern Africa around 1950 demonstrated a respect for humans who, at the time, lived in relatively close proximity. Later, these humans, the Bushmen, were forced out of the area. In 1986, when Thomas returned to the region, she found that the lions no longer showed the same deference. She concludes that the lions' behavior was a tradition that lions learned from each other (*Tribe* 109–86). If animals do have culture, however minimal or primitive, they must be able to represent to each other what is passed on from generation to generation, representations that can be lost the way hard-wired instincts could not.

Dogs and cats do not speak in the abstractions that would allow them to be taken seriously by philosophers. This poses a problem for animal-rights advocates and liberationists because, as Soper puts it, "No one stressing what is common between humans and other species devotes much attention to persuading those other species of the truth of their claims. Nor can anyone calling upon us to appreciate our affinities with other animals really deny that they are calling upon us to perform an act of cognition of which other beings are incapable—and which therefore renders them different from us" (40).[8] However, just because animals do not behave like philosophers (or practitioners of cultural studies) does not mean that they do not "talk" to us. According to Hearne, trainer "Hubert Wells's lions are not anything like so reticent as Wittgenstein's. Their otherness is not so absolutely unalterable. They have personalities, temperaments, moods, and they can be voluble about all this, sometimes chatty, sometimes (when they are working) radiating a more focused informativeness" (172–73). Trainers—especially of large, dangerous animals like big cats or elephants—come to understand their animals' attitudes, desires, and intentions even if they are never reported in propositional form. A misunderstanding could be fatal. Pet owners also, if they are at all attentive, know when their animals are happy, frightened, in pain, focused, bored, or playful.

Hearne, an animal trainer herself, puts the problem as a paradox: "There are enormous problems in attributing language to animals, of course, even greater than the problems involved in talking to them" (174). In my view, the paradox is explained by what I would call the partial incommensurability of human and animal worlds. Companion, domestic, and captive animals all share with humans not only a physical space, but a semiotic one as well. Within those spaces, there is commensurability, meanings that humans and animals both understand well enough for there to be companionship or a horse race or a circus act. However, there are also aspects of each other's worlds that we do not understand. I presume that my abyssinian, Mrs. Rutledge, who sees me to the door when I go out and greets me there when I return, does not understand where I go or what possible reason I could have for going. However, if it is obvious that humans know a great deal that animals apparently do not, it is also the case that animals know much that we do not. We have good evidence that dogs can hear sounds that human ears cannot and can discriminate among scents in ways that humans are unable. In a fictional work, *Certain Poor Shepherds,* Elizabeth Marshall Thomas invents a dog consciousness in which the world is elaborately represented by scents. This seems plausible, but the story is in human language. Surely scents mean things to dogs they cannot mean to us. These meanings are not translatable into our language because they are represented in a system of differences that we cannot perceive. We can imagine how a dog might represent the world, but we cannot represent it that way ourselves.

Pets are animals that we are socially licensed to anthropomorphize. We project our world on to them, but only if we are myopic do we not realize that they do not reflect it back to us like a mirror. Anthropomorphism is a trope or a model, a way of representing something we cannot represent more directly. Moreover, it is obvious that anthropomorphism only becomes total in the case of those few individuals who literally see their pets as humans—individuals we would probably take to be mentally impaired. We value our dogs for their dogness and cats for their catness and not just for their "humanity." Recognizing this allows us to see that to keep a pet really is to keep nature, defined as what is the other of humanity, in the apartment. To have a relationship with a pet is to encounter radical difference and to discover that it is not utterly different. This seems to me to be the lesson that should be learned from what one could call "other talk." Human others, despite their very real cultural differences, are never radically other in the way animals are. All human languages can be translated. However, even those beings with whom we can talk only in very limited ways are still not utterly alien. I conclude from this that pets—if treated with love, respect, and attention—can teach tolerance for human and natural difference. They can help city dwellers to understand the value of beings and ecosystems with which they can have no direct contact.

This is not to say that pets can teach everything that needs to be known about nature. Anthropomorphism about pets could mislead us about the character of the nonhuman by making us think that it is in fact human after all. Was it the pet paradigm that led visitors to Yellowstone National Park to feed the bears? This practice continued until wildlife specialists figured out that once in the habit of receiving such handouts, bears would expect them and become dangerous to humans and thus to themselves. Clearly feeding bears suggests a certain level of sympathy for the creatures, but it is also another instance of human manipulation of the environment. Yellowstone still must warn visitors not to feed bears, not to pet the buffalo, etcetera, though it does seem that many more people today do understand that wildlife needs autonomy if it is to remain wild. This is a lesson that must be taught more formally because it goes against the assumptions that humans normally have about their place in the world. Our physical supremacy and presumption of rationality lead us to believe that we ought to control nature.

One could argue that this is an expression of a desire for domination that Tuan sees as at the heart of pet-keeping itself. He denies that sympathy is an important element in human-animal relationships, and, like the liberationists, treats them as an instance of master and slave. James Serpell has provided an effective rebuttal to this claim. Some humans undoubtedly do enjoy such domination, he acknowledges,

> But it is still inaccurate to argue that the thrill of dominating others is necessarily the most important thing that humans, rich or poor, derive from pet ownership. True, pets are dependent on their owners for care and protection and this creates a fundamental inequality in the relationship. But inequality does not always entail domination. Children, after all, are dependent on their parents, but the rewards of parenthood are surely more to do with the responsibility of caring for and nurturing another individual than with domination. (41)

Buell, correctly I think, describes an important body of American nature writing as defined by an "aesthetics of relinquishment." This fits nicely with the program that identifies nature with the wilderness and animal welfare with severing human and animal relationships. However, we should remember that Faulkner's Ike McCaslin relinquishes not merely his gun and compass in the successful effort to encounter Old Ben, but the land itself which is, as a result, not preserved. Humans can stop eating other animals (which would not be in the least "unnatural"), thus giving up their literal place in the food chain, but it is hard to imagine a future in which our technology does not dominate all other beings. Given that reality, relinquishment is never a real possibility. If we want to save nature, we will have to continue to intervene in it for that purpose because intervention for other purposes will also continue. Of course, humans need to understand that our domination of nature is limited and will be temporary. We now know that nature is not the regular, orderly system for which Leopold's biota might be a synecdoche. New work in geology and paleontology suggests that natural history is a history of catastrophes (Davis). Humans will ultimately not be able to control all of these events, but it seems obvious that we will and should try to protect ourselves. However powerful the aesthetic of relinquishment might seem, it is unlikely to lead humans to give up trying to survive.

The point of this seeming digression is that any environmentalism with a chance to succeed will have to make its case in terms of human good. We value others—whether they be people, animals, or biota—for, among other things, their otherness. However, value can only be humanly defined and accounted. Although rooted in our physical being, what we value is not inherited but learned. We can teach people to value "nature," but only if we can show it to be a real value to them.

I have been arguing that people who keep pets do value their otherness and can on that basis learn to value the similar otherness in wild animals and ecosystems, in part because all of these are only partially other, only partially incommensurable. However, I also want to insist that keeping pets in urban households is a way of bringing "nature" into the city. Pets are of interest ecologically not just for what they might encourage people to feel or believe about distant ecosystems, but because they represent the continuation of the historically existing mixed community. This community has been not the whole of *Homo sapiens'* ecosystem, but a very important aspect of it nonetheless. Modern cities have increasingly excluded plants and other animals, and urban dwellers have thus been deprived of relationships that earlier human societies fostered and valued. In the past several decades, strong evidence has been presented that relationships with pets help keep people healthy and can be therapeutic for those suffering from emotional disorders (Robinson). Simply bringing dogs regularly to nursing homes has been shown to help some patients, while those in mental hospitals and prisons have also benefited from regular contact with animals. Pet-owning heart attack victims have been shown to have better survival rates than those without pets (Serpell 74–99).

Serpell argues persuasively that it is the friendship that pets and their owners often share that makes pet-keeping therapeutic. Clearly, loneliness is a major problem in institutions such as nursing homes and mental hospitals, but it is more generally a problem in postindustrial societies. As we increasingly spend our time "relating" to televisions and computers, we find less time for personal relationships, especially face-to-face relations with friends. I think it is obvious that the increasing popularity of pets is a response to this condition. Of course, it is sometimes suggested that animal lovers must care less about other people. Although there is no good reason to believe this, substituting animal for human relationships cannot be a positive trade-off. However, even if pet ownership is in some sense a symptom of social disintegration, it may also be part of the solution. There is anecdotal evidence to suggest that in the city dogs are sometimes kept because they seem to promote interaction with other humans. More important, however, is the consideration that pets—along with trees, shrubs, flower and vegetable gardens, robins, pigeons, falcons, and other wild creatures that share our urban spaces—ought to be understood as elements of a healthy human society. Some of these beings could be understood as part of a context or background environment that can nurture healthy social relations. However, if humans have typically lived in a mixed community with animals, then our definition of "society" should be expanded to reflect the fact that not all of the subjects to whom we relate are human.

The phenomenon of pet-keeping and its therapeutic value are powerful arguments against the antisocial atomism of current right-wing ideology. That humans keep pets is evidence of the very strong sense in which we are social animals. Unfortunately, a great deal of American nature writing contributes to right-wing ideology by making society itself the evil other of nature. Instead of the nature experienced by Thoreau in his cabin or Muir wandering in the Sierra Nevada, we need an ecological perspective that begins with the assumption that human communities are as natural as those of wolves. Environmentalists ought to be as concerned with designing cities that support human society as they are with preserving other ecosystems. Of course, in this era of that all-powerful idol, the market, it is hard to imagine cities actually being designed, much less designed for the good of the many. However, if we take seriously the value of human-animal relations, there are more modest things that can be done. Most leases for apartments and houses routinely prohibit pets. In the past few years, public housing authorities in Pittsburgh and New York City have decided to prohibit residents from keeping pets. That pet prohibitions in private housing are equally routinely flouted suggests that such regulations fail even to serve the purposes for which they were designed. Also, given the social problems of public housing, one might well argue that residents of such spaces ought to be *encouraged* to keep pets. The failure of public housing is blamed by the Right on the lack of a property interest of the residents in their dwellings. However, a much better case can be made that such projects failed because their spaces encouraged social division and that they did so in part by failing to provide for the existence of any beings besides human ones. "The environment" has become an important abstraction in the effort to make humans realize that they depend on what is not human. However, we need to remember that we all live in particular environments that are equally important to our health and well-being.

NOTES

1. See Nash for an analysis of this tradition.

2. Soper's otherwise excellent discussion fails to recognize the degree to which the environmental conception of nature depends on what she treats as an opposing conception of nature, one that mediates "access to the 'reality' it names" (3).

3. The more recent campaign to preserve tropical rain forests is an important counter-example. However, it differs from earlier movements for wilderness preservation precisely in its focus on consequences for the general health and well-being of humanity.

4. There is some question about whether dolphins may be called domestic animals, but "liberating" even species that typically live in the wild is often a death sentence because captive creatures may not have the requisite survival skills.

5. This is not to deny that some animals (e.g., orcas) should not be kept in captivity.

6. For a useful representation of this debate from an environmentalist perspective, see Hargrove. Callicott's "Animal Liberation: A Triangular Affair" sets out the differences among the three positions most starkly.

7. Although Davidson is not a behaviorist in the traditional sense, his position on animal thought also seems to stem from an epistemological dogma: "Unless there is behavior that can be interpreted as speech, the evidence will not be adequate to justify the fine distinctions we are used to making in the attribution of thoughts. If we persist in attributing desires, beliefs or other attitudes under these conditions, our attributions and consequent explanations of actions will be seriously underdetermined in that many alternative systems of attribution, many alternative explanations, will be equally justified by the available dat[a]" ("Thought" 164). Davidson claims that "On the moral issue of how we should treat dumb creatures, I see no

reason to be less kind to those without thoughts or language than to those with; on the contrary" ("Rational" 474, fn. 1). However, see Masson and McCarthy for evidence that denying an emotional life (i.e., desires, attitudes, etc.) to animals has allowed for all manner of cruelty in their treatment.

8. Because animals cannot state such propositions, it is hard to imagine that they can think them either. I can imagine that my cat desires to go outside, but cannot imagine that she desires freedom, because freedom is a moral and ethical abstraction. While behaviorism has allowed cruelty by denying consciousness to animals, liberationists perpetrate cruelty by granting to animals thoughts they give no evidence of having.

WORKS CITED

Buell, Lawrence. *The Environmental Imagination: Thoreau, Nature Writing, and the Formation of American Culture.* Cambridge, Mass.: Harvard UP, 1995.

Callicott, J. Baird. "Animal Liberation and Environmental Ethics: Back Together Again." Hargrove. 249–61.

———. "Animal Liberation: A Triangular Affair." Hargrove. 37–69.

Cavalieri, Paola, and Peter Singer, eds. *The Great Ape Project: Equality Beyond Humanity.* New York: St. Martin's Press, 1993.

Davidson, Donald. "On the Very Idea of a Conceptual Scheme." *Inquiries into Truth and Interpretation.* Oxford: Oxford UP, 1984. 183–98.

———. "Rational Animals." *Actions and Events: Perspectives on the Philosophy of Donald Davidson.* Eds. Ernest LePore and Brian P. McLaughlin. Oxford: Basil Blackwell, 1985. 473–80.

———. "Thought and Talk." *Inquiries into Truth and Interpretation.* Oxford: Oxford UP, 1984. 156–70.

Davis, Mike. "Cosmic Dancers on History's Stage: The Permanent Revolution in the Earth Sciences." *New Left Review* 215 (January–February 1996): 48–84.

Faulkner, William. "The Bear." *Go Down, Moses.* New York: Random House, 1942. 191–331.

Fisher, John. "Taking Sympathy Seriously: A Defense of Our Moral Psychology Toward Animals." Hargrove. 227–48.

Hargrove, Eugene C., ed. *The Animal Rights / Environmental Ethics Debate: The Environmental Perspective.* Albany: State U of New York P, 1992.

Hearne, Vicki. *Animal Happiness.* New York: HarperCollins, 1994.

Leopold, Aldo. *A Sand County Almanac.* New York: Oxford UP, 1987.

Masson, Jeffrey Moussaieff, and Susan McCarthy. *When Elephants Weep: The Emotional Lives of Animals.* New York: Delacorte, 1995.

Midgley, Mary. *Animals and Why They Matter.* Athens: U of Georgia P, 1983.

Nash, Roderick. *Wilderness and the American Mind.* Rev. ed. New Haven, Conn.: Yale UP, 1973.

Regan, Tom. *The Case for Animal Rights.* Berkeley: U of California P, 1983.

Robinson, I., ed. *The Waltham Book of Human-Animal Interaction: Benefits of Pet Ownership.* New York: Pergamon, 1995.

Serpell, James. *In the Company of Animals: A Study of Human-Animal Relationships.* London: Blackwell, 1986.

Soper, Kate. *What is Nature? Culture, Politics, and the Non-Human.* London: Blackwell, 1995.

Thomas, Elizabeth Marshall. *Certain Poor Shepherds: A Christmas Tale.* New York: Simon, 1996.

——. *The Tribe of the Tiger: Cats and Their Culture.* New York: Simon, 1994.

Thoreau, Henry David. "Walking." 1862. *The Portable Thoreau.* Ed. Carl Bode. New York: Penguin, 1983. 592–630.

Tuan, Yi-Fu. *Dominance and Affection: The Making of Pets.* New Haven, Conn.: Yale UP, 1984.

Wittgenstein, Ludwig. *Philosophical Investigations.* Trans. G. E. M. Anscomb. New York: Macmillan, 1953.

15

COSMOLOGY IN THE CASINO
Simulacra of Nature in the Interiorized Wilderness
Michael P. Branch

A place is above all a territory of meanings.
Edward Relph ("Modernity" 36)

PLACE STUDIES AND INTERIORIZED WILDERNESS

The Silver Legacy Resort Casino in Nevada, which was completed in 1995, is the newest and largest spectacle in Reno's downtown casino district. The central architectural feature of the $350 million project is the world's largest composite dome: a 180-foot-diameter, white fiberglass shell that rises up from the narrow streets like an immense igloo (fig. 15.1). Within the dome, which shelters a large part of the casino's expansive gaming floors, is a gigantic, arcing, artificial sky formed of a 75,000-square-foot painted mural depicting textured clouds floating listlessly in the cerulean vault of the heavens. Through the use of sophisticated technology including custom lighting, sound, and special effects, the sky is rendered with dynamic qualities that make it appear to change from first daybreak to rosy dawn to bright day to dramatic sunset to starry night. In addition, the movement of this artificial "day" is radically accelerated, such that a twenty-four-hour Earth day is made to pass in a mere two hours' time. Thus, to use a Disney term, the "illusioneered" sky represents an effective manipulation of both space (the creation of an artificial, interiorized sky) and time (the controlled recalibration of the celestial round otherwise known as a "day").

One's first experience of this domed immensity is overwhelming—

Figure 15.1. Exterior of the Silver Legacy Resort Casino, 1996. Photograph by the author.

perceptually intense, somehow exciting, and not a little bizarre. When entering this unusual urban space—which the casino public-relations people justly describe as a "unique environment" ("World's" 1)—one immediately marvels at the notion of a multimillion-dollar faux indoor sky constructed at the foot of the eastern slope of the northern Sierra Nevada, where the day and night skies towering above the high-elevation Great Basin desert are unusually clear and beautiful. This phenomenon leads me to ask several questions about the casino's artificial sky. What are the precedents for interiorized heavens in other architectural spaces? What purposes are served by this artificial sky? What might the "text" of this unusual artifact "mean," that is, what values does it express and what attitudes might it engender? Because this important third question ultimately subsumes the previous questions, we might simply restate the entire inquiry as, "What cultural work does this place do?"

A Brief History of Interiorized Heavens

In my search for precedents to the interiorized sky of the Silver Legacy, I thought immediately of the ambitious use of domes in the architecture and painting of the Italian Renaissance. However, the controlled use of vertical elements in monumental architecture appeared long before Bramante designed the vault of St. Peter's Cathedral in Rome. Sumerian and Neo-Babylonian cities made extensive use of ziggurats, towers, obelisks, minarets, spires, and other pointed architectural elements to invoke the *axis mundi*—the vital connection between the Earth and heaven—and to suggest the transcendent relationship between the earthly edifice and the celestial sphere. The dome, which is an architecturally sophisticated representation of the *axis mundi,* transformed the two-dimensional spire-form into a three-dimensional symbolization of heaven. Because domes both rise skyward and simultaneously resemble the vault of the sky itself, they induce what Edward S. Casey calls "a double action of enclosure and transcendence" (135).

The association of domed architectural spaces with the dome of the heavens is ancient and widespread. Egyptian tombs and Babylonian palaces featured blue ceilings with ornamental stars, and Greek and Roman temples were frequently adorned with star-studded coffers. In Asian architectural traditions, the dome of the tent was understood to represent the cosmic house. Likewise, Achaemenid Persian kings held sacred festivals in a divine tent, and pre-Islamic Arabs believed that domelike, leather structures enclosed sacred space. Of course, the dome has been of essential symbolic importance in Christian architectural traditions.[1]

The designers of Renaissance cities tended to secularize the Christian iconography of the dome while perfecting the illusionistic techniques that would allow ceiling paintings to enhance, amplify, or simulate the celestial qualities of architectural domes. Andrea Mantegna's ceiling fresco in the *Camera degli sposi* ("Room of the Newlyweds") in the Ducal Palace at Mantua (fig. 15.2) is an example of how the ancient tradition of dome construction and painting prefigures the interiorized heavens of postmodern urban spaces such as the Silver Legacy Resort Casino.[2] Executed in 1474 for the Gonzaga family of Mantua, the *Camera degli sposi* is the first consistent illusionistic decoration of an entire room. Mantegna's master achievement here is the first *di sotto in sú* perspective of a ceiling—the trompe l'oeil *oculus,* a tour de force of illusionism by which the ceiling of the room has been painted away, effectively simulating an apertured dome standing open to the sky. Surrounding the simulated *oculus* is a balustrade occupied by servants of the House of Gonzaga and a retinue of cherubs, all poised to welcome the Marquess and his wife into the newlywed chamber.

Figure 15.2. Andrea Mantegna, ceiling of the Camera degli sposi, *fresco, 1474. Ducal Palace, Mantua, Italy. Illustration from Helen Gardner's* Art through the Ages, *7th ed. Used by permission of Scala / Art Resource, NY.*

Apse mosaics, painted domes, and illusionistic ceiling frescos—as well as representations and simulations of the heavens as they appear in modern and postmodern architectural spaces—have in common three thematic or foundational principles, which I refer to as "nature," "time," and "control." In terms of nature, Mantegna's *Camera* ceiling fresco is rich with such naturalistic details as the vaulted sky, puffy clouds, colorful peacock, tub of citrus, and garlands of leaves and fruits. The scene is refreshing because it brings the eye up and "out," beyond the conventional perspectival limitations of the structure itself, while welcoming the natural world into the architectural space. Time in the painting is represented both by the time of day—the bright, sunny blue of the midday "sky," as well as by the time of ritual celebration and blessing so appropriate to the wedding and honeymoon of a member of the House of Gonzaga. Unlike the *Camera,* comparable works from periods earlier than the fifteenth century feature overtly Christian iconography, with representations of time tending toward the apocalyptic time of revelation, theophany, second coming, final judgment, or eternal salvation. Finally, control is the medium rather than the subject of the painting. Mantegna has successfully accomplished what I would call a technological innovation in the illusioneering of an urban architectural space. Using unprecedented perspectival techniques by which to charm and trick the eye, he has effectively controlled the perceptual experience of the audience for whom the painting is intended. As earlier church domes symbolized heaven and mediated between divine and human realms, the *Camera* ceiling fresco depicts the sky in a way that removes the barrier between domestic and celestial space. However, Mantegna's painting is not only *not the sky,* it is also pointedly *not a dome.* Instead, it is an illusioneered experience of spatial depth masterfully created by a thin layer of paint on the ceiling—a wonderful work of second-order artifice by which an interiorized sky is made to simulate not only the sky but also the architectural dome that would simulate the sky.

A modern manifestation of second-order celestial artifice is the planetarium. The first modern planetariums were built in the early 1920s, but the perfection of optically projected heavens came in the late 1920s and early 1930s, with the development and subsequent improvement of the Zeiss "universal" planetarium projectors. For their time, the Zeiss projectors were sophisticated machines designed not only to simulate the night sky, but to do so according to measurements, magnitudes, and movements that were astronomically accurate to a remarkable degree. Like the precursor globes of the seventeenth century, the modern planetarium required that viewers enter the hollow sphere of the dome, the planetarium itself. Unlike those globes, however, the revolution of the heavens was now accomplished by moving the stars rather than by moving the globe.

By the mid-1930s astronomically precise, Zeiss-equipped planetariums were being built and operated by urban research universities and science museums around the world. By the 1950s the white dome of the planetarium had become a familiar sight on the skyline of many American cities. At the Adler Planetarium and Astronomical Museum in Chicago, for example, urbanites of the 1930s, 1940s, and 1950s flocked to the museum's "Star-Theatre" to see presentations that were part science education and part entertainment.

Like Mantegna's *Camera* ceiling in Mantua, the dome of the Adler Planetarium in Chicago (and those of other planetariums) served as a giant canvas upon which a sophisticated illusionistic representation of the sky could be created. Zeiss technology replaced the artist's brush and the medium of optical projection replaced the paint, but the cultural work done within the two spaces is remarkably similar. Just as the accomplishment of Mantegna's fresco is to "open" the architectural space by effectively simulating the sky beyond it, the domed "Star-Theatre" of the Adler thrilled urbanites by replacing the perspectival limitations of narrow streets and crowded avenues with a simulated view of the limitless space beyond the city. Indeed, the heyday of urban planetariums was approximately coincident with the rise of the substantial air and light pollution that were beginning to obscure the stars in the night skies over large American cities. Chicago might be crowded and oppressive, but the Edenic heavens of the Adler's "Star-Theatre" were not. The actual sky may have become hazy with the effluents of an expanding urban-industrial population, but the simulated cosmos within the planetarium remained perpetually clear and deep.

The themes of nature, time, and control that characterized Mantegna's *Camera* fresco are also important in the planetarium. Obviously, the nature being represented in the planetarium is the wilderness of the stars, a heaven replicated with the scientific accuracy befitting a technological age. Whereas Mantegna used perspective to make the clouds appear real, the planetarium projector uses mathematical calibrations to render the movements of the stars with astronomical precision. Time in the planetarium is astronomical time, the harmonious, orbital, synchronous music of the spheres. Whereas Mantegna represented both the time of day and the celebratory time of marriage, the planetarium show simulates time of day and time of year, while also valorizing a particular time in human history—the "space age" in which our technological inventions allow us to simulate the heavens and, eventually, to explore the stars. Control in the planetarium, as in the *Camera degli sposi,* is control of the viewer's perspective, a control so perceptually seductive that it results in an illusionistic work of science and art that charms and tricks people into *feeling* (although of course not *believ-*

ing) that they are gazing into outer space. Control in the planetarium is control of time, space, and human perception, because in addition to simulating the time of day and year, the calibrations of the Zeiss projector allow spectators to move backward and forward in time (to depict such distinctive astrological phenomena as the star of Bethlehem or Halley's comet, for example), as well as allowing them to see the heavens from any simulated geographical position on Earth.

Even inexpensive and unsophisticated planetarium projectors attempt an imaginative transcendence of time and space. Consider an advertisement for the Spitz Model A home planetarium, first published in *Sky and Telescope* magazine in October 1947 (fig. 15.3). In it, the manufacturer suggests that the lucky owner of this microcosmos will be able to "watch the stars rolling across the sky in classroom, church, living room or bedroom." The rhetoric of the advertisement effortlessly erases distinctions between domestic and cosmic space: The stars are not said to roll across the ceiling of the church or living room, but across the "sky" that will be created within these rooms. Once plugged in, the Spitz Model A becomes an illusionistic device that imaginatively erases the conventional perspectival boundary of the bedroom ceiling and replaces it with a view "out" into the cosmos. The viewer is offered an imaginative escape from both now and here, because the owner of the Model A will be empowered to "set the planets for any date" and see the stars "as viewed from home, North Pole, Equator, or Southern Hemisphere." Although such a transcendence of time and space might offer welcome relief to any city dweller, in the wake of a world war and the first use of nuclear warfare, the prospect must have appeared even more appealing in 1947.[3] As Mantegna's *Camera* fresco and the Spitz home planetarium both suggest, the "final frontier" is perhaps not space, but the ability to simulate space without leaving the comfort of one's own home.

Having briefly examined the artificial skies rendered by ancient art and modern planetariums, we might also consider a uniquely postmodern precursor of the casino's artificial sky: atmospheric simulations. Although most atmospheric simulations (i.e., attempts to create a stable balance of ambient gases that simulates the actual gaseous atmosphere of Earth) occur in laboratory settings, the single ambitious example of the Biosphere 2 project will suffice. The structure was designed and built by a private corporation called Space Biospheres Ventures and funded at a cost of over $150 million by

Figure 15.3. Advertisement for the Spitz Model A home planetarium. From Sky and
Telescope *magazine, October 1947.*

*Figure 15.4. View from inside the west "lung" of Biosphere 2, circa 1990. Photograph ©
Gill C. Kenny. Used with permission.*

Texas billionaire Edward Bass. Biosphere 2 was the "largest totally enclosed
ecosystem ever constructed" (Warshall 22; fig. 15.4), with an airtight foot-
print covering 13,000 square meters and enclosing 204,000 cubic meters
(Cohen and Tilman 1150). The hermetically sealed structure, which is
located in the Sonoran Desert outside of Tucson, Arizona, was intended to
be a prototype space station and a working model of Earth's biosphere (in
the lexicon of the "Biospherians" the Earth is casually referred to as "Biosphere 1"). The project received extensive media coverage in 1991 and again
in 1993, when eight Biospherians respectively began and ended their two-
year experiment in domesticity within the sealed building. This microcosmos they inhabited contained a tiny ocean, marshland, rainforest, desert,
and agricultural area, complete with thirty-eight hundred species of introduced flora and fauna ("Bad" 1). Although the setting of the structure is
hardly urban, John Allen and the other directors of the project clearly view
what they call "Bios2" as a model mini-city of the future, a "micropolis"
that they assume will eventually "travel throughout space" (Allen 95, 11).

Rather than creating the *illusion* of day or night sky, as did Mantegna's
Camera fresco and the Zeiss planetarium projector, Biosphere 2 attempts to

create the illusion of Earth's atmosphere by actually *creating* Earth's atmosphere, albeit apart from the Earth in sealed domes built upon the planet's surface. Thus, the illusionistic challenge is no longer representational: The point is not to depict a cloud or a constellation, but to recreate the Earth's atmosphere for the eventual purpose of transplanting sealed bubbles of that atmosphere (the Biospheres 3, 4, 5, etc. that will presumably supplant the "Biosphere 1" that is our earthly home) to Mars and other planets. Biosphere 2 is an Earth-simulation that aspires not only to resemble, but to imitate and eventually to supersede the Earth. However, the cultural work of the project is quite similar to that of the *Camera* fresco and the planetarium. Because the enclosed, artificial environment of Biosphere 2 is both firmly fastened to Earth and yet designed to be transportable into space, the bright domes of this monumental cultural artifact partake of the same "double action of enclosure and transcendence" that has long been associated with domes and domed spaces (Casey 135).

Thus, concepts of nature, time, and control are as important within Biosphere 2 as they were within ancient domes and modern planetariums. However, it is control—absolute and total—that constitutes the central and indispensable organizing principle of Biosphere 2. One could hardly find a more poignant cultural monument to the fantasy of human control over nature than a hermetically sealed dome through which even the movement of atmospheric gasses is prohibited. The only plants and animals in this technological Eden are those placed there by the Biospherians, and a plethora of technological controls are daily employed to maintain the lived fantasy of a cybernetic universe in which everything from snails to skies are manipulated for the use and satisfaction of human masters. In its escapist utopianism, emphasis upon social control, dependence upon technology, even in its sometimes comical theatricality, Biosphere 2 is the type of cultural space Jean Baudrillard identified as "a world of simulation . . . a world completely cataloged and analyzed, then *artificially resurrected under the auspices of the real*" (*Simulacra* 8; original emphasis).

THE HEAVENLY NATURE OF THE CASINO

Having examined the long tradition of interiorized heavens as it is manifested in the precursor "texts" of ancient illusionistic domes, modern planetariums, and the postmodern atmospheric simulation of Biosphere 2, I return to Reno's Silver Legacy Resort Casino to ask what cultural work is being done by the artificial heavens domed within this monumental civic space. As noted, the casino's sky-mural occupies the entire 75,000-square-foot interior surface of the 180-foot-diameter dome. Executed by REALLYBIGSKIES™ of Hollywood, California, it took a five-man crew forty-two days to complete and required the use of twenty-three hundred gallons of paint. The mural, which also includes white light and ultraviolet paint pigments, is illuminated by twenty-five hundred specialized lighting units and is enhanced by an advanced audio and digital filing system ("World's" 1; Cashill 33). The combined result of this ambitious experiment in painting, lighting, audio, and special-effects technology is a simulated heaven that a casino public-relations press release describes as "the perfect sky . . . an image as precise as the sky outside" ("World's" 1).

Although the spectacle of the casino's fake sky appears unique to visitors, it is in fact a culturally precedented phenomena with a rather venerable history. Like Mantegna's painted *oculus* in the *Camera,* the sky of the Silver Legacy is simply a ceiling fresco, albeit one executed on a colossal scale. Indeed, casino public relations demonstrate some awareness of the connection between ancient and postmodern ceiling paintings in a press release that begins, incredibly, "Michelangelo step aside" ("World's" 1). One of the designers of the dome extends this connection between art and artifice in his comparison of the mural's "deep purples and pinks" to those of "a Maxfield Parrish sky" (Cashill 33).

Like atmospheric simulations such as that attempted within Biosphere 2, the Silver Legacy uses technology and spectacle to constitute a themed, overdetermined civic space. The casino's artificial sky is a hybrid cultural artifact that combines business enterprise, amusement park, tourist attraction, engineering feat, and technological experiment to produce a controlled environment within a monumental urban space. The dual imperative of containment and transcendence is in evidence: By sealing out the world and then interiorizing its simulation for the benefit of patrons, the casino's architectural design seems to suggest that the outside world has been obviated, transcended, or replaced. Like Biosphere 2, the casino secedes from nature to recreate nature in (and within) its own image.

Although the artificial sky of the Silver Legacy may be understood

Figure 15.5. Interior of the Silver Legacy Resort Casino, with dome perimeter, sky, and mining rig, 1996. Photograph by the author.

within a trajectory of comparable simulations, the iconography of the casino's architectural space is complicated by the presence of the Baron's Rig, a 130-foot-tall, 198-ton "replica" of a mining rig that towers beneath the dome (fig. 15.5). Casino brochures notwithstanding, the Baron's Rig is *not* a replica, a representation, or even a simulation of a nineteenth-century mining rig, because no rig of this design or scale existed before the casino's construction of the would-be "replica" in the 1990s. Thus, the rig is not only not real, it is also not a real simulation. Rather, it is a *simulacrum,* which the *Oxford English Dictionary* defines as a "mere image, a specious imitation or likeness, of something," but which might be simply glossed as "a model of something that never actually existed." The silver mine beneath the casino is entirely fictional, with the accompanying legend and personage of Sam Fairchild likewise spurious. Thus, both the "silver" and the "legacy" of the Silver Legacy Resort Casino are fantastic fabrications—not simply imitations, but "specious imitations," or what we might call faux fakes. Having acknowledged that silver was mined in Nevada during the mid-nineteenth century, one has exhausted the authentic connection between this contrived spectacle and the historical reality it claims to represent.

It is perhaps best to view the casino's sky and mining rig not as either real or fake, but instead as *hyperreal*.[4] Consider the casino spectacle in light of Jean Baudrillard's claim that "today abstraction is no longer that of the map, the double, the mirror, or the concept. Simulation is no longer that of a territory, a referential being, or a substance. It is the generation by models of a real without origin or reality: a hyperreal. The territory no longer precedes the map, nor does it survive it" (*Simulacra* 1). Alternatively, using Umberto Eco's neosemiotic terminology, we might describe the casino as a "masterpiece of reconstructive mania" or as a "place of absolute iconism" in which the "imagination demands the real thing and, to attain it, must fabricate the absolute fake" (16, 48, 8).[5] Eco contends that "the public is meant to admire the perfection of the fake," and further proposes that a hyperreal construction (such as that of the Silver Legacy) "not only produces illusion, but—in confessing it—stimulates the desire for it" (44).

Not authenticity, but signification, is most important in examining the spatial and ideological narrative articulated in the interiorized, urban wilderness of the Silver Legacy. The relationship of the artificial mining rig to the artificial sky dramatizes the tension Leo Marx refers to as "the machine in the garden," the tension between human technological artifice and the pastoral world of nature. The mining machine—an apt embodiment of technological and industrial force—is so gigantic as to barely fit beneath the artificial cosmos, which seems built only to house it. Despite the presumption of its advertisement as the "world's largest" sky ("World's" 1), the dome of the casino is not only tiny in relation to the Earth's real sky, but is made to seem even more diminutive above the overwhelming gigantism of the rig, as if the universe were but a small garage in which one were obliged to park a large car. While the would-be wilderness of the "world's largest" sky remains pathetically small, the hyperreal machine is a simulacrum literally larger than life. The narrative embodied in this carefully themed space idealizes a distorted relationship, one in which human technological artifacts assume exaggerated importance relative to the natural world within which they must be produced and maintained. Furthermore, although the machine in the casino's garden is very much a machine, the garden itself is also a machine: Both the mining rig *and* the sky are artificial productions maintained by human technology. Unsimulated nature has been entirely banished from this cultural space and is now represented only by the iconographic surrogate of the simulated heavens that shelter the rig.

What relationship of culture to nature is dramatized in the elaborate narrative of the mining rig and "How It Works"? The imagined mine is, quite simply, a simulacrum of a nineteenth-century mine—a model of a sort of mine that never existed. Unlike most nineteenth-century mines, this hyperreal mine does not depend for its profitability upon the exploitation of miners—indeed, it does not require miners at all, because it exists as an artifact of pure cybernetic automation. Also, of course, it need not reckon with the complications and expense of environmental impact statements. In effect, the simulacrum of the mine offers a parable of prelapsarian ecological harmony in which human actions appear to have no deleterious environmental consequences.

There is a roundedness and elegance to this remarkable system, by which simulated mining is made to generate real capital. The ore that is supposedly mined need not be sold or even converted into something to be sold, but is made directly into money—a gesture of pure, unmediated commodification by which the imaginary silver is minted into the very coins that, seen through the glass face of the slot machine, keep patrons feeding and pulling, pulling and feeding.[6] Project manager Kirk Kennedy describes the mining machine as "a power source—and a gigantic toy . . . developed to feed the casino constantly and automatically" (Cashill 31). However, this too is an illusion, because it is not the machine that feeds the patrons, but the patrons who feed the machine. Beneath the surface of the themed narrative is a commercial flow running in the opposite direction. The process of "How It Works" actually *begins* when patrons feed money into slot machines and *ends* in the multimillion-dollar simulacrum that is purchased with their quarters and "silver" dollars. The only *real* elements of the factitious narrative are the consumers of the fantasy who purchase its extravagance with their losses. The extractive industry operating beneath the faux sky is not mining but gaming.

Recalling our examinations of illusionistic domes, planetarium domes, and the geodesic domes of Biosphere 2, we might again invoke the three primary ideas of nature, time, and control and ask how these ideas are expressed beneath the composite dome of the Silver Legacy Resort Casino. The simulacrum of the casino sky is so pervasive and seductively illusioneered, however, that it is impossible to discuss nature or time outside the context of control. For what idea of the universe is being expressed in this cultural space—what cosmology is in the casino—if not that of total human control of nature?

Henry Thoreau's observation that "the universe is wider than our views of it" (368) is nowhere more poignantly accurate than in this entirely artificial and scripted urban cultural space. The simulation of nature here is not on the order of silk plants and plastic flamingos—instead it mounts to the very vault of the heavens, to the movement of the stars, to the time of night or day, to the coming of storms. A visitor to any casino will notice that clocks are absent from gaming spaces and that windows are usually nonexistent or heavily curtained, with the obvious objective of preventing the time of day (time to eat, time to sleep, time to cut one's losses) from distracting patrons who are otherwise engaged in revenue-generating behaviors. However, the themed Silver Legacy gaming environment effectively controls the experience of time to a degree unprecedented in an urban architectural space. First, the appropriation, co-opting, and subsequent distortion of nineteenth-century American history is a way of controlling and marketing the time of the past by substituting an anachronistic fantasy for a very real and often very disturbing body of historical fact. Likewise, the godlike recalibration of the artificial heavens to a two-hour cycle involves the co-opting and replacement of an Earth day with an intensely accelerated "hyperday" during which the natural procession from dawn to dusk to dawn occurs twelve times faster than it does outside the casino. The rotation of the heavens is not only artificial (a simulation), but is also programmed according to a schedule that is purposefully and substantially deviant from naturalistic detail (i.e., a simulacrum).

To what end are the casino's remarkably elaborate and fantastically expensive simulacra finally devoted? They are calculated to recalibrate and control a particular kind of nature: *human* nature. The ultimate objective of any casino design is to attract people inside, to dissuade them from leaving, and to encourage them to engage in revenue-generating behaviors. Thus, the first function of the simulacra of sky and mining machine is simply that of attraction—people come to see the spectacle (particularly because both sky and machine are advertised as the "world's largest") and are likely, once there, to spend money. Second, this artificial environment is carefully designed to hold the visitors' interest. The novelty of perceptually intense simulated dawns, sunsets, and storms keeps spectators in rapt attention, while the constant change of the accelerated hyperday means that a new thrill is always impending and that the insatiable desire for novelty can be immediately satisfied even as it is constantly inspired. Finally, the controlled space of the casino also strikes visitors (however subconsciously) as a refuge, an attractive alternative to the chaotic and threatening world outside. As one expert on theme parks explains, "People feel secure coming to an artificial destination where they don't need passports, visas, where it's spotlessly clean and secure, so this is probably what our society wants, a mini cosmos" (Milman). Or, to quote Walt Disney, the father of American simulated space, "I don't want the public to see the world they are living in. . . . I want them to feel they're in another world" (Wilson *Culture* 161).[7]

Recognizing that space within the casino is organized so as to control human behavior, we might inquire into the possible consequences of such manipulation.[8] As current studies in environmental health and psychology demonstrate, "our ordinary surroundings, built and natural alike, have an immediate and a continuing effect on the way we feel and act, and on our health and intelligence. . . . This means that whatever we experience in a place is both a serious environmental issue and a deeply personal one" (Hiss xi).[9] Although gambling is by nature a test of luck, very little is left to chance in the design of the casino's physical space. Lights and buzzers draw patrons' attention (but only to currently paying slot machines); banks of gaming tables are positioned so as to obstruct direct exit from the gaming floor (thus offering additional enticement to customers who might otherwise depart); and extravagant attractions (circuses, aquaria, simulated historical sites) are used to lure customers into the establishment.

What, then, are we to make of a multimillion-dollar artificial sky that replicates, controls, and distorts the celestial cycles of light and dark? It is well known that circadian rhythms, the body's evolved responses to the cyclic and seasonal periodicity of the twenty-four-hour Earth day, are among the most powerful determinants of human physiology and emotion. The work of chronobiologists—scientists who study the ways in which light cycles affect human health and behavior—has demonstrated that light exposure is closely linked to mood, mental activity, alertness, sleep, rest, hunger, digestion, sex drive, body temperature, aging, and numerous other organismic processes. Dawn and sunrise have long functioned as human symbols of hope, renewal, and rebirth in part because the breaking of day is anticipated and accompanied by substantial hypothalamic secretions of various stimulant hormones, including epinephrine. Because our "biological clocks" are coevolved and synchronized with the regular periodicity of the twenty-four-hour day, disturbances in this regular cycle of dark and light often induce attendant disturbances in human physiology and emotion (as anyone who has experienced "jet lag" knows), which can result in fatigue, depression, mania, disorientation, and dangerously poor judgment.[10]

Let us imagine a gambler who, after sustaining substantial losses while playing blackjack, begins to contemplate returning to his hotel room. The artificial sky above him is purplish black and pebbled with stars. He has been playing for nearly four hours since dinner, and his wallet and eyelids both suggest that enough is enough. At this precise moment he begins to hear the sound of birds chirping in the distance. Within moments the sky above him turns pink with the glory of daybreak, and soon he is bathed in the effulgent light that pours down from the bright dome above. Although the real nighttime of the Earth day outside the casino is irrelevant to the design of the themed simulation inside the casino, the man's body responds (albeit with some difficulty) to the breaking dawn. Feeling suddenly refreshed and optimistic, he continues to play for several more hours before retiring.

Thus, the seemingly unique phenomenon of the Silver Legacy's artificial sky—which is actually interpretable in terms of a long tradition of related celestial simulations—serves the profit motive of the gaming industry by which it was designed and built. However, where do American culture's exponentially proliferating simulacra of nature finally leave and lead us? What attitudes or values will be expressed and consequently conditioned by such cultural spaces in the future? Will the dominant spatial relations of America's urban environments simply become a hyperreal Foucauldian "heterotopia" in which the meaning of all places is infinitely contested and contestable (Chidester and Linenthal 19)?

Although these fascinating questions are not yet answerable, I wish to offer a concluding observation that may serve as a prolegomenon to the study of fake nature in American cities of the twenty-first century. The ways in which nature has historically been engaged in urban environments suggests the following trajectory: *inclusion representation simulation simulacrum displacement*. Let me illustrate the process with a simple example. Wishing nature to be *included* in our urban spaces, we plant a tree in the foyer of an urban edifice. When the tree requires too much maintenance or dies, we opt for an elegant mural *representing* the same tree. Realizing, however, that we can have a fully three-dimensional tree without the complications of the earlier tree, we replace the mural with a plastic tree exactly *simulating* the original tree. However, becoming bored with the tree we seize the opportunity to replace it with a *simulacrum* of a tree, let us say a tree of a fantastic species that never actually existed, but that holds beautiful silk blossoms all year while requiring no maintenance. Finally, we find the convenience and handsome appearance of the tree so satisfying that, as real trees still growing elsewhere in the building die, we simply *replace* them with synthetic copies of this tree. We could extend this trajectory to a particularly dark conclusion by assuming not only that the species of tree originally growing in the foyer will go extinct, but also that the next generation of Americans in this city will have no knowledge that real trees once existed here, and when told of the original living trees will fail to value—or perhaps even to fully comprehend—the distinction between real and artificial trees.

This is an extreme example of a process that, thankfully, will always be mitigated by what Yi-Fu Tuan calls "topophilia" and what E. O. Wilson calls "biophilia": the love of place and of life, respectively. Still, the surreal experience of postmodern urban fantasyscapes and technological utopias such as the Silver Legacy Resort Casino suggests that Americans are all too willing to "buy" (in both senses of the word) artificial representations of the natural world and to do so in ignorance of the very real effects that these places (however artificial) have upon them. I agree with Eco's sense that the message of these simulacra is not "We are giving you the reproduction so that you will want the original," but rather, "We are [selling] you the reproduction so you will no longer feel any need for the original" (19). Indeed, Baudrillard's definition of the commodified "hyperreal" as "the disappearance of objects in their very representation" assumes the final stage I have called "displacement." Baudrillard thus refers to "simulation" as "an implosion of meaning" because it results, he believes, in a world in which it is "*impossible to isolate the process of the real,* or to prove the real" (*Simulacra* 31, 21; original emphasis).[11] Or, to conclude as did a waitress whom I overheard answering a patron's sincere question one "day" beneath the interiorized wilderness of the casino's domed sky: "Well, yeah, it's *real* . . . but not, like, *really* real."[12]

NOTES

1. I am indebted to Yi-Fu Tuan for the substance of this paragraph on the history of domes (*Topophilia* 168–70). For a fascinating study of how contemporary urban civic constructions (especially the shopping mall) function as sacred space, see Zepp.

2. See Gardner (521). Although examples from many periods and artistic traditions might be chosen to illustrate my argument here, a few outstanding works suggest themselves: the anonymous apse mosaic, *Christ between Angels and Saints,* circa A.D. 547, in the Church of San Vitale, Ravenna (Gardner 238); Giovanni Guercino's 1621–23 ceiling fresco *Aurora,* in the Villa Ludovisi, Rome (Gardner 646); and Giambattista Tiepolo's 1761–62 ceiling fresco *Apotheosis of the Pisani Family,* in the Villa Pisani, Stra (Gardner 695).

3. The highly controlled simulation of nature and time within the planetarium is evident not only in astronomical programs, but also in other programs such as the Imax films that are so often shown in planetariums. Both the star programs and the perceptually intense Imax films use optical projections on a domical surface to create an illusionistic transcendence of the barriers of time and space. Most Imax films—such as *Grand Canyon: The Hidden Secrets,* which recently played in the "Skydome 8/70" at the University of Nevada, Reno's Fleischmann Planetarium— are accompanied by advertisements promising that the film "takes viewers where they can never go" and "shows them things they can never see" (Fleischmann). Again, the emphasis is upon a technological transcendence of time and space experienced within the highly controlled "Skydome." Even the Pink Floyd and Pearl Jam laser shows that remain a staple of planetarium fare employ optical projections on a domical screen for the purpose of illusioneering a perceptual experience for the viewer-customers.

4. Recently, the *Utne Reader* devoted an issue to the question "Is Real Life Possible Anymore?" In an introductory essay, Jon Spayde prefers the term "hyper-fake" to the term "hyperreal" (49).

5. For a fascinating application of semiotics to the study of urban places, see Gottdiener and Lagopoulos.

6. The Baron's Rig machine recirculates $114 thousand worth of one-dollar coins each hour as part of the "show."

7. The idea that themed fantasy worlds satisfy by cosmeticizing and compressing

the otherwise inconvenient and time-consuming experience of reality is aptly conveyed by a Disney publicist's description of the "Jungle Cruise" at Disneyland: "It compacts into ten minutes the highlights, mystique, fun and excitement of an adventure that could only be duplicated through weeks on a safari. Best of all, it has none of the mosquitoes, monsoons, and other misadventures of the 'not always so great' outdoors" (Wilson *Culture* 161).

8. Of course all civic spaces—including schools and churches—are designed to "manipulate" or influence human behavior. Edward Relph argues that the difference between traditional communal architectural spaces and modern "illusioneered" architectural spaces is "that the latter are deliberately manufactured and manipulated, often solely for economic and political ends" (*Modern* 130).

9. Although designers in the West have recognized the "psychological ecology" (Gallagher 127) of places since the time of such influential Greek and Roman architects as Hermogenes and Vitruvius, American culture has been slow to recognize the vital importance of "environmental context" to human physical and psychological well being. As Winifred Gallagher notes, "while we readily accept that a healthy seed can't grow into a plant without the right soil, light, and water . . . we resist recognizing the importance of environment in our own lives" (16). For studies of the influence of environmental design upon human behavior, see Broadbent et al.; Canter and Lee; and Krasner.

10. My discussion of circadian rhythms and the effects of their disturbances is derived from Brown and Graeber; Mills; Moore-Ede; and Moore-Ede et al.

11. Baudrillard goes so far as to assert that a simulated world such as Disneyland "is presented as imaginary in order to make us believe that the rest is real, whereas all of Los Angeles and the America that surrounds it are no longer real, but belong to the hyperreal order and to the order of simulation" (*Simulacra* 12). For further discussions of cultural simulation, see Mander and Schwartz.

12. The author wishes to thank Michael P. Cohen, Terrell Dixon, Eryn Hoagland, Richard Hunt, Gaye McCollum, Daniel J. Philippon, David Robertson, and David Teague for their helpful responses to earlier versions of this article.

WORKS CITED

Allen, John. *Biosphere 2: The Human Experiment*. Ed. Anthony Blake. New York: Viking, 1991.

"Bad Odour: Biosphere Two." *The Economist* (newspaper) 1 February 1992: 1.

Baudrillard, Jean. *Simulacra and Simulation*. 1981. Trans. Sheila Faria Glaser. Ann Arbor: U of Michigan P, 1994.

Broadbent, Geoffrey, Richard Bunt, and Tomas Llorens, eds. *Meaning and Behavior in the Built Environment*. New York: John Wiley, 1980.

Brown, Frederick M., and R. Curtis Graeber, eds. *Rhythmic Aspects of Behavior*. Hilldale, N.J.: Lawrence Erlbaum, 1982.

Canter, David, and Terrence Lee, eds. *Psychology and the Built Environment*. New York: John Wiley, 1974.

Casey, Edward S. *Getting Back into Place: Toward a Renewed Understanding of the Place-World*. Bloomington: Indiana UP, 1993.

Cashill, Robert. "Reno Strikes Silver." *TCI* (January 1996): 30–33.

Chidester, David, and Edward T. Linenthal, eds. *American Sacred Space*. Bloomington: Indiana UP, 1995.

Cohen, Joel E., and David Tilman. "Biosphere 2 and Biodiversity: The Lessons So Far." *Science* 274 (15 November 1996): 1150–51.

Eco, Umberto. *Travels in Hyperreality*. 1986. Trans. William Weaver. San Diego: Harvest, 1990.

Fleischmann Planetarium at the University of Nevada, Reno. Brochure advertising public programs for 1996. Fold-out advertisement for the Imax film *Grand Canyon: The Hidden Secrets*, which showed in the Fleischmann 18 June 1996–5 January 1997.

Gallagher, Winifred. *The Power of Place: How Our Surroundings Shape Our Thoughts, Emotions, and Actions*. New York: HarperPerennial, 1993.

Gardner, Helen. 1926. *Art through the Ages*. 7th ed. Rev. by Horst de la Croix and Richard G. Tansey. New York: Harcourt, Brace, Jovanovich, 1976.

Gottdiener, M., and Alexandros Ph. Lagopoulos. *The City and the Sign: An Introduction to Urban Semiotics*. New York: Columbia UP, 1986.

Hiss, Tony. *The Experience of Place*. New York: Random House, 1990.

Krasner, Lawrence. *Environmental Design and Human Behavior: A Psychology of the Individual in Society*. New York: Pergamon, 1980.

Mander, Jerry. *In the Absence of the Sacred: The Failure of Technology and the Survival of the Indian Nations*. San Francisco: Sierra Club, 1991.

Marx, Leo. *The Machine in the Garden: Technology and the Pastoral Idea in America*. Oxford: Oxford UP, 1964.

Mills, J. N., ed. *Biological Aspects of Circadian Rhythms*. London: Plenum, 1973.

Moore-Ede, Martin. *The Twenty-Four-Hour Society: Understanding Human Limits in a World That Never Stops*. Reading, Mass.: Addison-Wesley, 1993.

Moore-Ede, Martin, Frank M. Sulzman, and Charles A. Fuller. *The Clocks That Time Us: Physiology of the Circadian Timing System*. Cambridge, Mass.: Harvard UP, 1982.

Relph, Edward. "Modernity and the Reclamation of Place." *Dwelling, Seeing, and Designing: Toward a Phenomenological Ecology*. Ed. David Seamon. Albany: State U of New York P, 1993. 25–40.

———. *The Modern Urban Landscape*. Baltimore, Md.: Johns Hopkins UP, 1987.

Schwartz, Hillel. *The Culture of the Copy: Striking Likenesses, Unreasonable Facsimiles.* New York: Zone, 1996.

"The Secret of the Baron's Rig." Promotional brochure. Reno, Nev.: Silver Legacy Resort Casino, 1996.

Spayde, Jon. "A Way Out of Wonderland: Is Real Life Possible Anymore?" *Utne Reader* (July–August 1997): 49–54.

Thoreau, Henry David. *Walden*. 1854. New York: Penguin, 1986.

Tuan, Yi-Fu. *Topophilia: A Study of Environmental Perception, Attitudes, and Values.* 1974. New York: Columbia UP, 1990.

Warshall, Peter. "Lessons from Biosphere 2: Ecodesign, Surprises, and the Humility of Gaian Thought." *Whole Earth Review* 89 (Spring 1996): 22+.

Wilson, Alexander. *The Culture of Nature: North American Landscape from Disney to the Exxon Valdez*. Cambridge, Mass.: Blackwell, 1992.

Wilson, E. O. *Biophilia*. Cambridge, Mass.: Harvard UP, 1984.

"World's Largest Composite Dome Receives a Paint Job at the New Silver Legacy." Press release. Reno, Nev.: Silver Legacy Resort Casino, 19 May 1995.

Zepp, Ira G., Jr. *The New Religious Image of Urban America: The Shopping Mall as Ceremonial Center*. 2nd ed. Niwot: UP of Colorado, 1997.

About the Contributors

Michael Bennett is assistant professor of English at Long Island University, Brooklyn. He is the coeditor (with Vanessa Dickerson) of the forthcoming *Recovering the Body: Self-Representations by African American Women.* He has published essays on African American families and public policy, computers and composition, ecocriticism, and African American literary theory.

Michael P. Branch is associate professor of literature and environment in the Department of English at the University of Nevada, Reno, where he teaches courses in nature writing and American literature and helps to coordinate graduate studies in literature and environment. He is a founder and past president of the Association for the Study of Literature and Environment (ASLE) and is the current book review editor of the journal *ISLE: Interdisciplinary Studies in Literature and Environment.* He has published over sixty articles, chapters, and reviews on nature writing and environmental literature and is coeditor of *The Height of Our Mountains: Nature Writing from Virginia's Blue Ridge Mountains and Shenandoah Valley* (with Daniel J. Philippon; Johns Hopkins University Press, 1998) and *Reading the Earth: New Directions in the Study of Literature and Environment* (with Rochelle Johnson, Daniel Patterson, and Scott Slovic; University of Idaho Press, 1998). His current project, *John Muir's Last Journey: South to the Amazon and East to Africa* (Island Press/Shearwater Books), is a textually edited collection of Muir's late travel journals.

Terrell Dixon is associate professor of English at the University of Houston, where he served as departmental chair for fifteen years and directed the interdisciplinary Scholar's Community. He is coeditor (with Scott Slovic) of *Being in the World: An Environmental Reader for Writers,* guest editor of a special issue of *American Book Review* on urban ecocriticism, and the author of many articles on environmental literature and teaching. His current work is focused on American literature and toxicity.

Catherine Villanueva Gardner is assistant professor in the Department of Philosophy at the University of Michigan–Flint. Her interests are in feminist ethics, broadly conceived. She has published in *Hypatia*.

Joanne Gottlieb is a doctoral candidate in English at Princeton University. She lives in New York City, where she manages an HIV/AIDS information web site.

Richard Heyman is a doctoral student in the Geography Department at the University of Washington. He has published articles on Toni Morrison and on the social production of urban space in Los Angeles. He is currently working on a history of geographical thought.

Andrew Light is assistant professor of philosophy and environmental studies at the State University of New York at Binghamton. He has published over two dozen articles on environmental philosophy, political philosophy, and philosophy of film. He is the editor or coeditor of six books, in print or forthcoming, including *Environmental Pragmatism* (with Eric Katz) and *Social Ecology after Bookchin*. He is the founding coeditor (with Jonathan Smith) of the journal *Philosophy and Geography*. He has held positions at Texas A&M University, the University of Alberta, The University of Montana, and Tel Aviv University and has lectured widely in North America, Europe, Australia, and the Middle East.

Gary Roberts is a doctoral candidate at Brandeis University. He has published essays on Robert Frost, Allen Grossman, and Jane Kenyon. His dissertation topic is rhetorics of vulgarity and efficacy in twentieth-century poetry.

Andrew Ross is professor and director of the Program in American Studies at New York University. His books include *The Chicago Gangster Theory of Life, Strange Weather, No Respect,* and, most recently, *Real Love: In Pursuit of Cultural Justice.* He has also edited several collections, including *No Sweat: Fashion, Free Trade, and the Rights of Garment Workers.*

David R. Shumway is associate professor of English and literary and cultural studies at Carnegie Mellon University. He is the author of *Michel Foucault* and *Creating American Civilization: A Genealogy of American Literature as an Academic Discipline* and coeditor (with Ellen Messer-Davidow and David Sylvan) of *Knowledges: Historical and Critical Studies in Disciplinarity.* He is currently working on a book on the discourses of romantic love (film, fiction, songs, self-help, etc.) in twentieth-century America and coediting (with Craig Dionne) a collection entitled *Disciplining English.*

Laura L. Sullivan is a doctoral student in English at the University of Florida. Her research interests include Marxist and feminist media theory, women and technology, electronic pedagogy, hypertext, the politics of the World Wide Web, autobiography, and the discourse of beauty. She has published articles on several topics: linguistic and social developments in the wake of new electronic technology, gender and cyberspace, feminism and the theorization of hypertext, Cuba and the Internet, and electronic pedagogy.

Adam W. Sweeting is assistant professor of humanities at Boston University, College of General Studies. He is the author of *Reading Houses and Building Books: Andrew Jackson Downing and the Architecture of Popular Antebellum Literature.*

David W. Teague is associate professor of English at the University of Delaware Parallel Program. He is the author of *The Southwest in American Literature and Art* and the coeditor (with Peter Wild) of *The Secret Life of John C. Van Dyke.*

Kathleen R. Wallace is an independent scholar and the former assistant director of the First-Year Writing Program at The Ohio State University. Her publications include *Beyond Nature Writing* (with Karla Armbruster; forthcoming) and " 'Roots, Aren't They Supposed to Be Buried?': The Experience of Place in Midwestern Women's Autobiographies" in *Mapping American Culture,* edited by Wayne Franklin and Michael Steiner. Her research interests include ecocriticism, nature writing, and mapping.

Index

dualistic thinking, 193–94, 200–01, 227, 255–56, 258·

Earth Day, 15, 86
Earth First! 26
Earth Goddess, 7
ecocomposition, 77–78, 88
ecocriticism, 9, 10, 11nn. 2–5, 81, 169, 173, 184; definitions of, 3, 57; history of movement, 10n. 1; urban, 9, 15–16, 170
ecofeminism, 8, 25, 28, 191–210, 223–24, 226–27; and urban environment, 7, 199–209
ecological activism, 7, 22, 28, 197, 204, 207
ecological literacy, 58, 72, 73
ecology, culture and, 170, 256
ecomarketing, 214
economics; American, 175, 176, 178–79; changes in, 129–32, 178–79; contemporary cosmetics discourse's relation to, 213–29; global, 112, 227; impact of gentrification on, 182; inner city and, 170; of Seattle, 123
ecosystems, 4, 18, 285; suburban, 162, 163, 166; urban, 9, 166, 173, 256, 259, 261, 271
education. See schools
Eliot, T.S., "The Waste Land," 34
Emerson, Ralph Waldo, 94, 104, 107
employment, 16, 170, 172, 176–80, 183, 205, 208
environment: academic study of, 80, 88; anthologies/readers about, 3, 10–11 n. 2, 12n. 7; as concept, 273; cultural/political aspects of, 59, 60,

166–67; graduate programs in, 11n. 4; legislation of, 16, 69, 70; literature of reform of, 96, 105, 106; sociopolitical construction of, 9, 87
environmentalist rhetoric, 214, 215, 217, 221, 222, 262, 271
environmental movement, 7, 15, 22, 27, 28, 56, 71, 81, 173, 195, 255, 257, 259
Environmental Protection Agency (EPA), 131, 185n. 1
environmental racism, 7, 169, 180, 184, 185n. 1, 205
ethics. See morality
ethnicity. See race
eugenics, 25
European Americans, 65, 192, 203–05; beliefs and practices of, 138–40, 142–43, 154, 172, 174, 202, 204, 228; in city, 6, 7, 170, 151, 173, 175–77, 183, 204; in green movement, 169; policymaking and, 152, 196; in suburbs, 16, 141, 150, 165, 176, 177, 181–82, 185n. 2. See also whiteness
evolution, 233–52. See also social Darwinism

Fair Housing Act of 1968, 181
Falling Down, 137, 141–49, 150, 151, 153, 154, 155, 172
farming, 257–58
feminism, 55, 71, 206, 192–93, 196–97, 207–08, 215, 222, 225, 226, 228
feminist criticism, 3, 26
First National People-of-Color Environmental Leadership Summit, 204

162, 181; racial minorities in, 162; vs. cities, 18, 19, 24, 147, 177, 179; white flight to, 157–67, 176, 181, 182, 185n. 2; wildness in, 77–89

Sullivan, Laura, 8, 25

sweatshops, 22–23, 129, 130

Sweeting, Adam, 5

Swift, Jonathan, 36, 37–40, 42, 43, 49, 52

taxation, 18, 19, 23, 165, 177, 179, 182

Teague, David, 6, 7, 169

technoculture, 29, 226, 233–52, 282

teenage childbearing, 172

Thoreau, Henry David, 70, 77, 85, 88, 89, 94, 104, 255, 257, 261, 272, 291

towns, medieval and Renaissance, 35

toxic poisoning, 30, 185n. 1, 191, 195, 227

toxic sites, 7, 87, 88, 131, 180, 185n. 1, 195–97, 203–04, 210n. 11, 222

traffic, 16, 19, 159, 162, 163

trees, 79, 98, 102, 159, 163, 202, 294

trendy neighborhoods, 182

Tucson, Ariz., 285

unemployment. *See* employment

Updike, John, 159–60, 163, 166

urban, concept of, 121

urban cultural sites, 281

urban culture, 20

urban decay, 200, 203, 248

urban ecology, 8, 15, 16, 17, 259

urban green space: as backyard garden, 198; as civilizing agent, 22. *See also* parks

urbanicity: philosophical traditions of, 10n. 1; sociological traditions of, 10n. 1

urbanization, 18, 35, 82, 223, 234, 248

urban literature, 33, 34, 35, 46; in Audre Lorde's writing, 55–73; by people of color, 57, 67; rhetorics of, 36, 37, 39, 40, 42, 43, 49, 51, 52

urban nature, 4, 93–109, 246

urban nature writing, 4, 81, 82, 88, 89n. 2, 89n. 3, 93

urban planning, 171

urban poetry, 33–52. *See also* urban literature

urban policy, 7, 81, 150, 172, 173, 183–84

urban reform, 22, 99, 154

urban renewal, 22, 181, 182, 183

urban sociology, 4, 12n. 7

urban Western consumers, 214, 216, 221, 226, 227

urban wilderness, 137–55, 185n. 3

utopia, 8, 215–16, 221, 233, 235–37, 241–51, 286, 294

Vaughn, Henry, 51–52

Vaux, Calvert, 108

violence, 98, 153, 154, 174

Virgil, 37, 38, 47

walking, 47–52, 53n. 5, 84

Wallace, Kathleen, 5

War on Poverty, 7

waste disposal. *See* sanitation

water, 15, 96, 131. *See also* pollution

wealth, 18, 100, 143, 183; distribution of, 27, 247

welfare, 21, 23, 172, 184, 207

whiteness, 60, 174

whites. *See* European Americans

Whitman, Walt, 101

wilderness, 28, 48, 58, 83, 203, 261; activism, 26; classical view of, 137–41, 143, 145, 150, 152, 155; images of, 22, 66, 125, 126, 201, 255–58, 270, 282; loss of, 18; preservation of, 15, 81, 88, 169; Romantic view of, 137–38, 140, 145; urban, 6, 20, 22, 137, 140, 141, 145–55, 176, 185n. 3

wildlife, 78, 240, 269; protection of, 15

Williams, Joy, 5

Williams, Raymond, 3–4, 35, 36, 37, 46

Williams, Terry Tempest, 70

Wilson, Alexander, 29

women, 56, 58, 69, 207–09; and cosmetics industry, 213–19; in environmental activism, 26, 184, 191, 195–98, 205, 206; First World, 8, 216, 221, 223, 224, 226; and nature, 193, 194, 201–03; Third World, 8, 129, 202, 203, 216–17, 221, 223–27. *See also* sexism

women's liberation. *See* feminism

Wordsworth, William, 34, 36, 37, 39–40

workers, 107, 114, 123, 129, 132, 144, 165, 178, 223–27

workplace, 23, 24, 30, 70–71, 85, 100, 115, 169, 208, 222, 226

Wright, Will, 4